HELLBOY ™

STRANGE PLACES

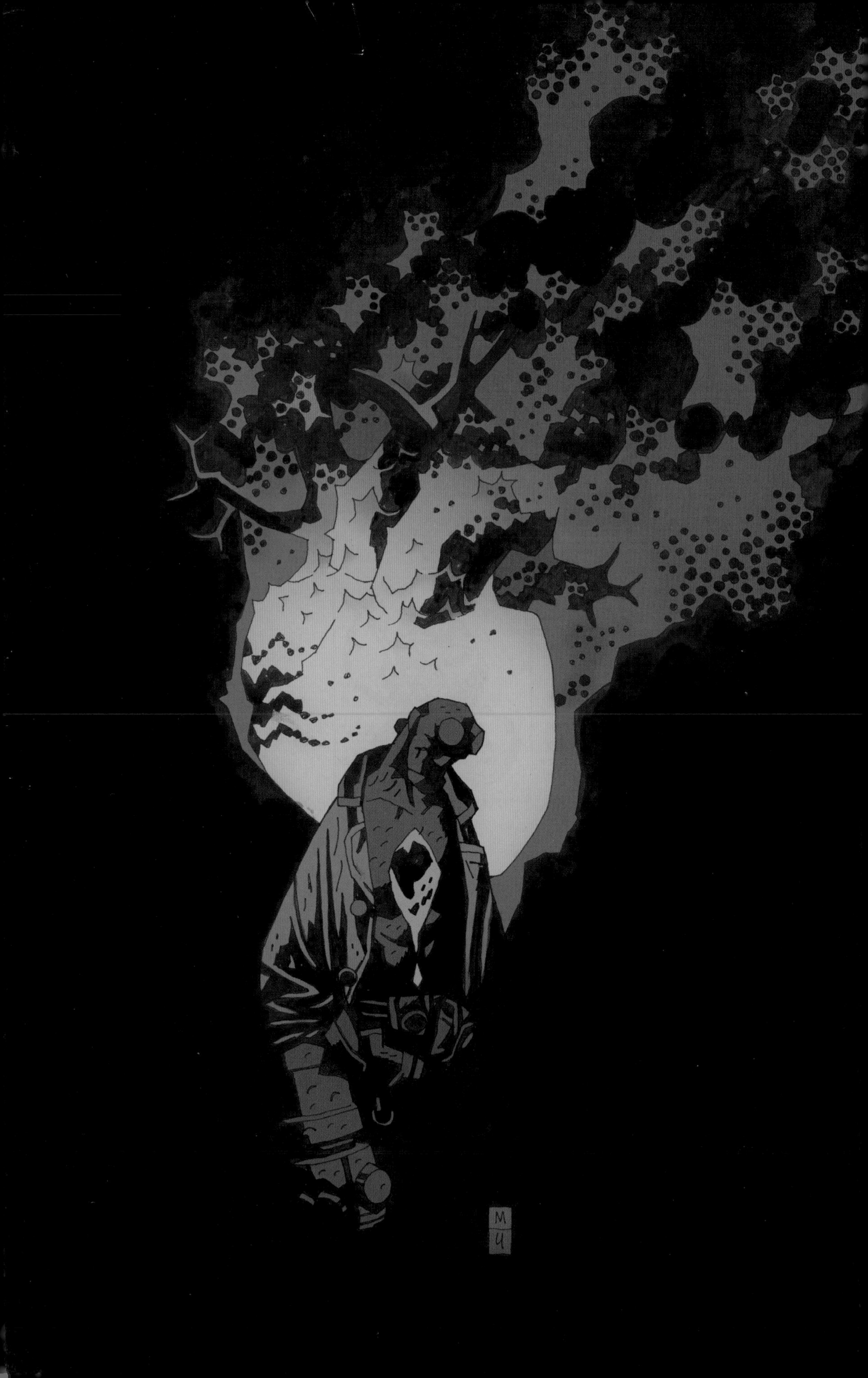

STRANGE PLACES

by
MIKE MIGNOLA

Colored by
DAVE STEWART

Lettered by
CLEM ROBINS

✠

Introduction by
GARY GIANNI

Edited by
SCOTT ALLIE

Hellboy logo designed by
KEVIN NOWLAN

Collection designed by
MIKE MIGNOLA & CARY GRAZZINI

Published by
MIKE RICHARDSON

DARK HORSE BOOKS™

Published by
Dark Horse Books
A division of Dark Horse Comics, Inc.
10956 SE Main St.
Milwaukie, OR 97222

First Edition
April 2006
ISBN: 1-59307-475-1

This book collects *Hellboy: The Third Wish* #1-2 and *Hellboy: The Island* #1-2, published by Dark Horse Comics.

5 7 9 10 8 6 4

PRINTED IN CHINA

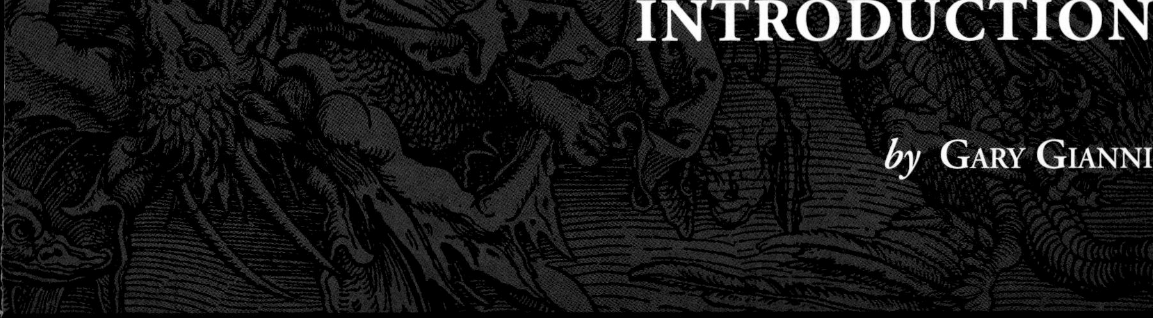

INTRODUCTION

by Gary Gianni

A few years ago I asked Mike Mignola to write an introduction for my comic-book adaptation of Jules Verne's *20,000 Leagues Under the Sea*. What sort of insight could the creator of *Hellboy* provide for the marvelous nineteenth-century adventure story? By nature, Mignola has an utterly unique, often zany viewpoint on every topic from abomination to Zarathustra, and, given his reverence for Victorian literature, I thought he'd find the offer worthy of his mettle.

Unfortunately, he declined.

His excuse? Well, that would have made an introduction in and of itself. The bizarre angle I had hoped he'd commit to paper was rendered verbally in the form of an inspired soliloquy which he delivered off the top of his head. It was a snapshot of a true storyteller—a portrait of the artist as a gifted madman.

"You want me to write an introduction?" Mignola's voice echoed incredulously over the phone. He paused a moment, considering the possibilities, and proceeded to launch into an imagined scenario which Charles Dickens, who thrilled audiences with his storytelling skills at public readings, would have greatly appreciated.

"Yeah, I can just picture it," Mignola mused. "The long-deceased Jules Verne smashing his way out of a tomb somewhere in France after he hears *I'm* writing an introduction for his *20,000 Leagues Under the Sea.* He'll look like he's grinning, but he's not, because he doesn't have any lips—he'll just be mad."

I could easily see the black-and-white shapes Mignola would use in rendering an illustration for his whimsical nightmare. One of his chief attributes as an artist is the ability to create poetic imagery from material which, in the hands of others, would be vulgar and tasteless.

The artist continued: "Verne is yelling, 'That bastard, Mignola, I'll find him and tear his heart out.' Verne will *try* to say this, but by now his jaw unhinges and falls down around his collar bones. He shambles half-way 'round the world, and winds up at my front door. *Boom! Boom! Boom!* 'C'mon down here, Mignola! Open Up! Ya hear me? C'mon down here and I'll beat the crap out of ya!'"

I cracked up laughing, but when I realized this comic narrative was Mignola's polite way of bowing out of my request, I knew there was no hope of arguing. On the contrary, I began to wonder if adapting *20,000 Leagues* into a comic book had any merit at all.

I describe the phone call, albeit in a paraphrased manner, because I think it illustrates—in a small way—Mike Mignola's modus operandi. He takes his work seriously, and yet he is acutely aware of the absurdity of the proceedings. (See *Screw-on Head* for further testimony.) The literary references which are often sprinkled throughout his stories allow Mignola to acknowledge his influences without being pedantic or ostentatious.

As entertaining as the *Hellboy* series is, I find an underlying sense of melancholy and pathos at the heart of it all. Mignola once admitted to me he regretted not having the skill as a writer to be able to move readers to tears—a difficult task for even the best among the Victorian writers to achieve.

Poetry, myth, and folklore are other interests which surface in his stories, but the high regard for classic foundations are mingled in a refreshing manner with pulp material from the '30s and '40s, as well as horror films and other comics. The pulp material in particular is a favorite area of exploration for Mignola. He has examined some of the lamest, hare-brained concepts anyone has ever laid eyes upon, and managed to develop even more grist worthy of his creative mill. I would go as far as to say Mignola never met a pulp idea he didn't like. Except perhaps for the dream detective—a paranormal investigator who has the ability to solve supernatural cases while he sleeps. "How many times can you hit the snooze alarm on that idea?" Mignola observed, to his credit. Over all, Jules Verne, Dickens, and even the pulp writers of their day entertained the reading public, and much of their work, enduring over time, is now recognized by modern critics as classic literature.

It's just possible, one hundred years from now, a scholar of twenty-first-century pop culture will compose a new introduction for this very book, and Mignola's *Hellboy* will be re-issued and appreciated by an as-of-yet unborn audience. Somewhere, dear reader, you and I will be grinning.

Gary Gianni
Goldstadt Medical University
2005

For Hans Christian Andersen,
King of Mermaids,
and
William Hope Hodgson,
Master of the Sargasso Sea.

THE THIRD WISH

THIS ONE STARTED OUT as a Sub-Mariner story.

Back in 1983, I'd just drawn my first story for Marvel Comics, a short Sub-Mariner story (written by Bill Mantlo) about a drowning horse. It was a nightmare. I didn't know how to draw boats or horses, or pretty much anything in the real world. I just wanted to draw rocks and monsters. So, as a possible follow-up to the horse story, I plotted something that would take place *entirely* underwater, with the Sub-Mariner captured by mermaid sisters and turned over to a demonic sea hag. Then I think I just filed it away in my head. I don't remember sending it to my editor (at that time, the great Al Milgrom). I don't remember it being rejected (seems like I'd remember that). I do remember that I liked the story. Ten years later, when I created Hellboy, I slid it over into the corner of my brain where I keep all my Hellboy stuff. It would need a better ending and some brilliant way to keep Hellboy breathing underwater, but I'd worry about that when the time came.

Cut to September 11, 2001.

I had just moved back to New York City and was about to start a new project, a non-Hellboy graphic novel set in a partially ruined New York City. How's that for timing? By the end of that day— I remember the air smelling like burnt wire—I'd shelved my "New York thing." Suddenly it seemed like a good time to do a cute little fairy tale about mermaids.

I had originally intended to follow *Conqueror Worm* with a story about Hellboy in Africa, so I had started doing some research: Mohlomi was a real person, and the haunted banana tree, the bat with the basket, and Ananse trading for stories are all taken from actual African folktales. The first half of the mermaid story is almost exactly the story I made up in 1983, inspired by Hans Christian Andersen's *The Little Mermaid*.

The overall tone of the story ended up much darker than I originally intended. Maybe it was 9/11 (the ghost father and souls in jars were all post 9/11 inventions), or maybe it's just that Beast of the Apocalypse thing catching up to Hellboy. Not sure. Probably a little bit of both. I had trouble drawing this one. I did four different covers for issue 2, and, for the first time, I drew and discarded whole pages. It was nothing compared to the trouble I would have with *The Island*, but we'll get to that later.

The Third Wish was published as a two-issue miniseries in 2002.

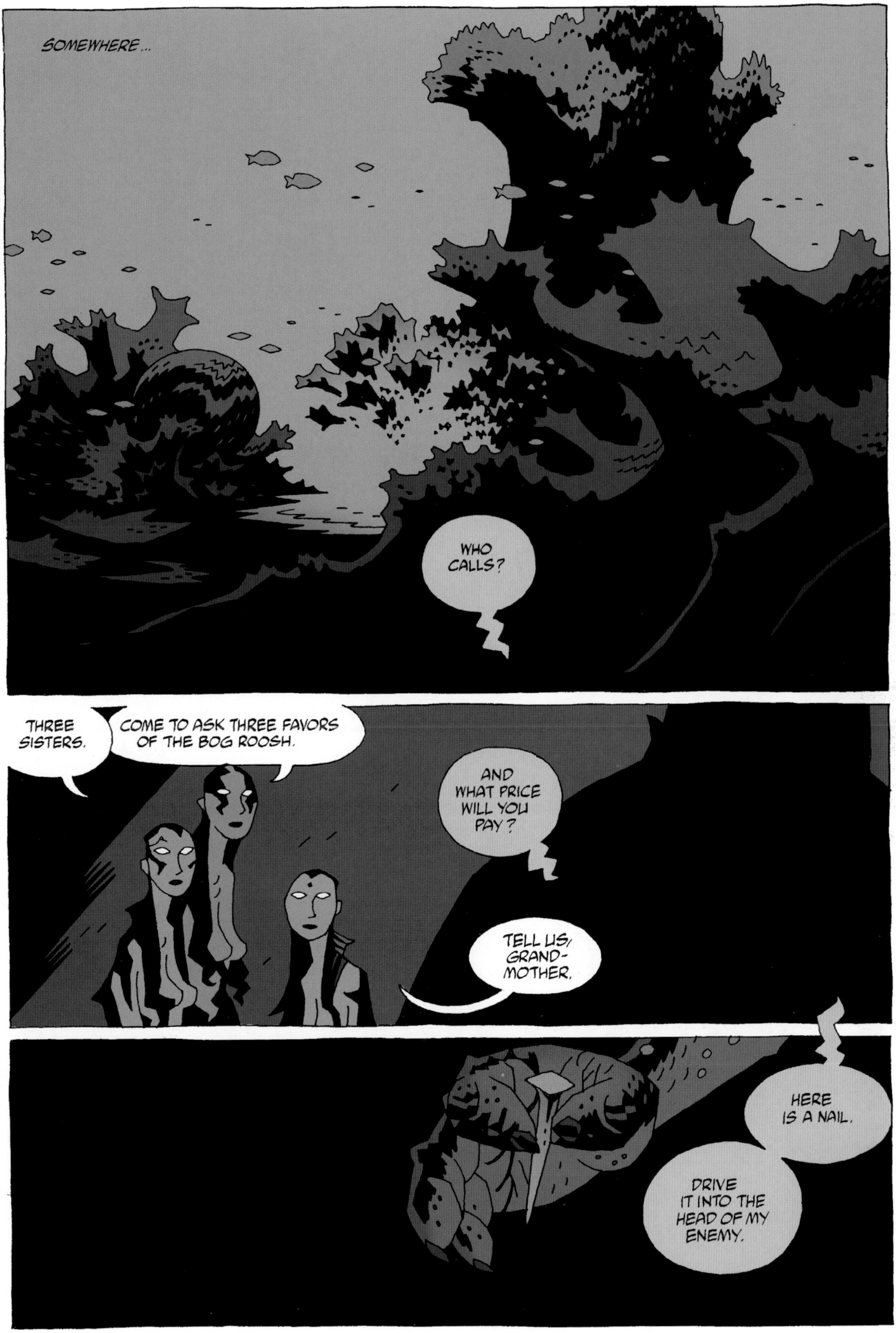
SOMEWHERE...
WHO CALLS?
THREE SISTERS.
COME TO ASK THREE FAVORS OF THE BOG ROOSH.
AND WHAT PRICE WILL YOU PAY?
TELL US, GRANDMOTHER.
HERE IS A NAIL.
DRIVE IT INTO THE HEAD OF MY ENEMY.

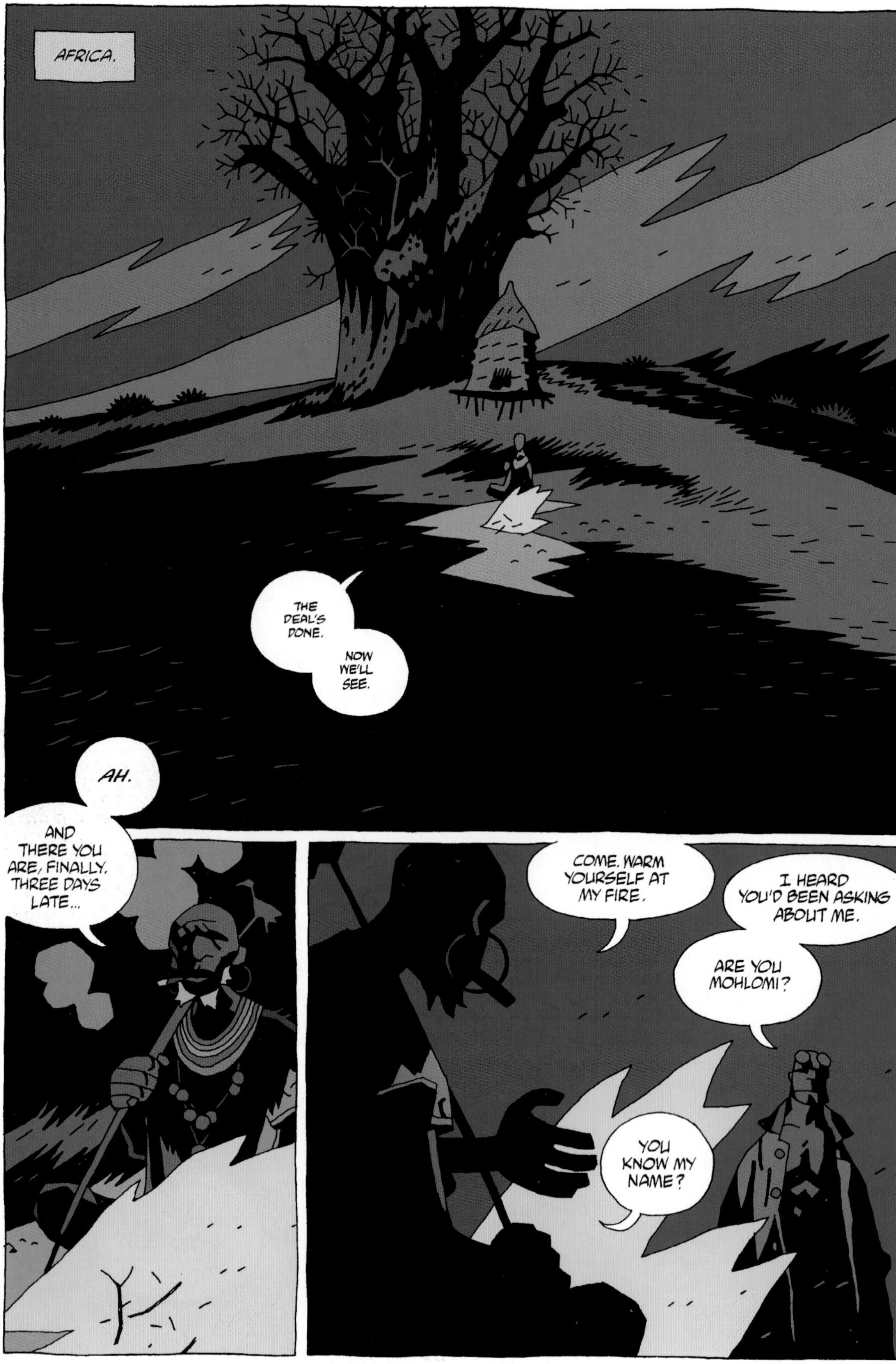
AFRICA.
THE DEAL'S DONE.
NOW WE'LL SEE.
AH.
AND THERE YOU ARE, FINALLY. THREE DAYS LATE...
COME. WARM YOURSELF AT MY FIRE.
I HEARD YOU'D BEEN ASKING ABOUT ME.
ARE YOU MOHLOMI?
YOU KNOW MY NAME?

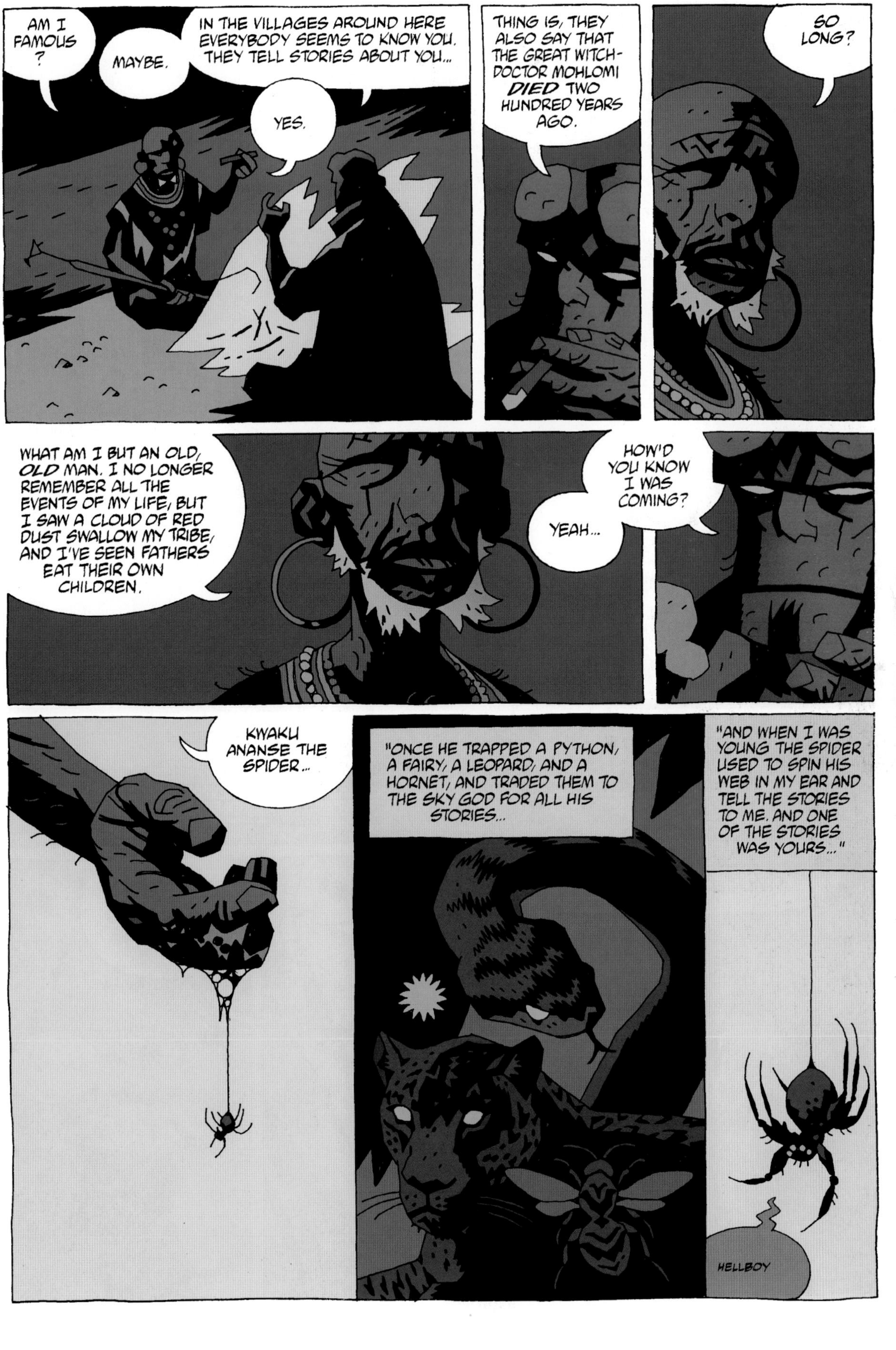
AM I FAMOUS ?
MAYBE.
IN THE VILLAGES AROUND HERE EVERYBODY SEEMS TO KNOW YOU. THEY TELL STORIES ABOUT YOU...
YES.
THING IS, THEY ALSO SAY THAT THE GREAT WITCH-DOCTOR MOHLOMI DIED TWO HUNDRED YEARS AGO.
SO LONG?
WHAT AM I BUT AN OLD, OLD MAN. I NO LONGER REMEMBER ALL THE EVENTS OF MY LIFE, BUT I SAW A CLOUD OF RED DUST SWALLOW MY TRIBE, AND I'VE SEEN FATHERS EAT THEIR OWN CHILDREN.
YEAH...
HOW'D YOU KNOW I WAS COMING?
KWAKU ANANSE THE SPIDER...
"ONCE HE TRAPPED A PYTHON, A FAIRY, A LEOPARD, AND A HORNET, AND TRADED THEM TO THE SKY GOD FOR ALL HIS STORIES...
"AND WHEN I WAS YOUNG THE SPIDER USED TO SPIN HIS WEB IN MY EAR AND TELL THE STORIES TO ME. AND ONE OF THE STORIES WAS YOURS..."
HELLBOY

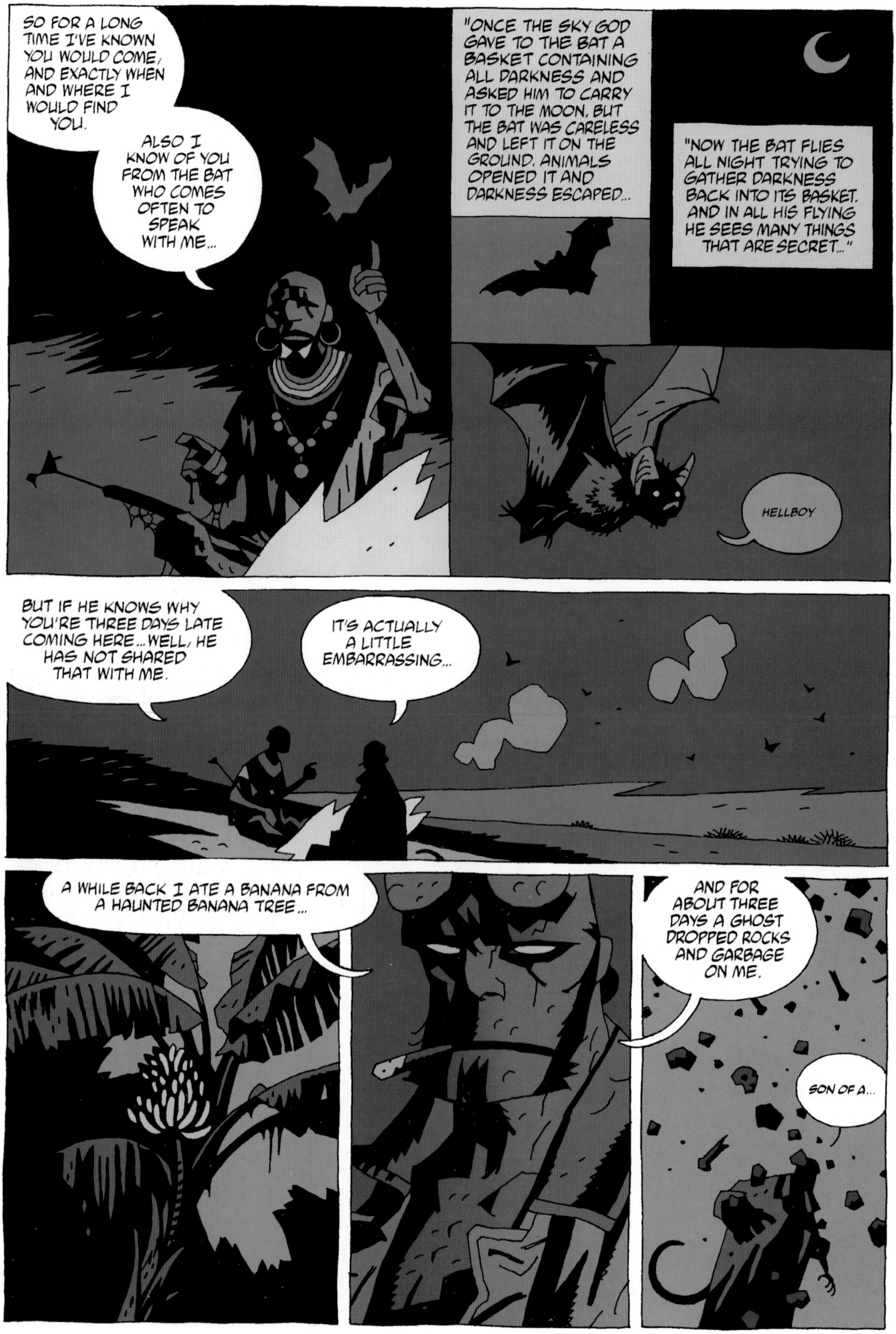

SO FOR A LONG TIME I'VE KNOWN YOU WOULD COME, AND EXACTLY WHEN AND WHERE I WOULD FIND YOU.
ALSO I KNOW OF YOU FROM THE BAT WHO COMES OFTEN TO SPEAK WITH ME...
"ONCE THE SKY GOD GAVE TO THE BAT A BASKET CONTAINING ALL DARKNESS AND ASKED HIM TO CARRY IT TO THE MOON, BUT THE BAT WAS CARELESS AND LEFT IT ON THE GROUND. ANIMALS OPENED IT AND DARKNESS ESCAPED...
"NOW THE BAT FLIES ALL NIGHT TRYING TO GATHER DARKNESS BACK INTO ITS BASKET. AND IN ALL HIS FLYING HE SEES MANY THINGS THAT ARE SECRET..."
HELLBOY
BUT IF HE KNOWS WHY YOU'RE THREE DAYS LATE COMING HERE...WELL, HE HAS NOT SHARED THAT WITH ME.
IT'S ACTUALLY A LITTLE EMBARRASSING...
A WHILE BACK I ATE A BANANA FROM A HAUNTED BANANA TREE...
AND FOR ABOUT THREE DAYS A GHOST DROPPED ROCKS AND GARBAGE ON ME.
SON OF A...

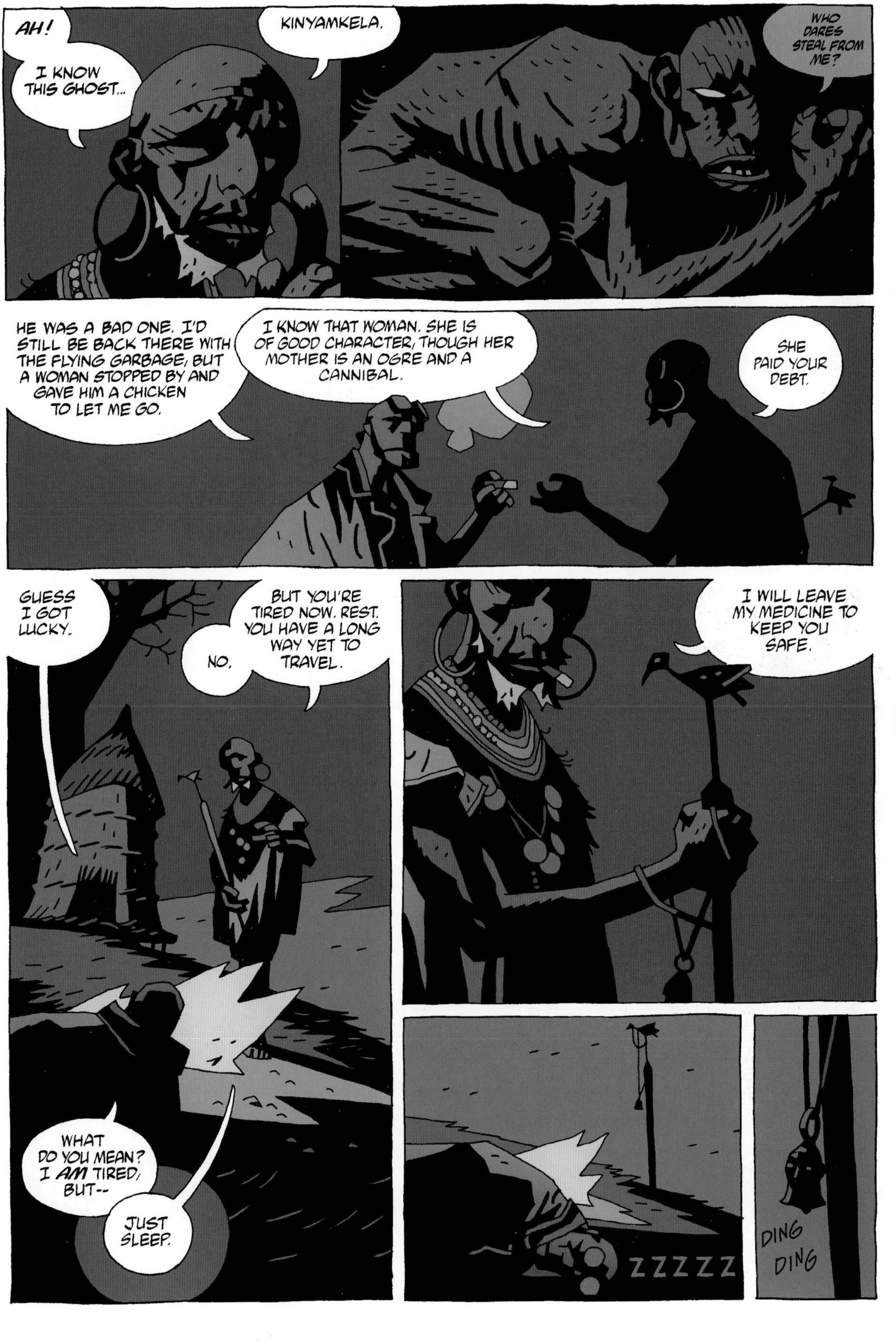

AH!
I KNOW THIS GHOST...
KINYAMKELA.
WHO DARES STEAL FROM ME?
HE WAS A BAD ONE. I'D STILL BE BACK THERE WITH THE FLYING GARBAGE, BUT A WOMAN STOPPED BY AND GAVE HIM A CHICKEN TO LET ME GO.
I KNOW THAT WOMAN. SHE IS OF GOOD CHARACTER, THOUGH HER MOTHER IS AN OGRE AND A CANNIBAL.
SHE PAID YOUR DEBT.
GUESS I GOT LUCKY.
NO.
BUT YOU'RE TIRED NOW. REST. YOU HAVE A LONG WAY YET TO TRAVEL.
WHAT DO YOU MEAN? I AM TIRED, BUT--
JUST SLEEP.
I WILL LEAVE MY MEDICINE TO KEEP YOU SAFE.
ZZZZZ
DING DING

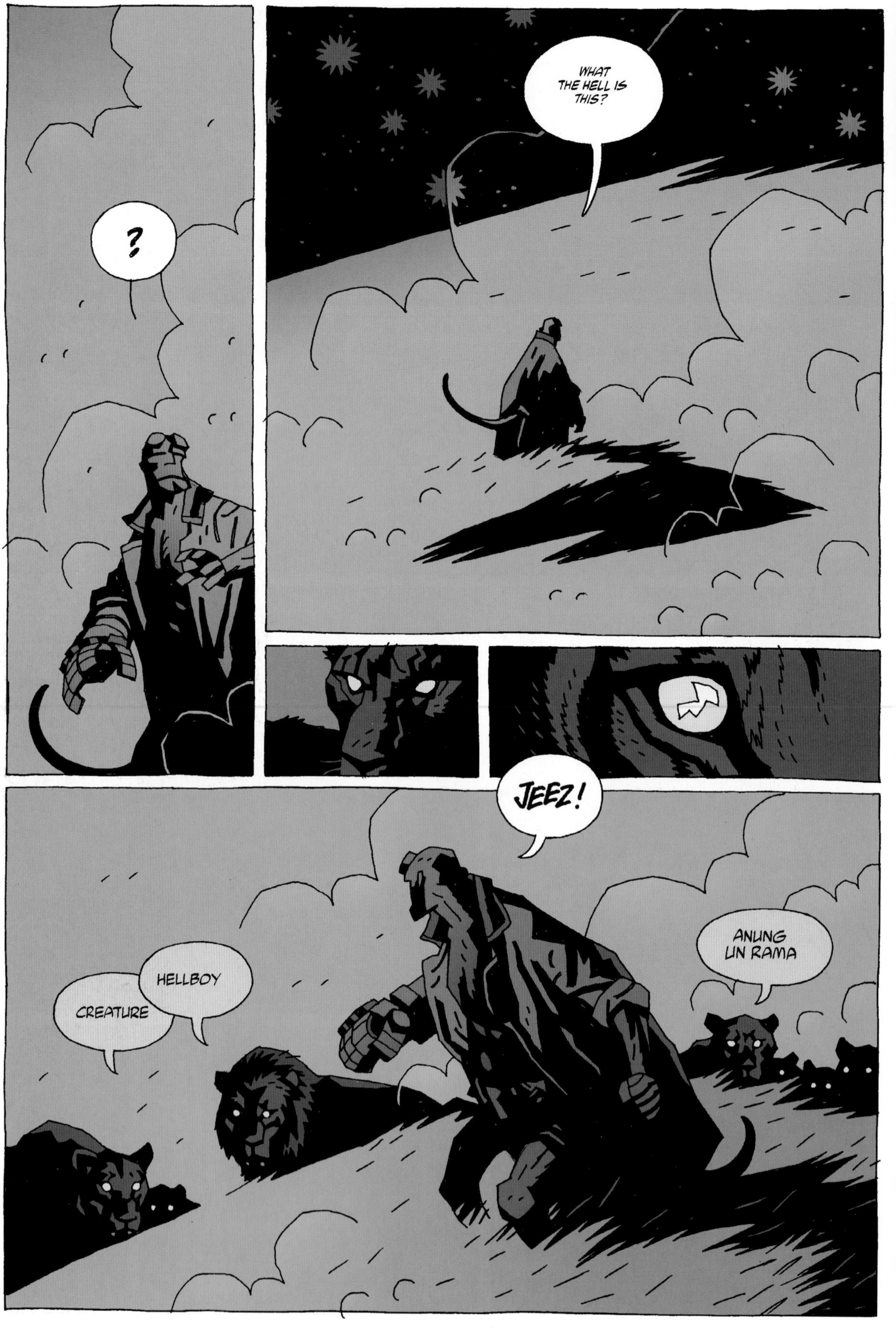
?
WHAT THE HELL IS THIS?
JEEZ!
HELLBOY
CREATURE
ANUNG UN RAMA

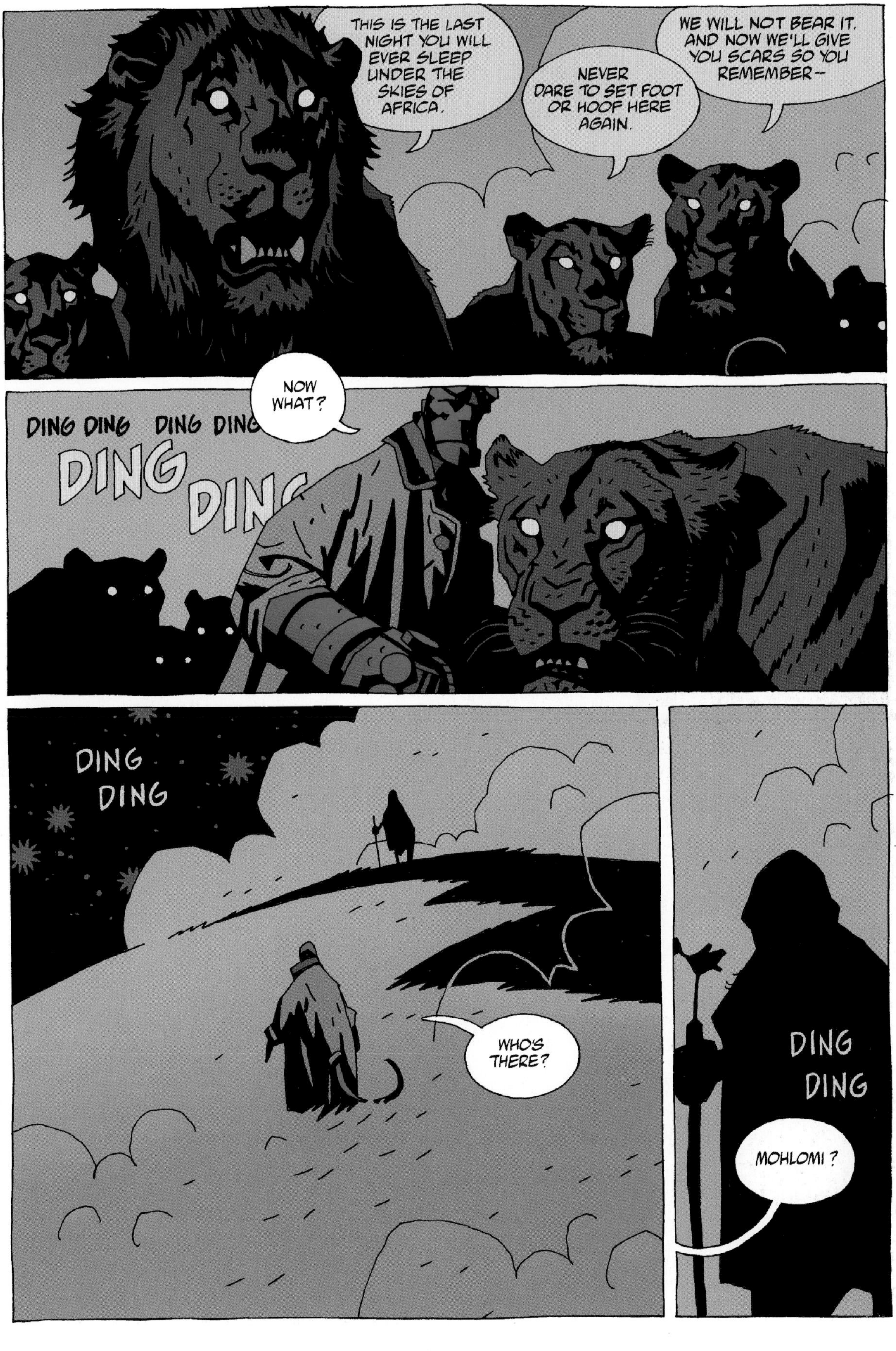
THIS IS THE LAST NIGHT YOU WILL EVER SLEEP UNDER THE SKIES OF AFRICA.
NEVER DARE TO SET FOOT OR HOOF HERE AGAIN.
WE WILL NOT BEAR IT. AND NOW WE'LL GIVE YOU SCARS SO YOU REMEMBER--
NOW WHAT?
DING DING DING DING
DING DING
DING DING
WHO'S THERE?
DING DING
MOHLOMI?

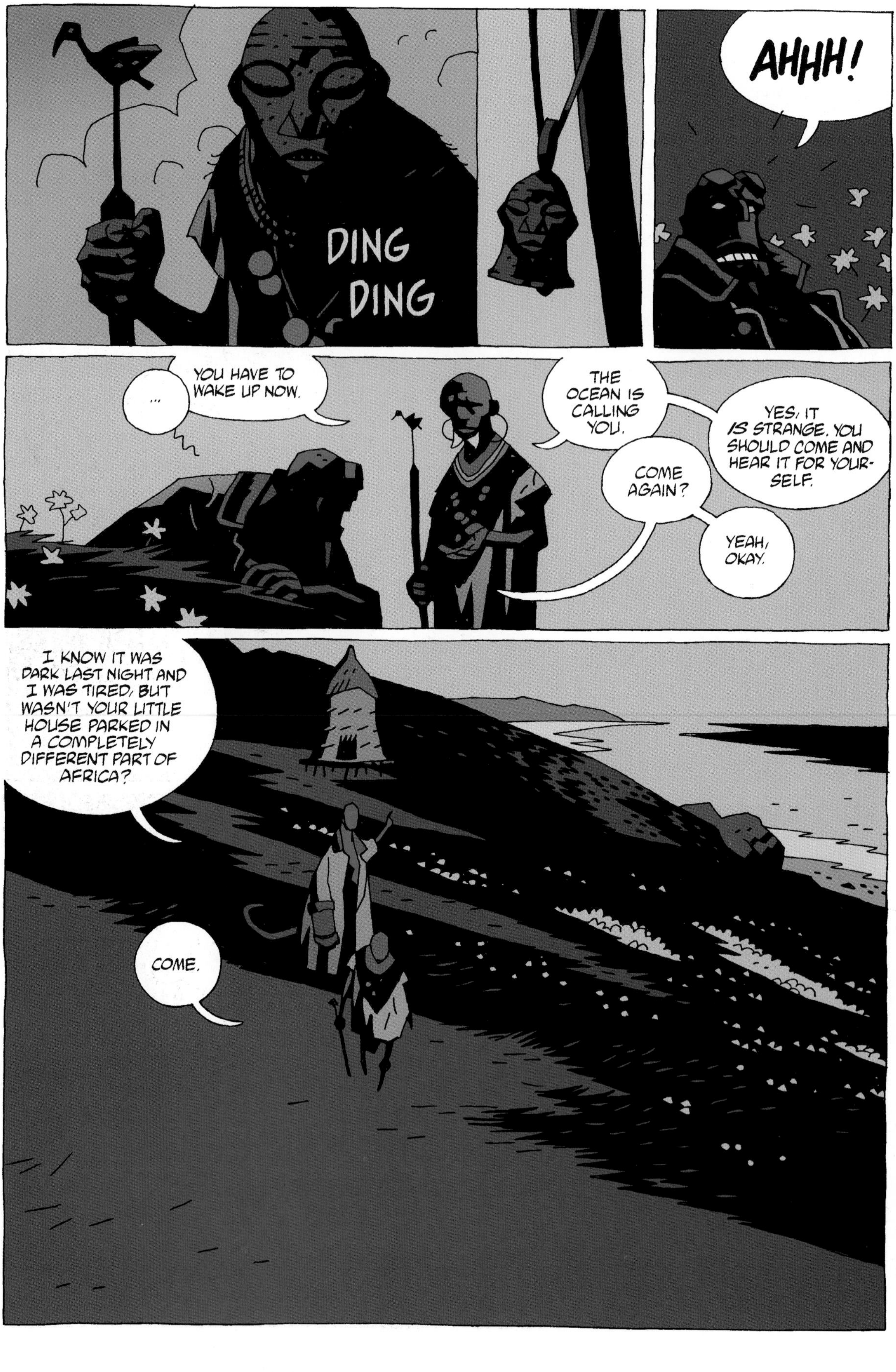
DING
DING
AHHH!
...
YOU HAVE TO WAKE UP NOW.
THE OCEAN IS CALLING YOU.
COME AGAIN?
YES, IT IS STRANGE. YOU SHOULD COME AND HEAR IT FOR YOUR-SELF.
YEAH, OKAY.
I KNOW IT WAS DARK LAST NIGHT AND I WAS TIRED, BUT WASN'T YOUR LITTLE HOUSE PARKED IN A COMPLETELY DIFFERENT PART OF AFRICA?
COME.

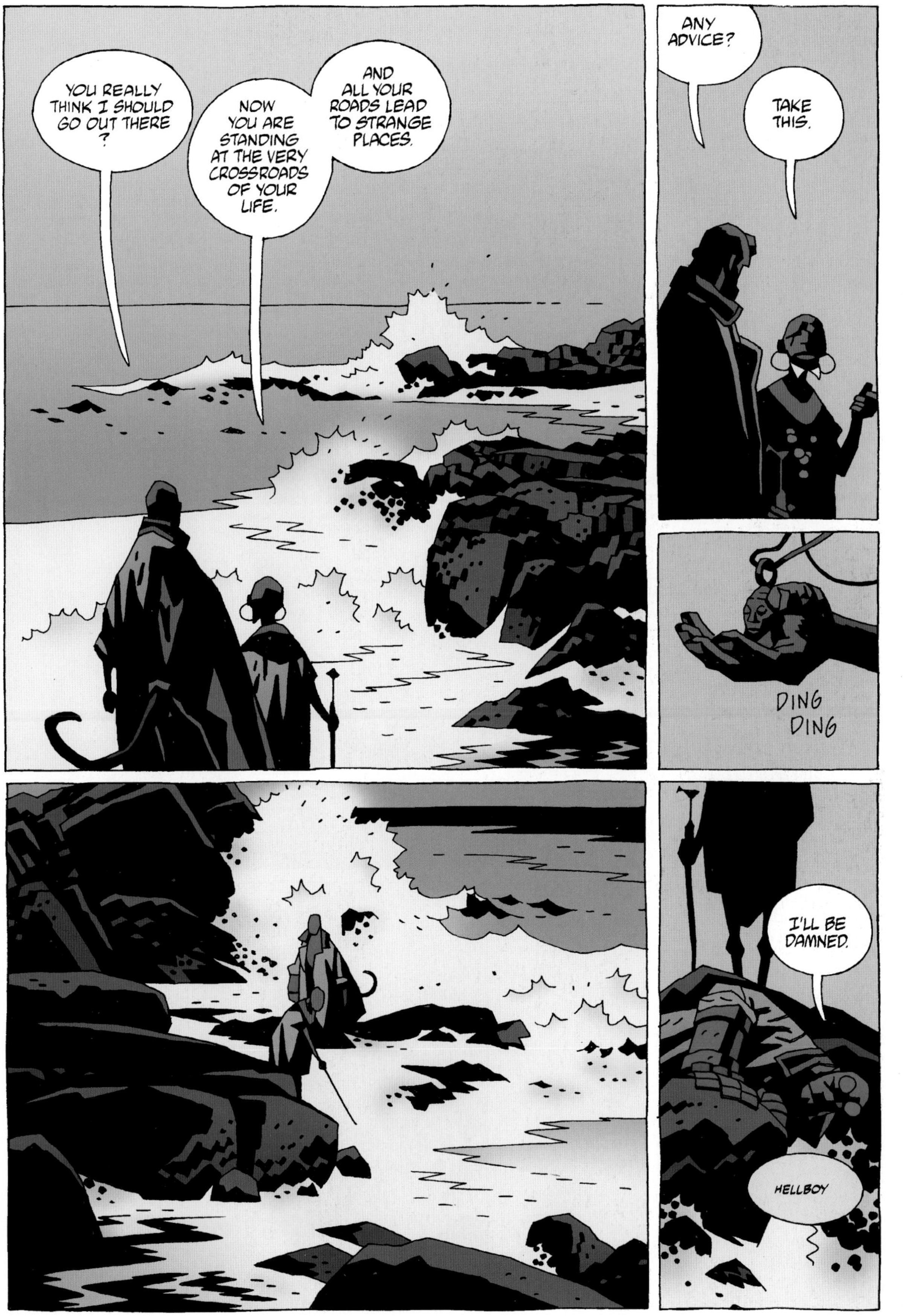
YOU REALLY THINK I SHOULD GO OUT THERE ?
NOW YOU ARE STANDING AT THE VERY CROSSROADS OF YOUR LIFE.
AND ALL YOUR ROADS LEAD TO STRANGE PLACES.
ANY ADVICE?
TAKE THIS.
DING DING
I'LL BE DAMNED.
HELLBOY

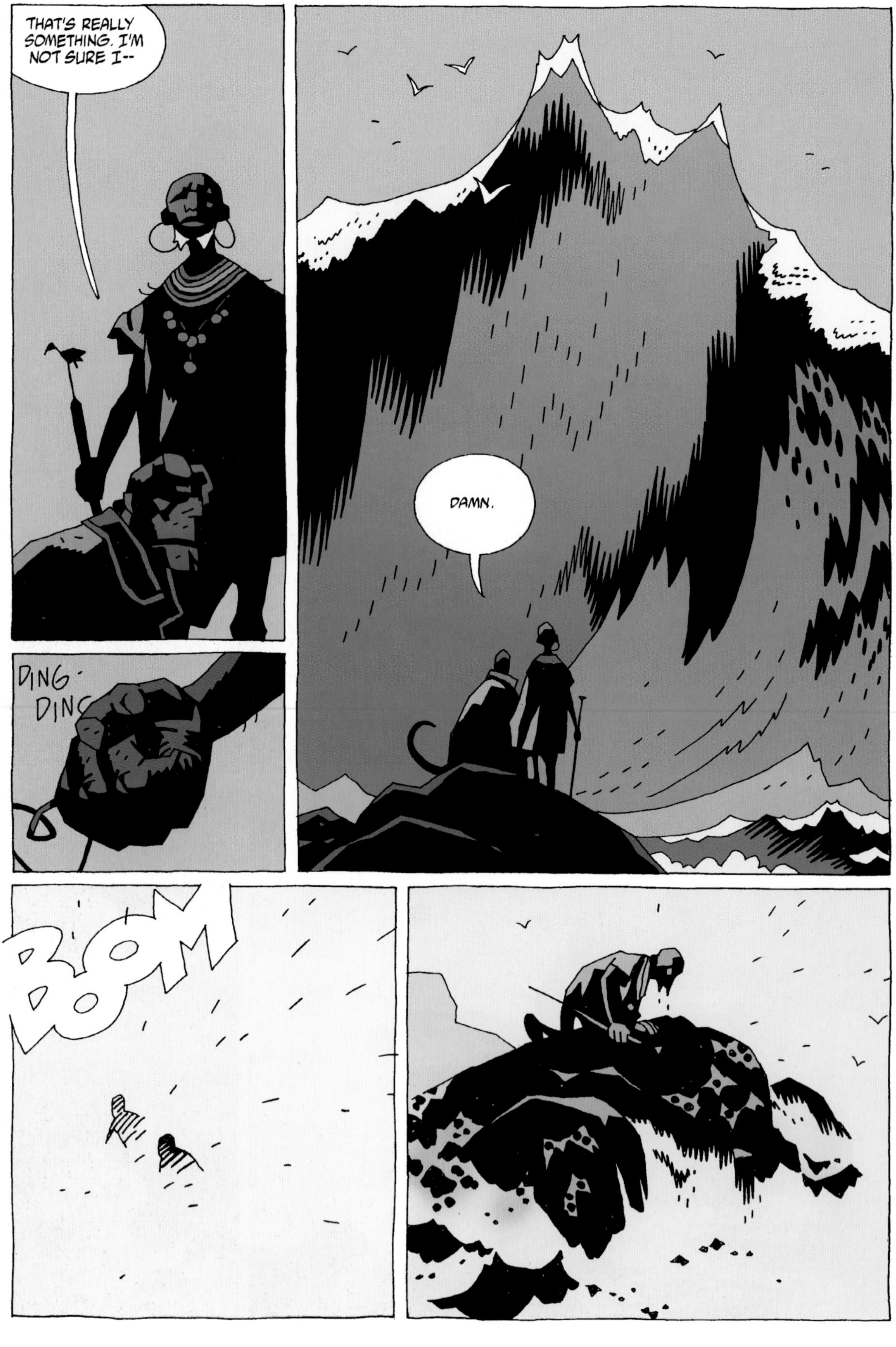

THAT'S REALLY SOMETHING. I'M NOT SURE I--
DAMN.
DING-DING
BOOM

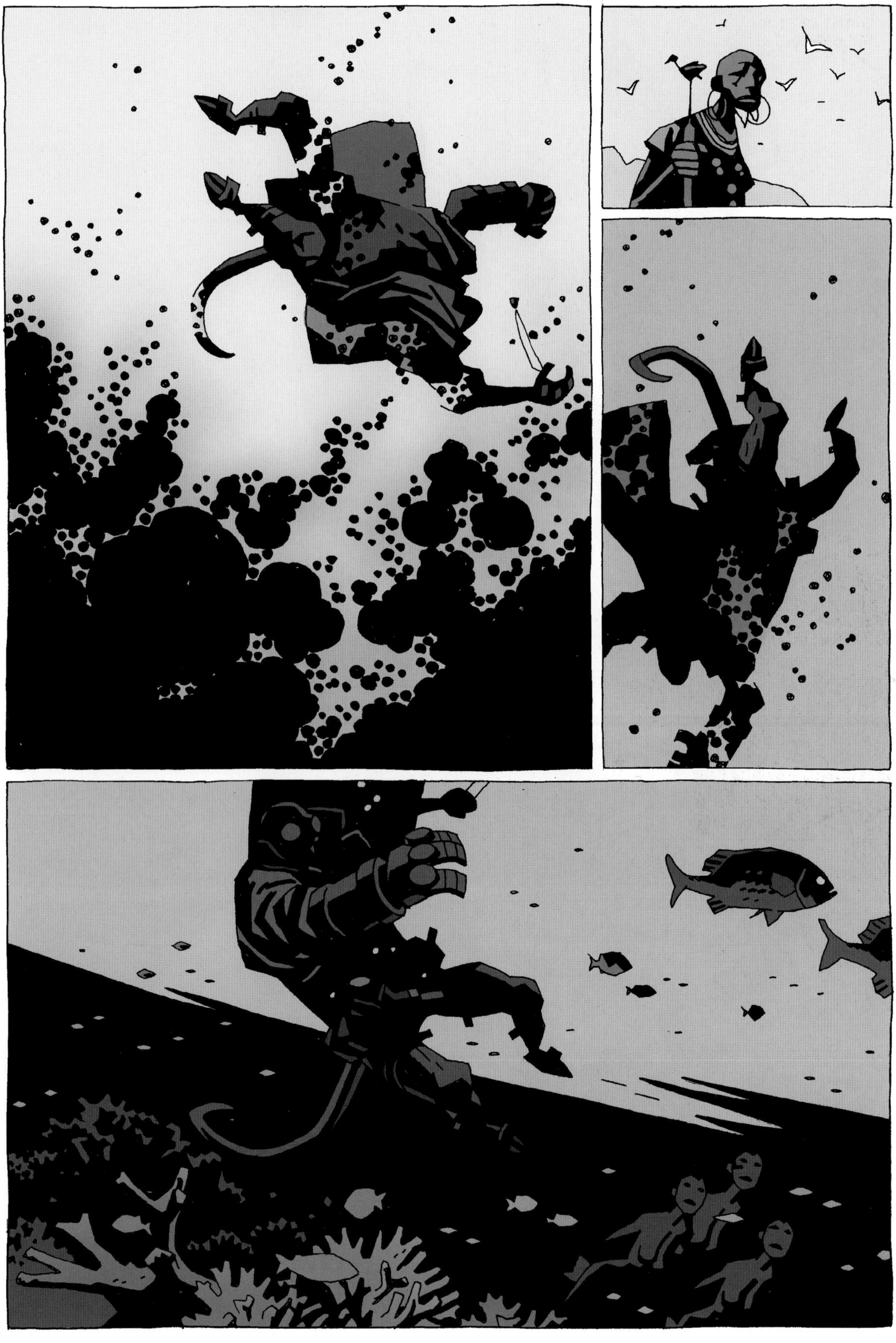

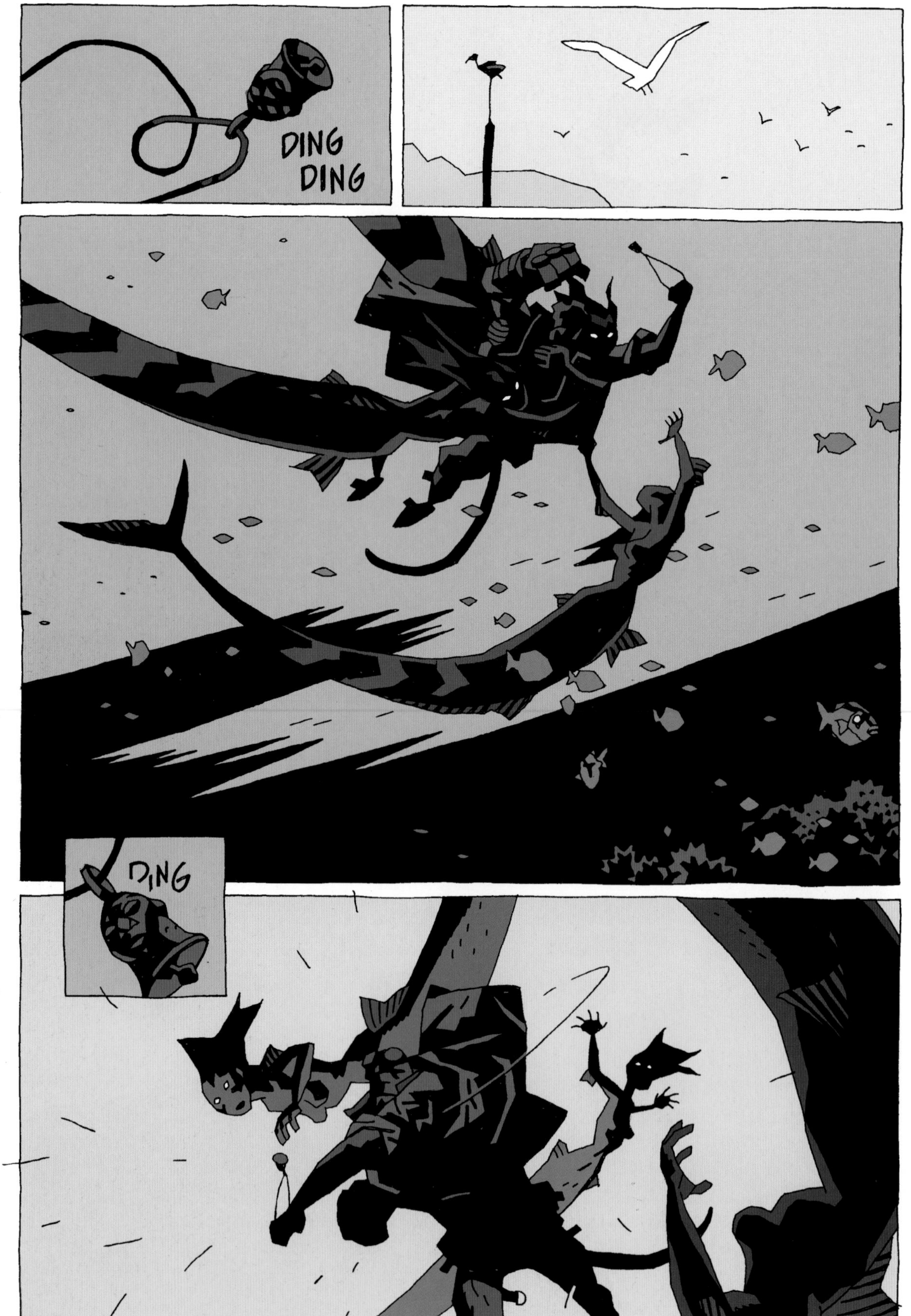
DING
DING
DING

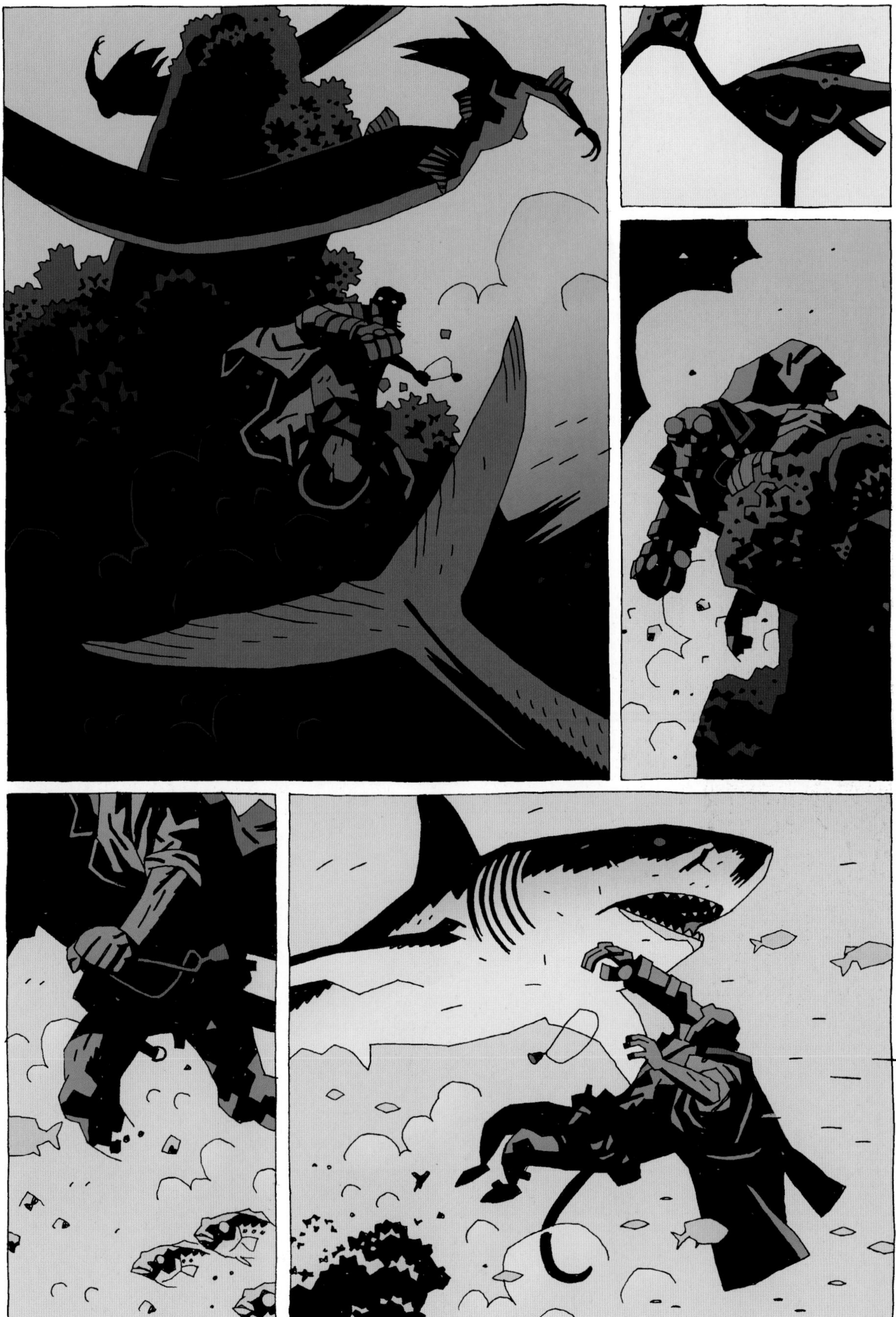

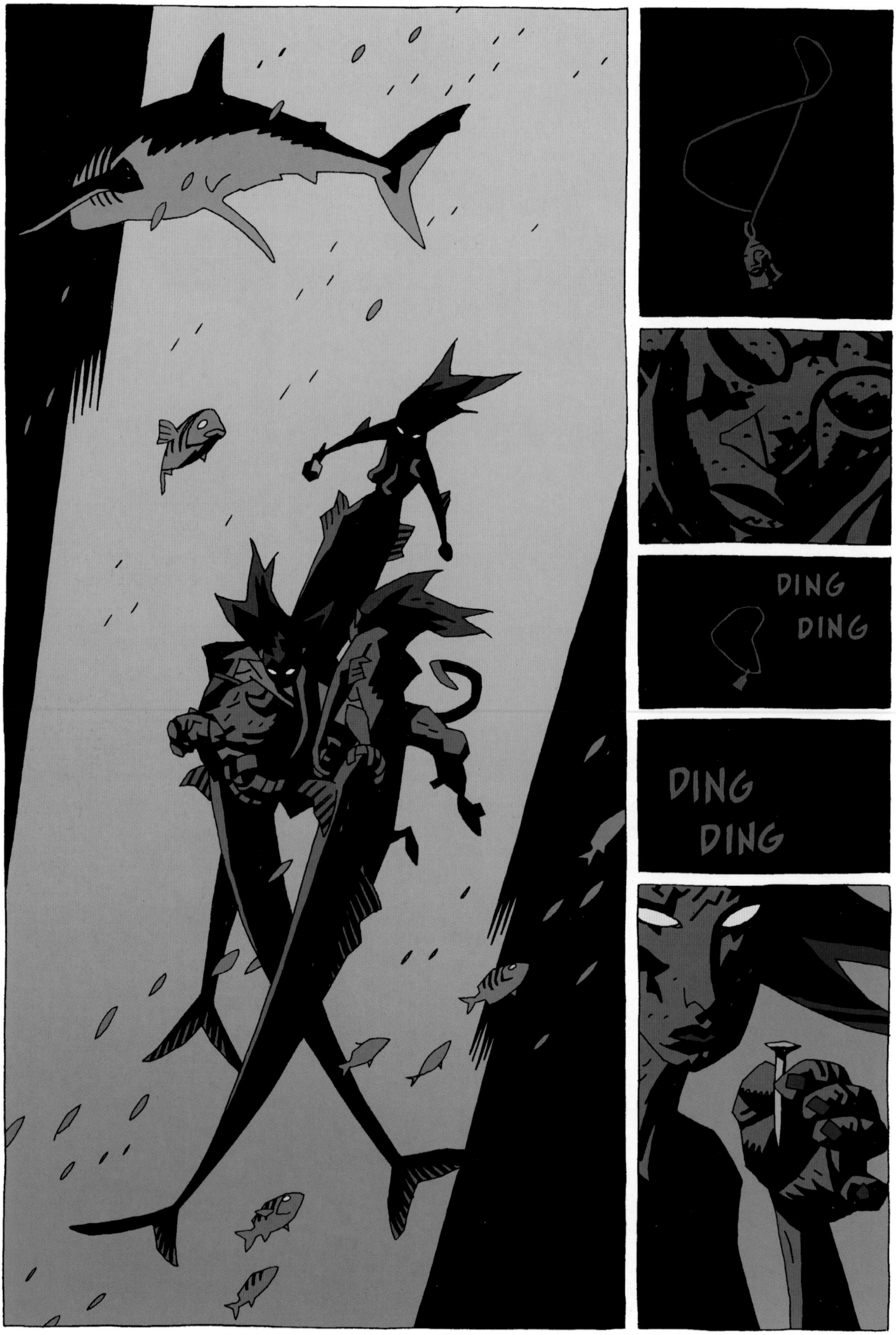
DING
DING
DING
DING

BRANG

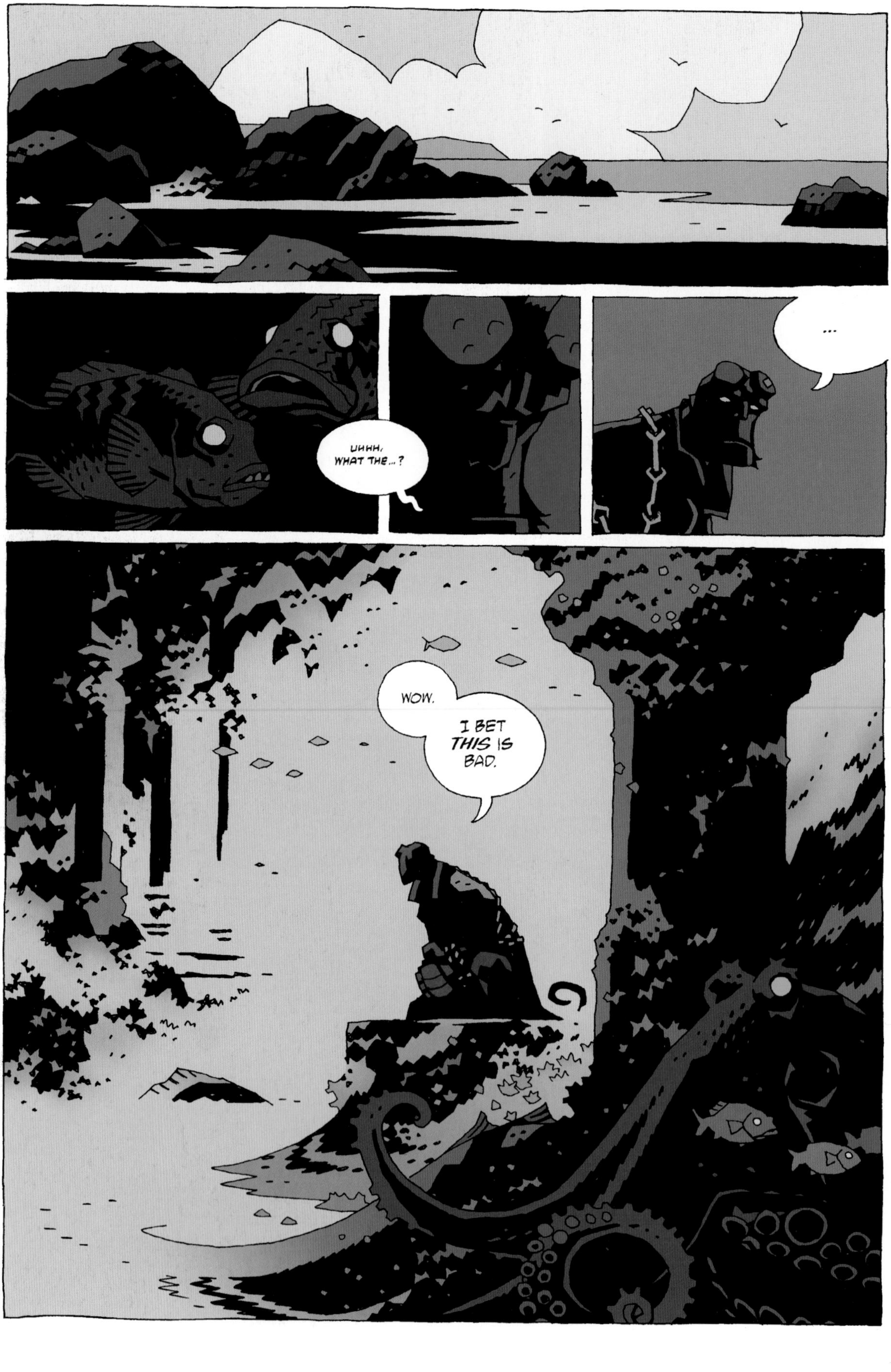
UHHH, WHAT THE...?
...
WOW.
I BET THIS IS BAD.

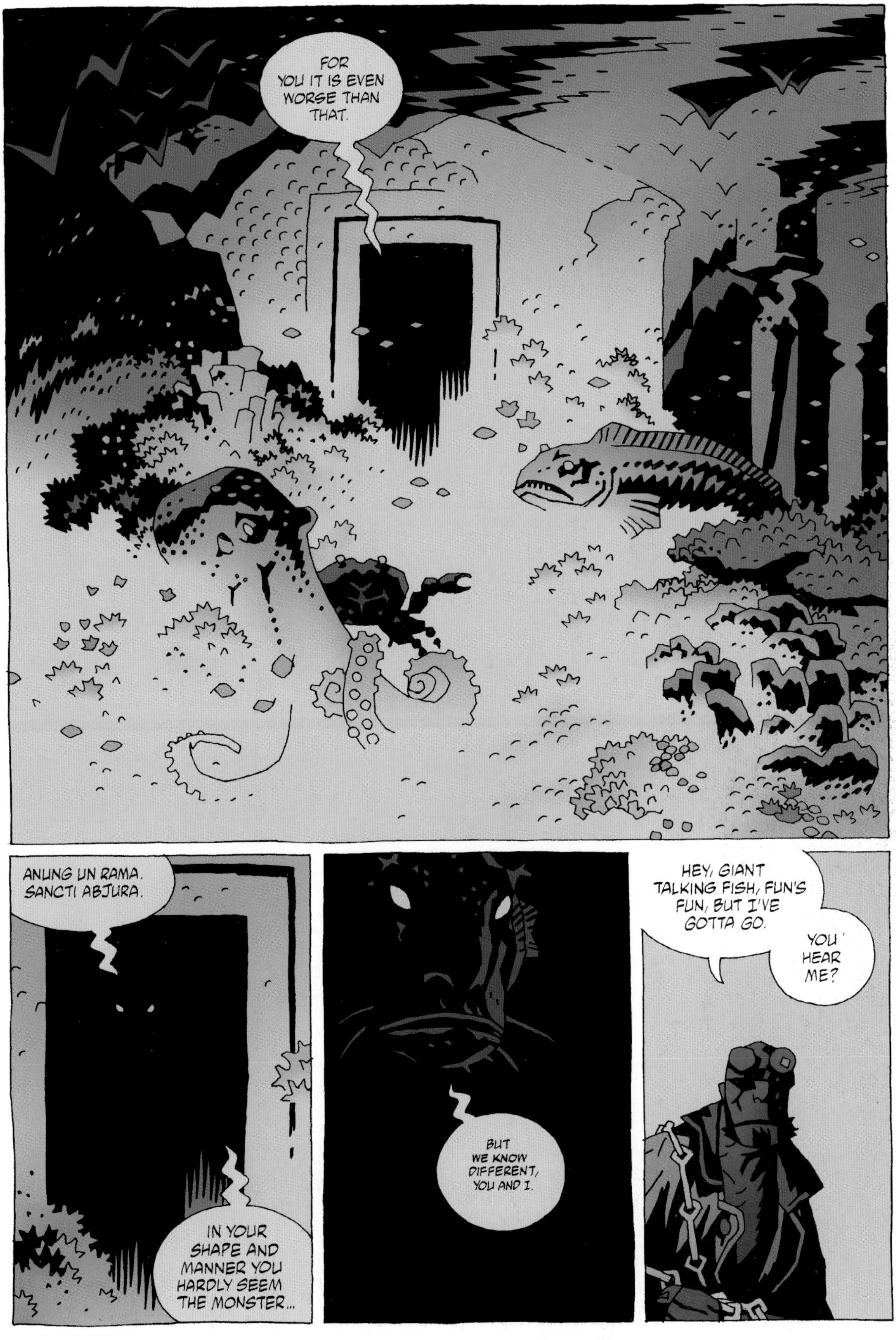
FOR YOU IT IS EVEN WORSE THAN THAT.
ANUNG UN RAMA. SANCTI ABJURA.
IN YOUR SHAPE AND MANNER YOU HARDLY SEEM THE MONSTER...
BUT WE KNOW DIFFERENT, YOU AND I.
HEY, GIANT TALKING FISH, FUN'S FUN, BUT I'VE GOTTA GO.
YOU HEAR ME?

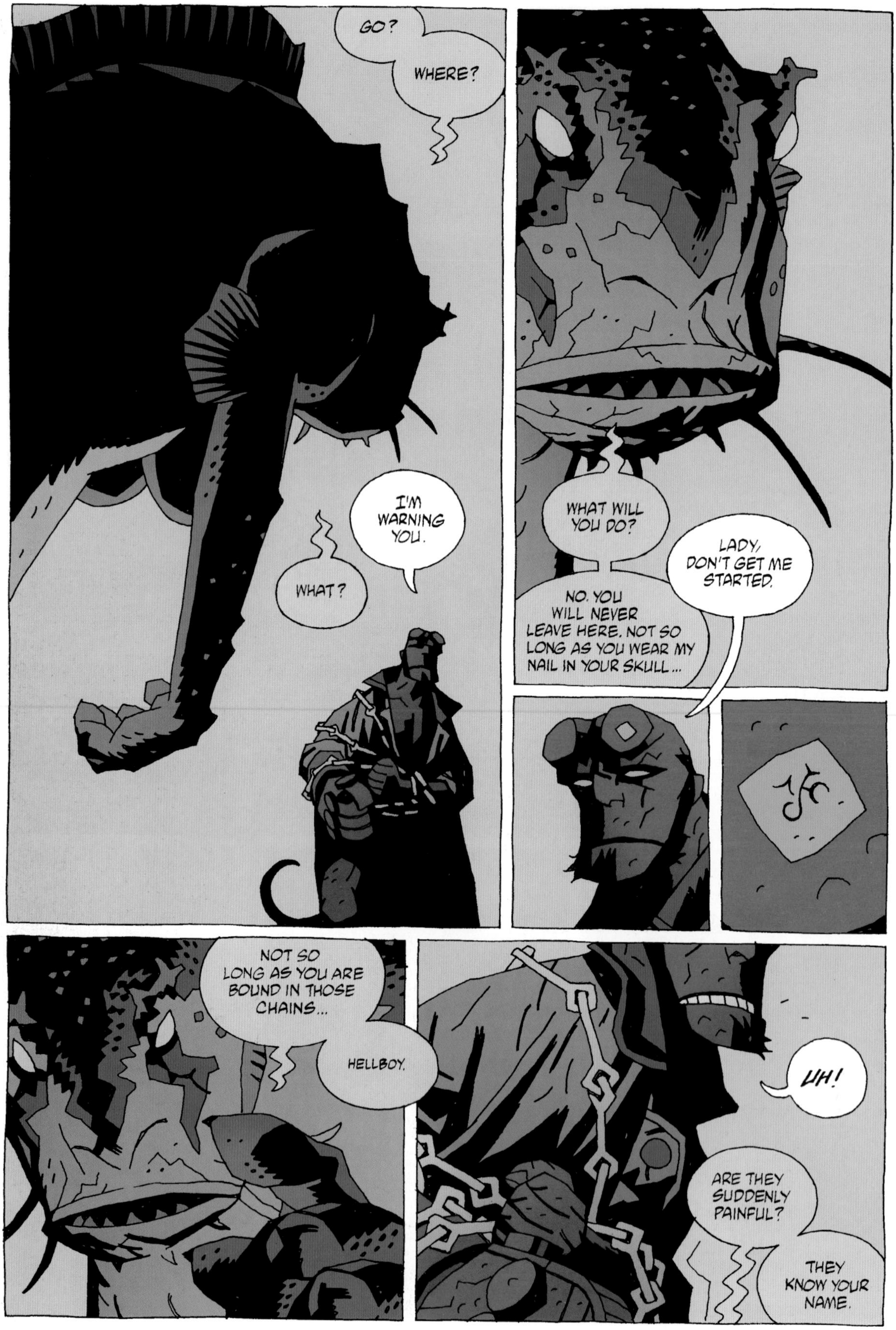
GO?
WHERE?
I'M WARNING YOU.
WHAT?
WHAT WILL YOU DO?
NO. YOU WILL NEVER LEAVE HERE. NOT SO LONG AS YOU WEAR MY NAIL IN YOUR SKULL...
LADY, DON'T GET ME STARTED.
NOT SO LONG AS YOU ARE BOUND IN THOSE CHAINS...
HELLBOY.
UH!
ARE THEY SUDDENLY PAINFUL?
THEY KNOW YOUR NAME.

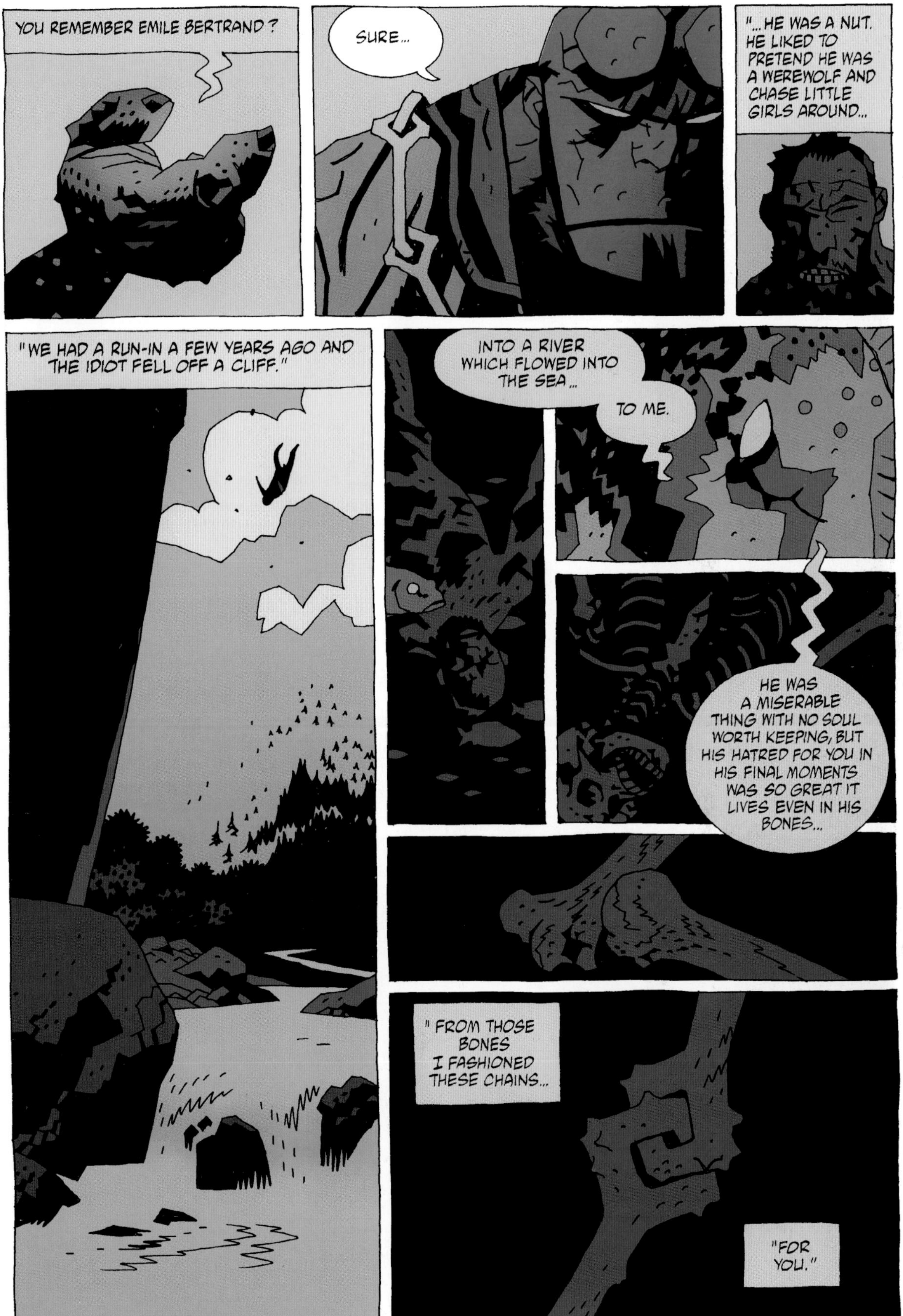
YOU REMEMBER EMILE BERTRAND?
SURE...
"...HE WAS A NUT. HE LIKED TO PRETEND HE WAS A WEREWOLF AND CHASE LITTLE GIRLS AROUND...
"WE HAD A RUN-IN A FEW YEARS AGO AND THE IDIOT FELL OFF A CLIFF."
INTO A RIVER WHICH FLOWED INTO THE SEA...
TO ME.
HE WAS A MISERABLE THING WITH NO SOUL WORTH KEEPING, BUT HIS HATRED FOR YOU IN HIS FINAL MOMENTS WAS SO GREAT IT LIVES EVEN IN HIS BONES...
" FROM THOSE BONES I FASHIONED THESE CHAINS...
"FOR YOU."

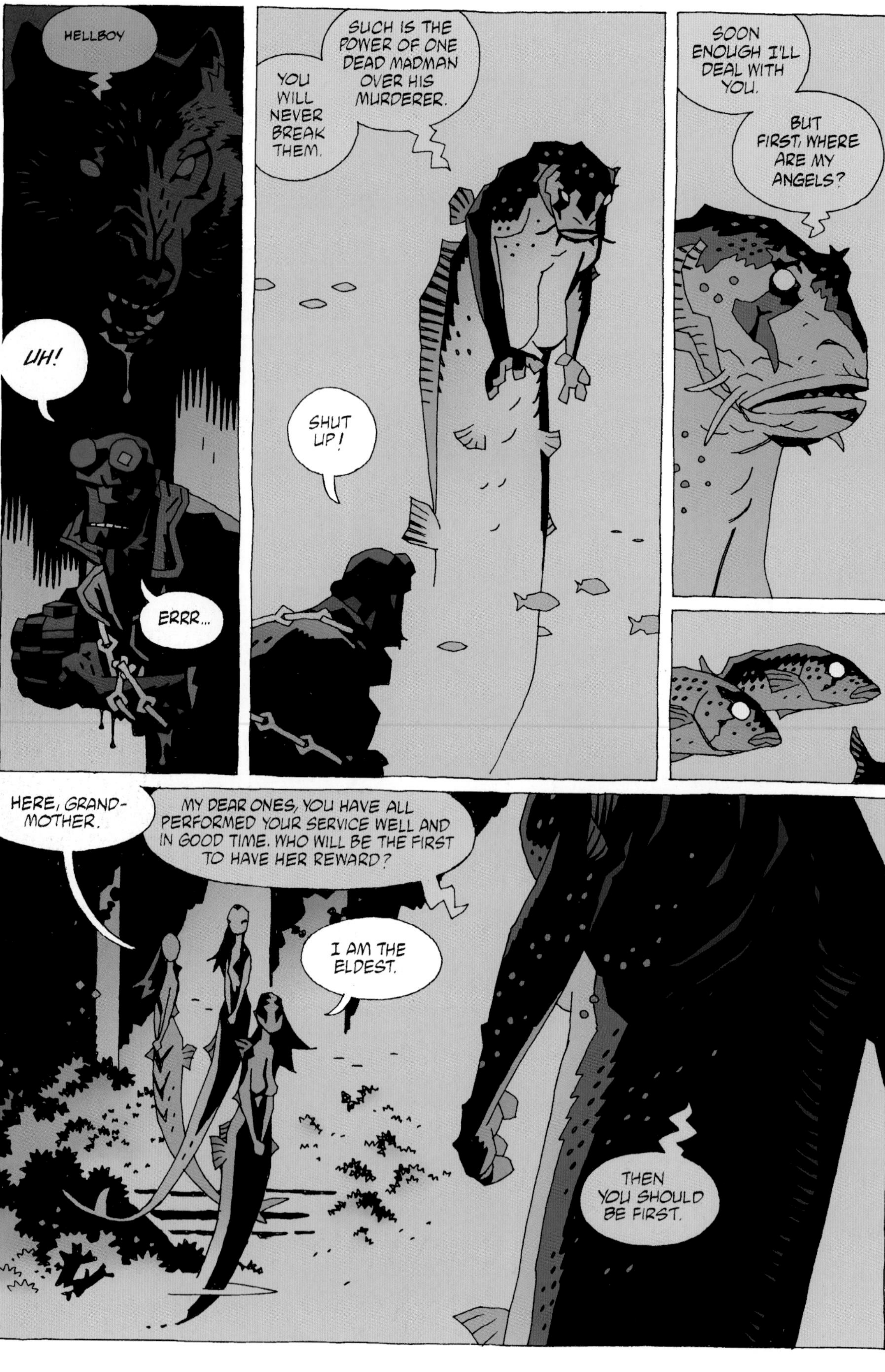
HELLBOY
UH!
ERRR...
SUCH IS THE POWER OF ONE DEAD MADMAN OVER HIS MURDERER.
YOU WILL NEVER BREAK THEM.
SHUT UP!
SOON ENOUGH I'LL DEAL WITH YOU.
BUT FIRST, WHERE ARE MY ANGELS?
HERE, GRAND-MOTHER.
MY DEAR ONES, YOU HAVE ALL PERFORMED YOUR SERVICE WELL AND IN GOOD TIME. WHO WILL BE THE FIRST TO HAVE HER REWARD?
I AM THE ELDEST.
THEN YOU SHOULD BE FIRST.

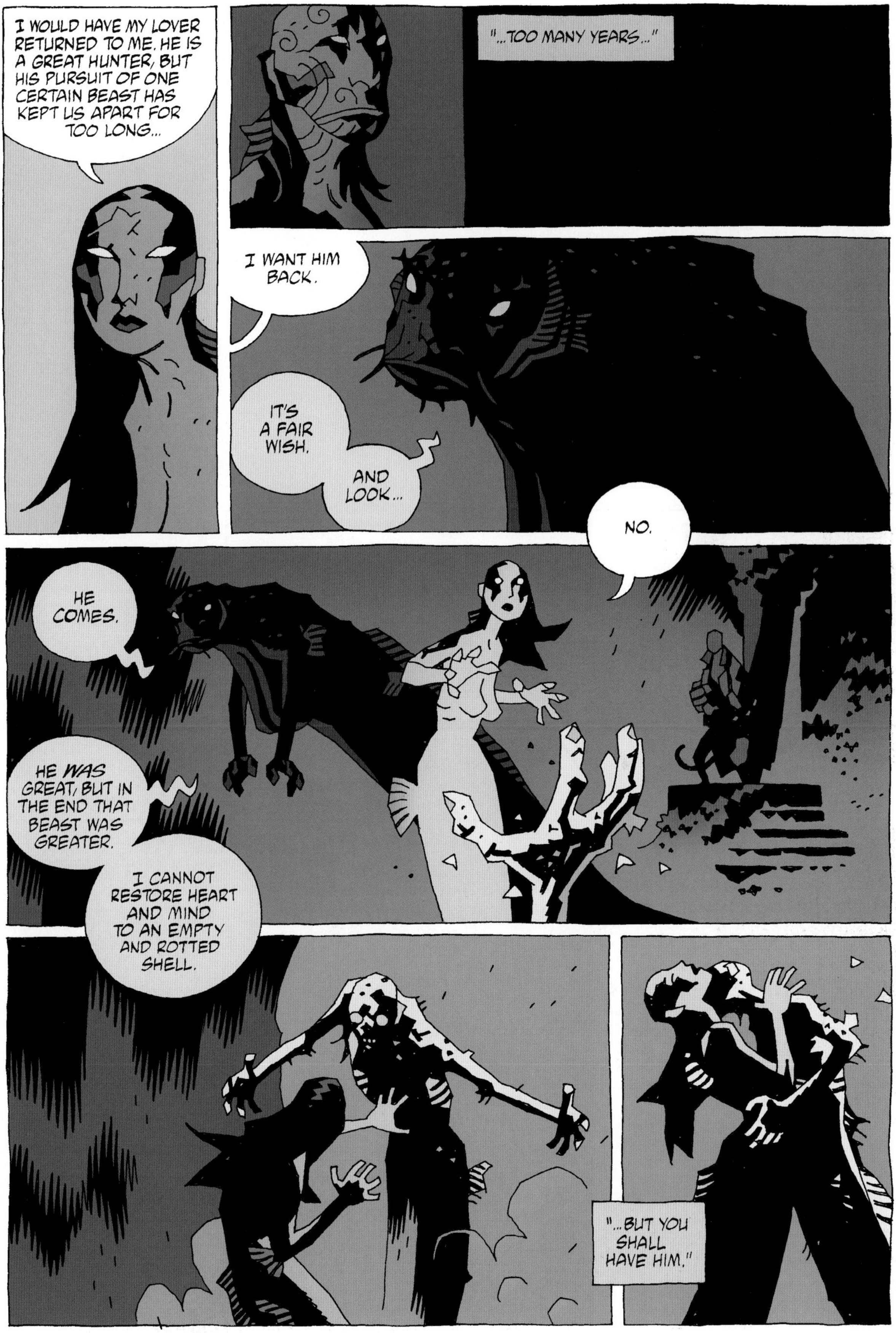
I WOULD HAVE MY LOVER RETURNED TO ME. HE IS A GREAT HUNTER, BUT HIS PURSUIT OF ONE CERTAIN BEAST HAS KEPT US APART FOR TOO LONG...
"...TOO MANY YEARS..."
I WANT HIM BACK.
IT'S A FAIR WISH.
AND LOOK...
HE COMES.
NO.
HE *WAS* GREAT, BUT IN THE END THAT BEAST WAS GREATER.
I CANNOT RESTORE HEART AND MIND TO AN EMPTY AND ROTTED SHELL.
"...BUT YOU SHALL HAVE HIM."

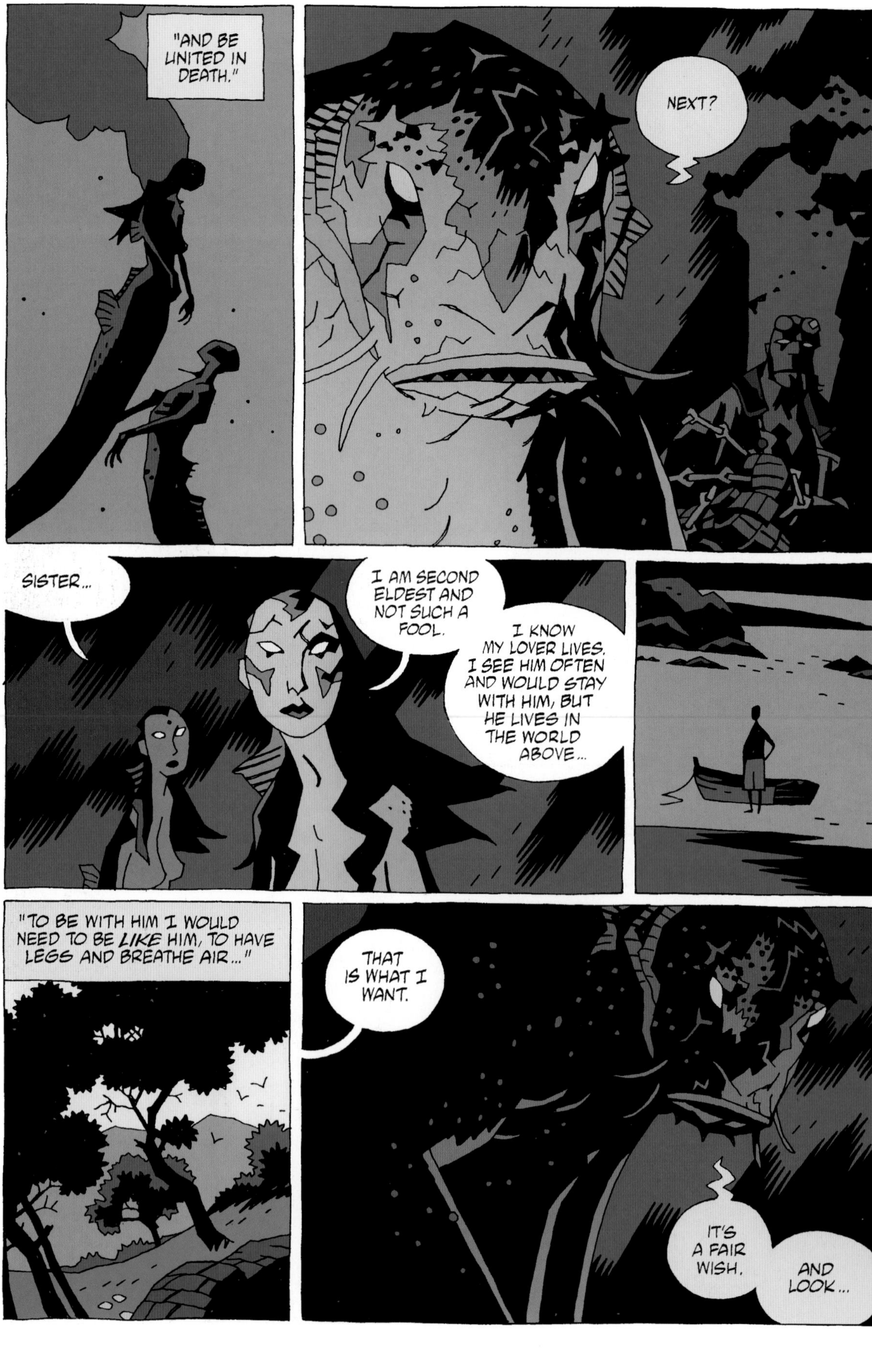
"AND BE UNITED IN DEATH."
NEXT?
SISTER...
I AM SECOND ELDEST AND NOT SUCH A FOOL.
I KNOW MY LOVER LIVES. I SEE HIM OFTEN AND WOULD STAY WITH HIM, BUT HE LIVES IN THE WORLD ABOVE...
"TO BE WITH HIM I WOULD NEED TO BE *LIKE* HIM, TO HAVE LEGS AND BREATHE AIR..."
THAT IS WHAT I WANT.
IT'S A FAIR WISH.
AND LOOK...

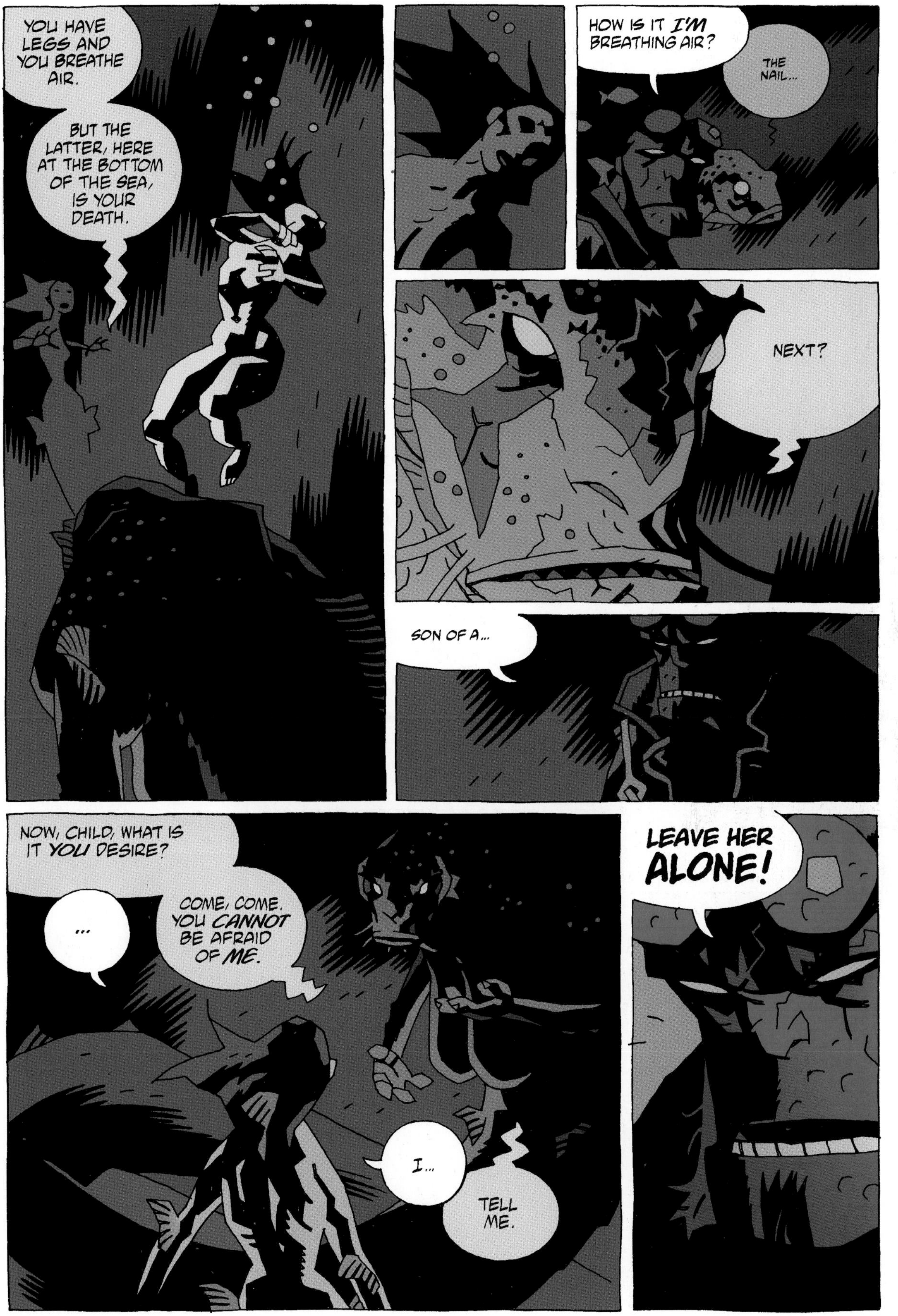
YOU HAVE LEGS AND YOU BREATHE AIR.
BUT THE LATTER, HERE AT THE BOTTOM OF THE SEA, IS YOUR DEATH.
HOW IS IT I'M BREATHING AIR?
THE NAIL...
NEXT?
SON OF A...
NOW, CHILD, WHAT IS IT YOU DESIRE?
...
COME, COME. YOU CANNOT BE AFRAID OF ME.
I...
TELL ME.
LEAVE HER ALONE!

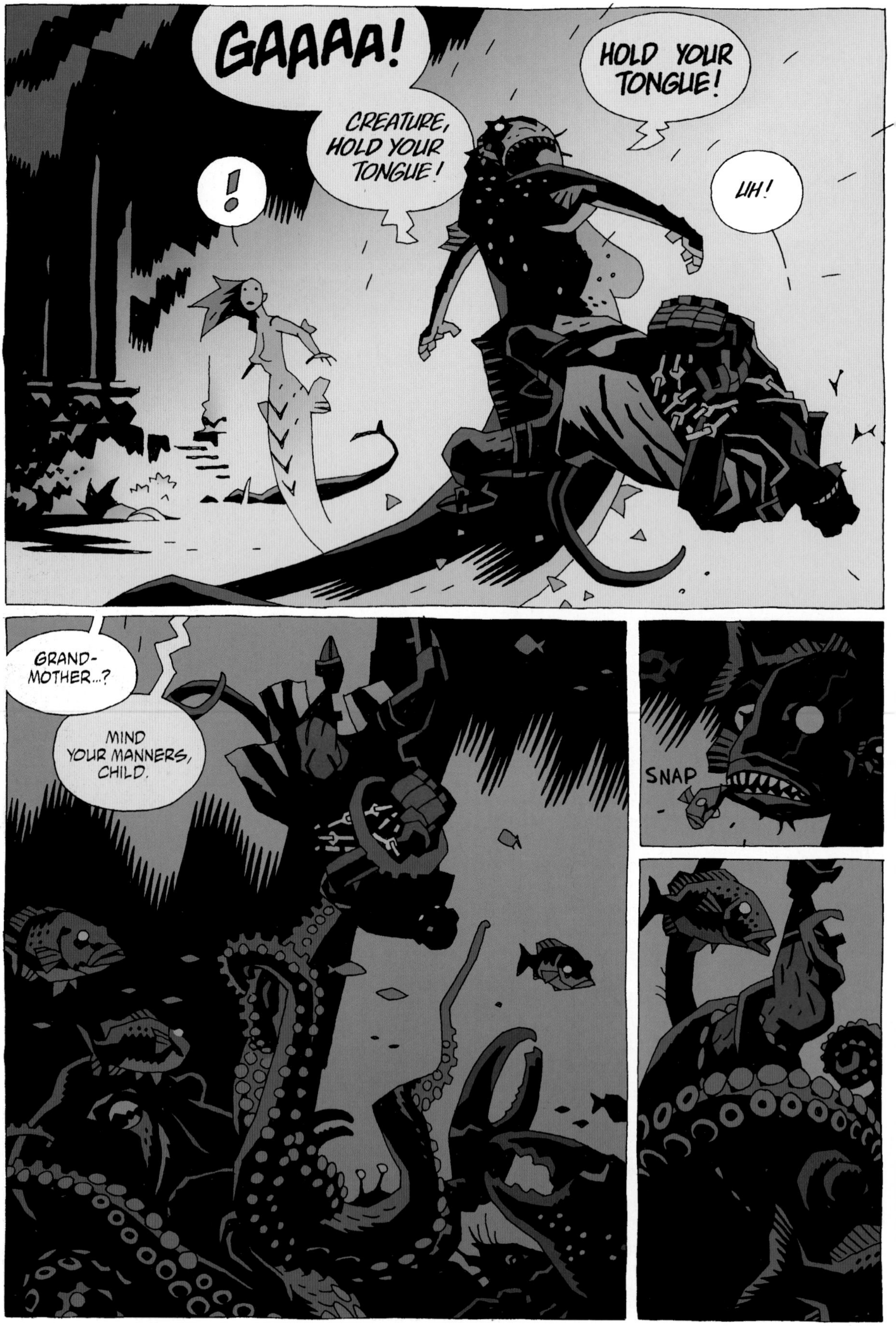
GAAAA!
CREATURE, HOLD YOUR TONGUE!
HOLD YOUR TONGUE!
!
UH!
GRAND-MOTHER...?
MIND YOUR MANNERS, CHILD.
SNAP

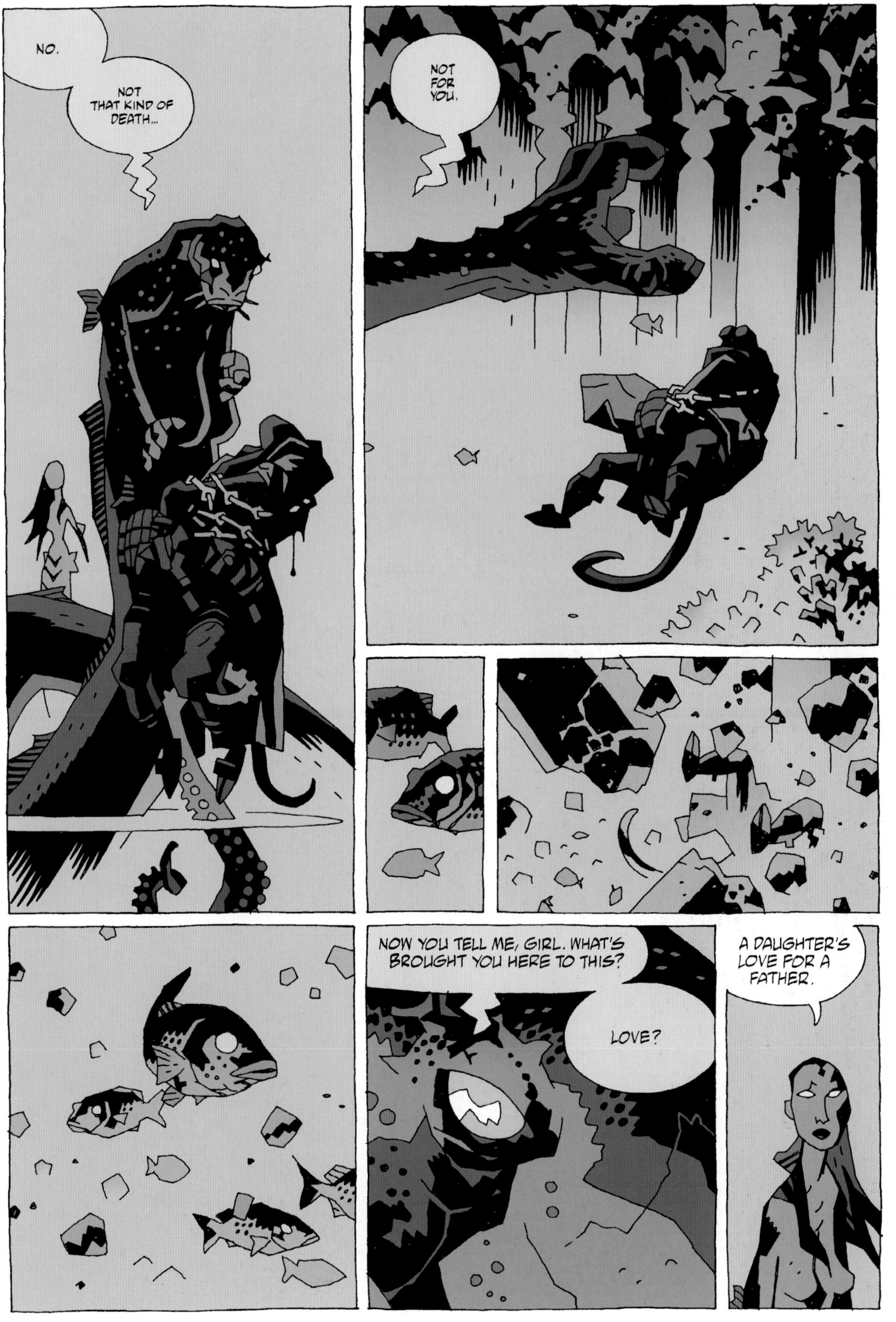
NO.
NOT THAT KIND OF DEATH...
NOT FOR YOU.
NOW YOU TELL ME, GIRL. WHAT'S BROUGHT YOU HERE TO THIS?
A DAUGHTER'S LOVE FOR A FATHER.
LOVE?

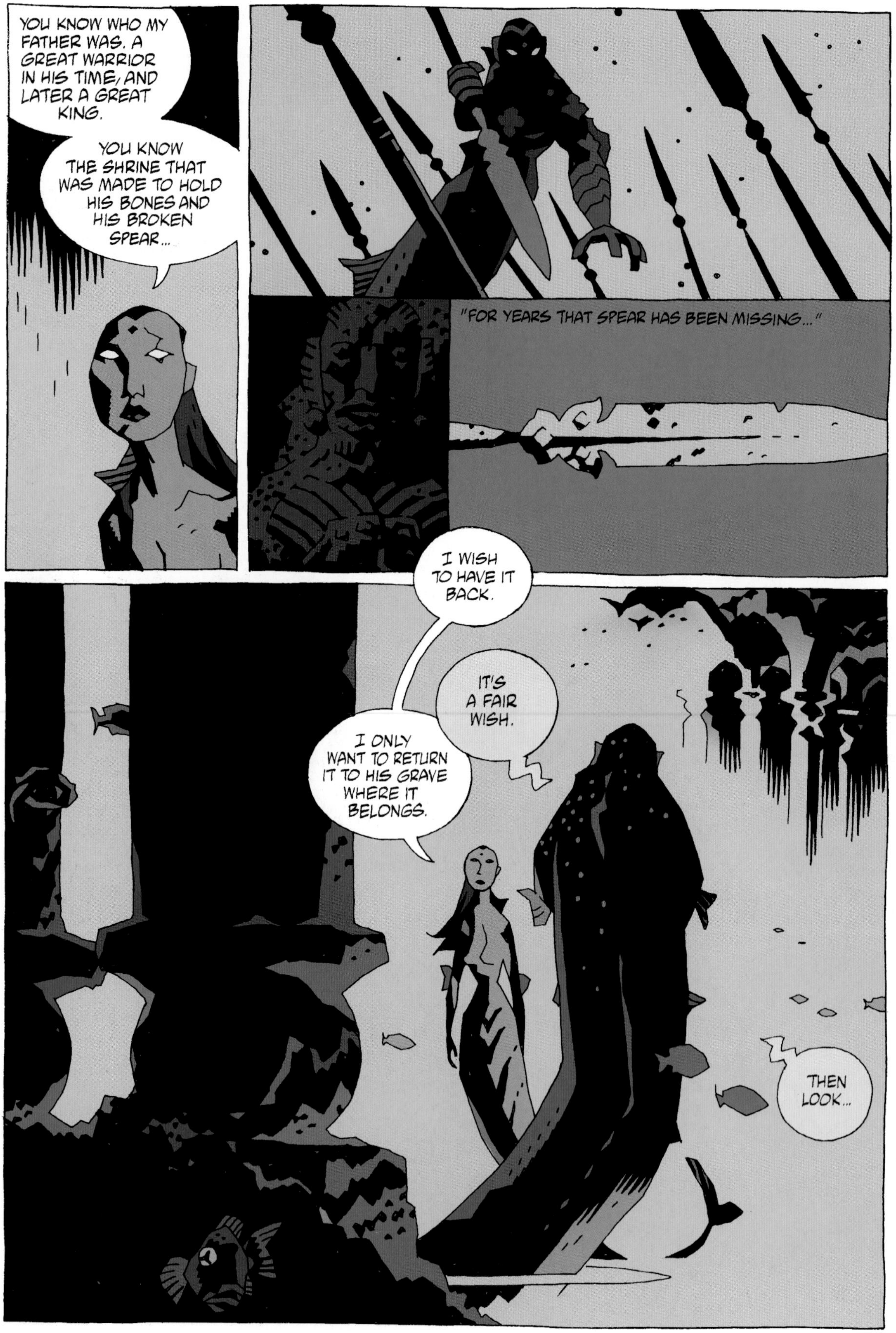
YOU KNOW WHO MY FATHER WAS. A GREAT WARRIOR IN HIS TIME, AND LATER A GREAT KING.
YOU KNOW THE SHRINE THAT WAS MADE TO HOLD HIS BONES AND HIS BROKEN SPEAR...
"FOR YEARS THAT SPEAR HAS BEEN MISSING..."
I WISH TO HAVE IT BACK.
I ONLY WANT TO RETURN IT TO HIS GRAVE WHERE IT BELONGS.
IT'S A FAIR WISH.
THEN LOOK...

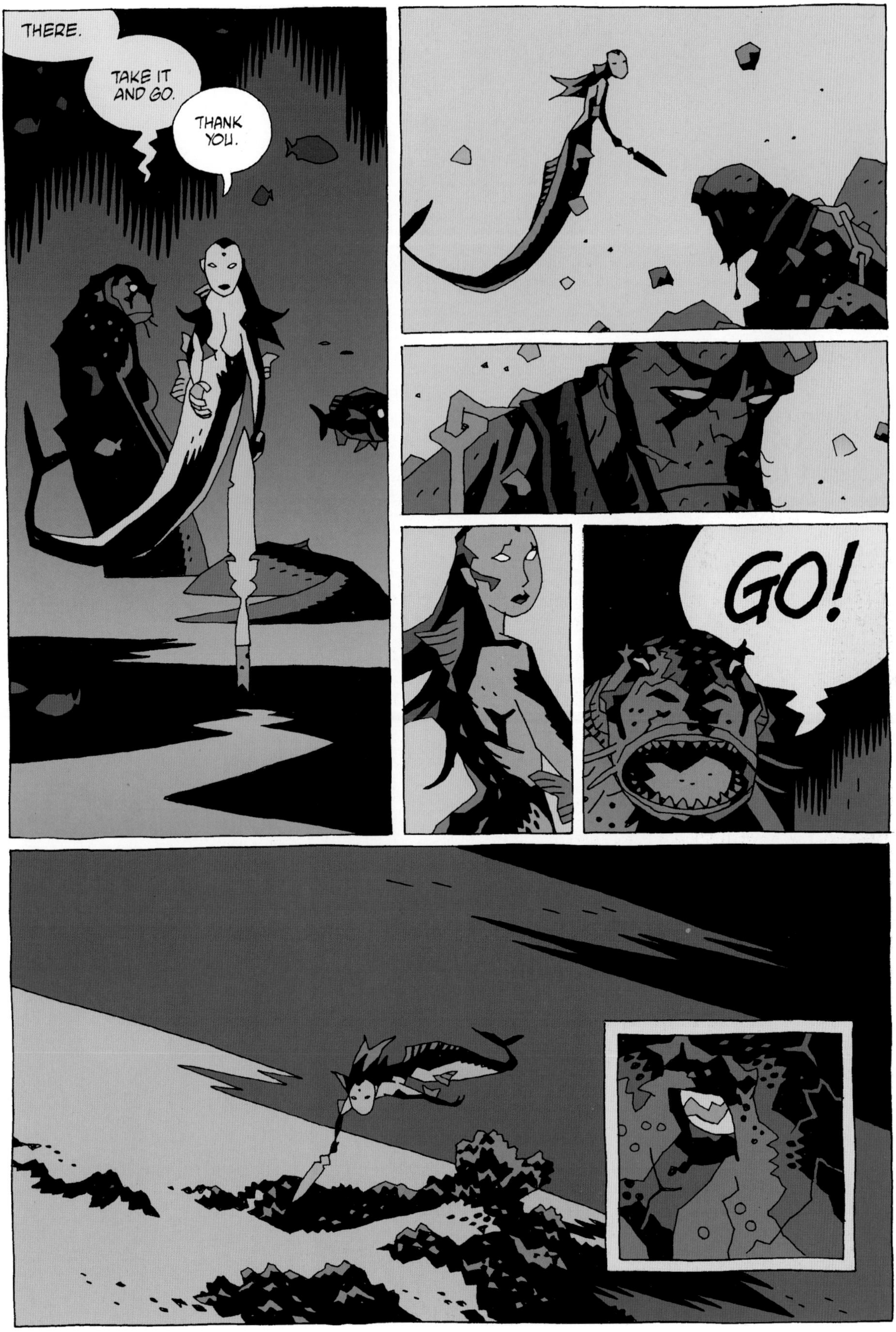
THERE.
TAKE IT AND GO.
THANK YOU.
GO!

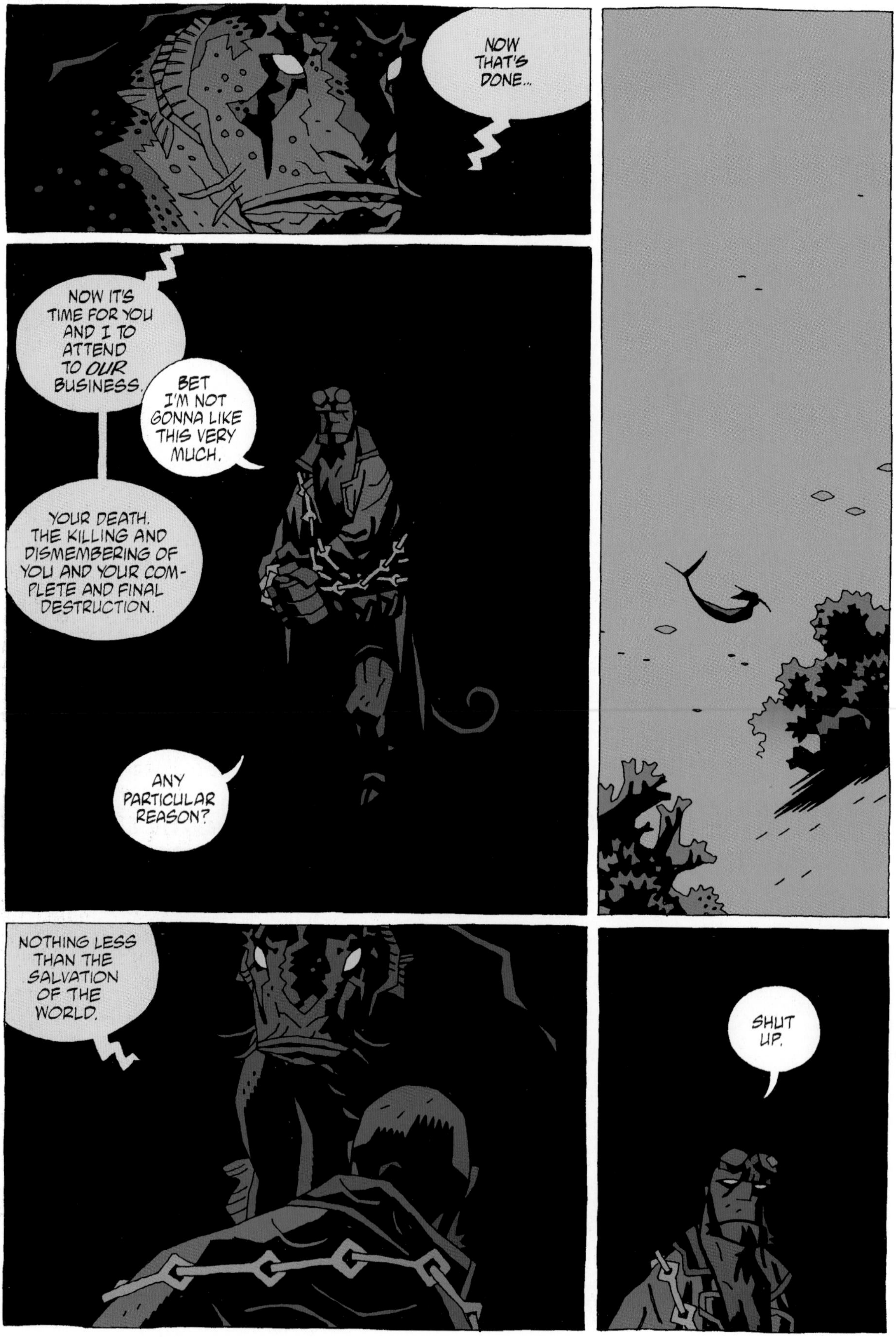
NOW THAT'S DONE...
NOW IT'S TIME FOR YOU AND I TO ATTEND TO OUR BUSINESS.
BET I'M NOT GONNA LIKE THIS VERY MUCH.
YOUR DEATH. THE KILLING AND DISMEMBERING OF YOU AND YOUR COMPLETE AND FINAL DESTRUCTION.
ANY PARTICULAR REASON?
NOTHING LESS THAN THE SALVATION OF THE WORLD.
SHUT UP.

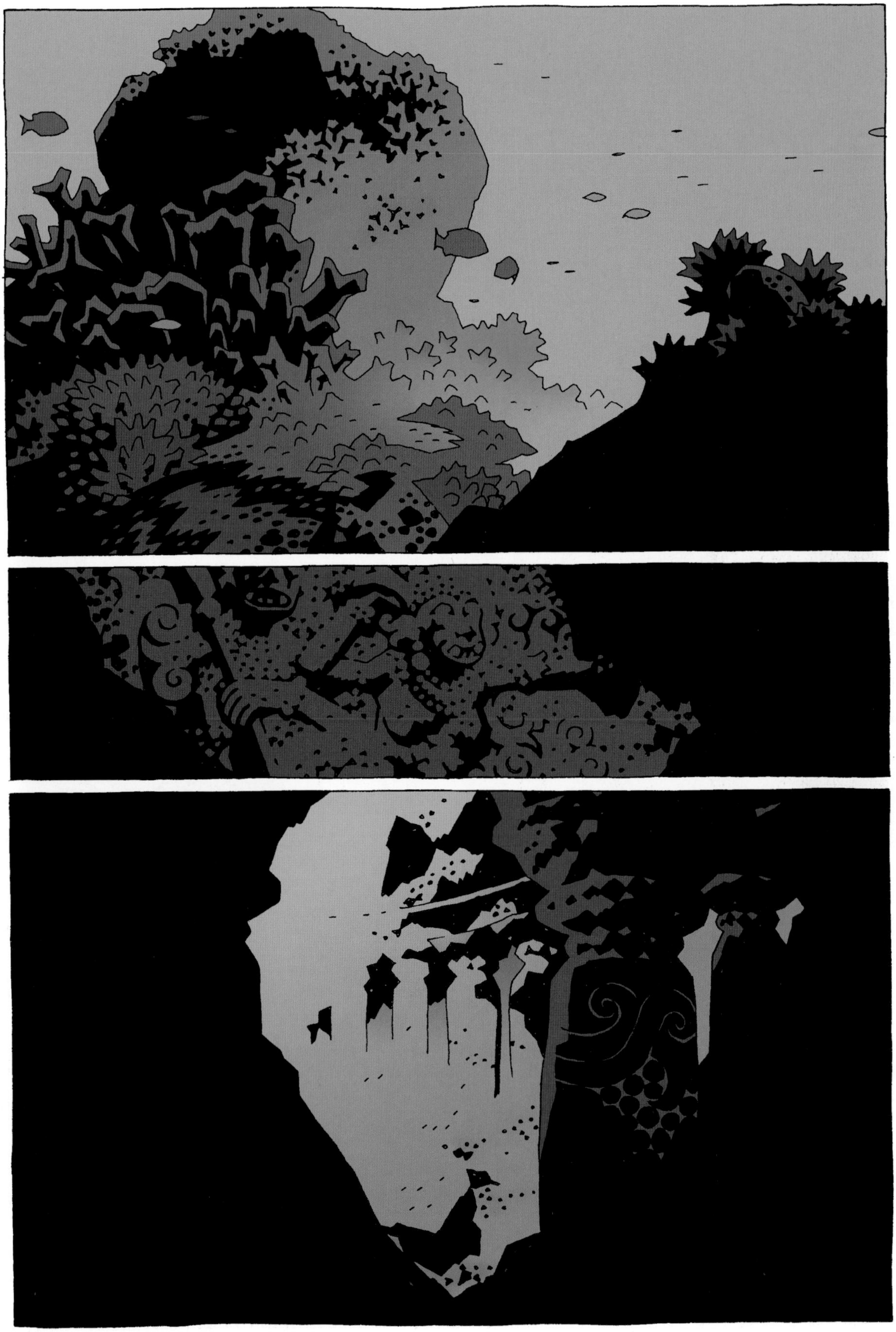

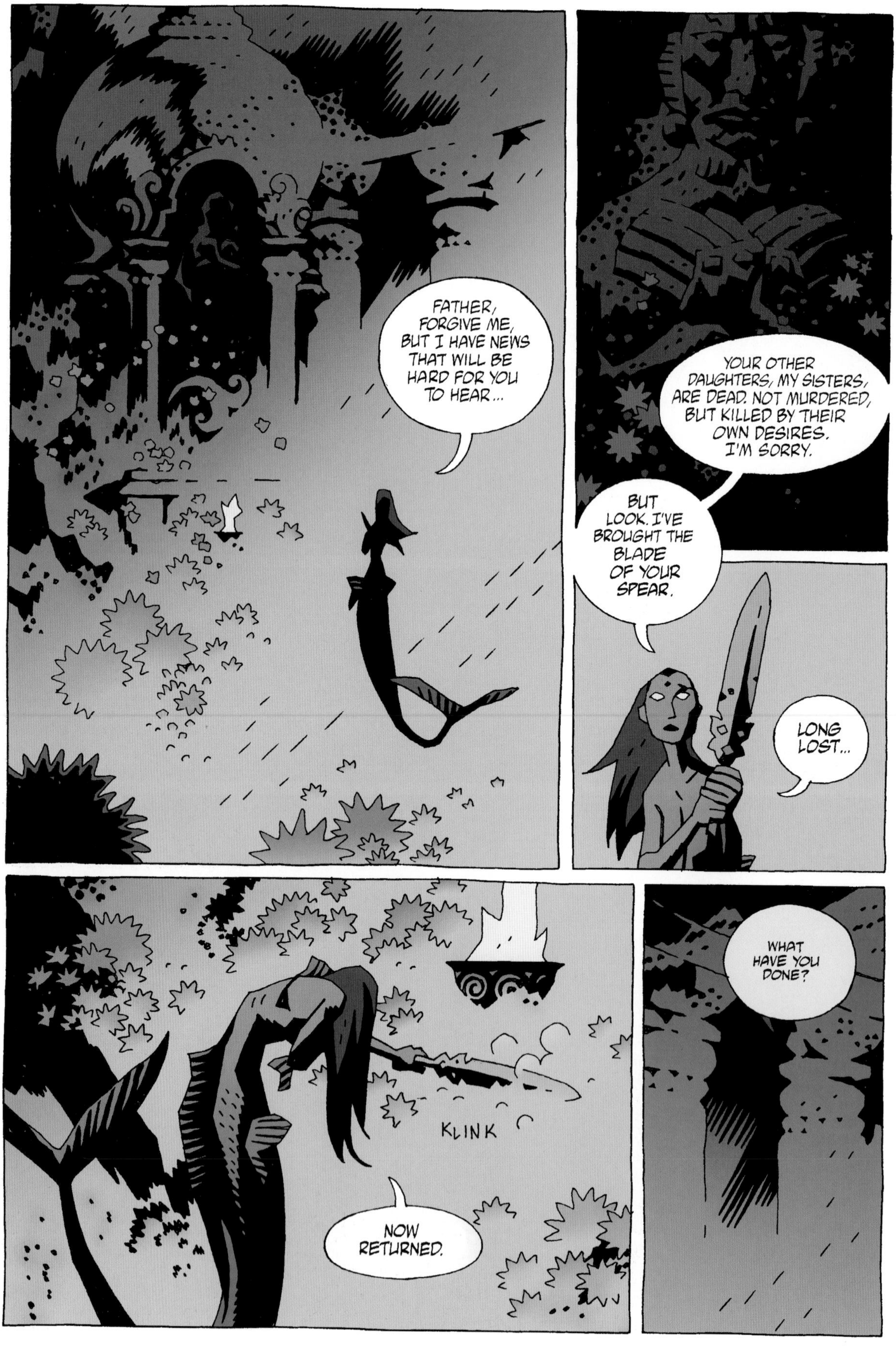
FATHER, FORGIVE ME, BUT I HAVE NEWS THAT WILL BE HARD FOR YOU TO HEAR...
YOUR OTHER DAUGHTERS, MY SISTERS, ARE DEAD. NOT MURDERED, BUT KILLED BY THEIR OWN DESIRES. I'M SORRY.
BUT LOOK. I'VE BROUGHT THE BLADE OF YOUR SPEAR.
LONG LOST...
KLINK
NOW RETURNED.
WHAT HAVE YOU DONE?

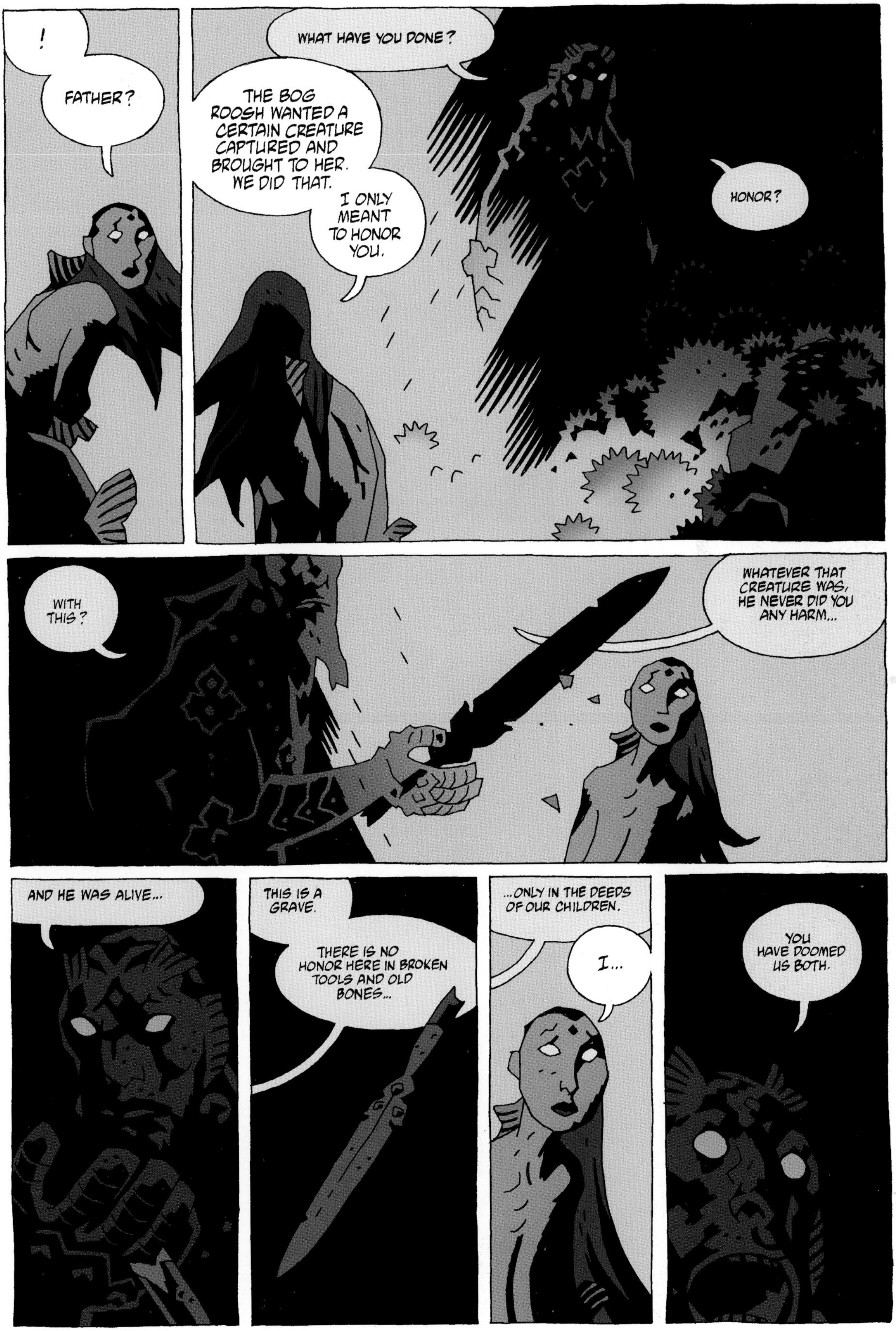
!
FATHER?
WHAT HAVE YOU DONE?
THE BOG ROOSH WANTED A CERTAIN CREATURE CAPTURED AND BROUGHT TO HER. WE DID THAT.
I ONLY MEANT TO HONOR YOU.
HONOR?
WITH THIS?
WHATEVER THAT CREATURE WAS, HE NEVER DID YOU ANY HARM...
AND HE WAS ALIVE...
THIS IS A GRAVE.
THERE IS NO HONOR HERE IN BROKEN TOOLS AND OLD BONES...
...ONLY IN THE DEEDS OF OUR CHILDREN.
I...
YOU HAVE DOOMED US BOTH.

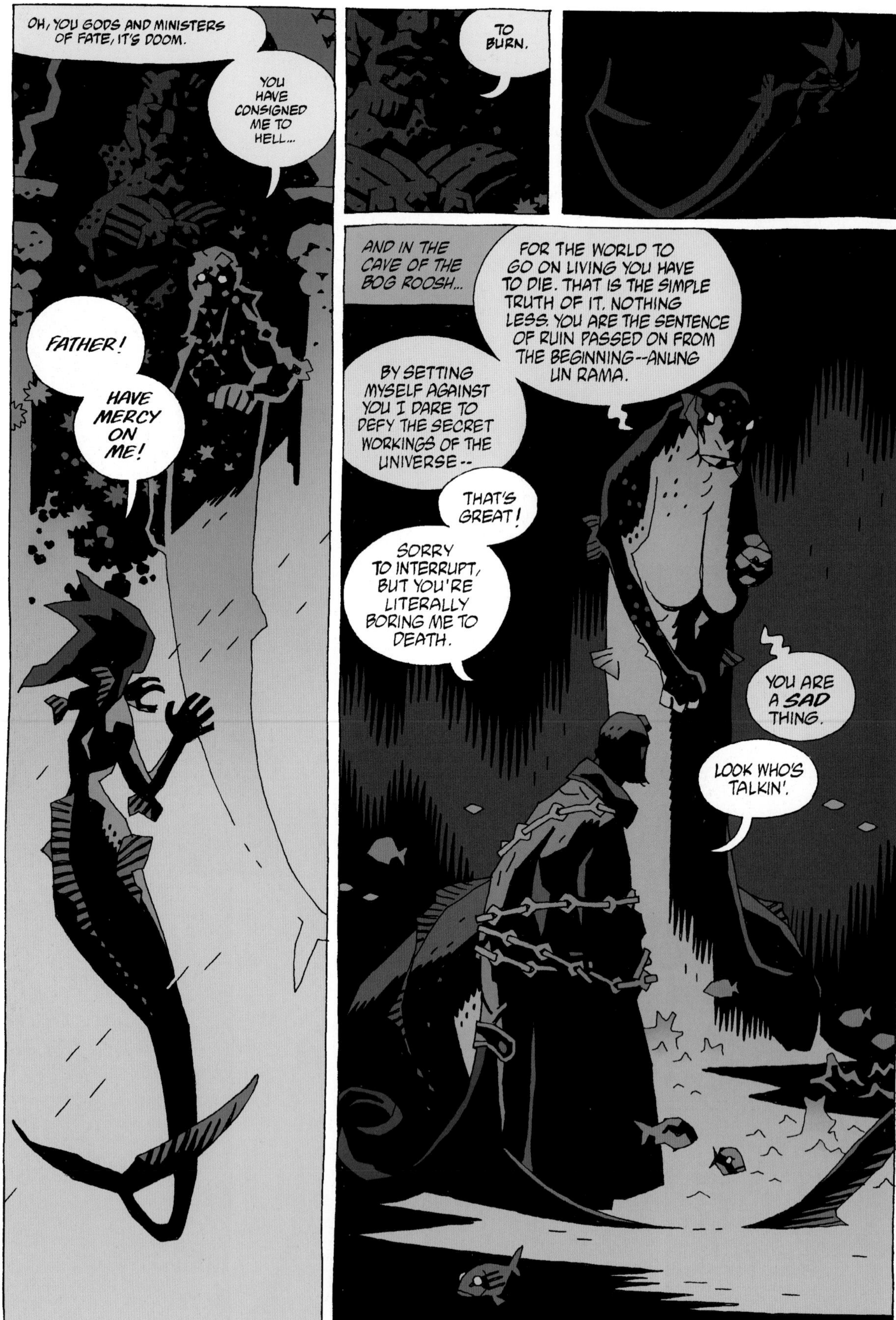
OH, YOU GODS AND MINISTERS OF FATE, IT'S DOOM.
YOU HAVE CONSIGNED ME TO HELL...
FATHER!
HAVE MERCY ON ME!
TO BURN.
AND IN THE CAVE OF THE BOG ROOSH...
FOR THE WORLD TO GO ON LIVING YOU HAVE TO DIE. THAT IS THE SIMPLE TRUTH OF IT. NOTHING LESS. YOU ARE THE SENTENCE OF RUIN PASSED ON FROM THE BEGINNING--ANUNG UN RAMA.
BY SETTING MYSELF AGAINST YOU I DARE TO DEFY THE SECRET WORKINGS OF THE UNIVERSE--
THAT'S GREAT!
SORRY TO INTERRUPT, BUT YOU'RE LITERALLY BORING ME TO DEATH.
YOU ARE A SAD THING.
LOOK WHO'S TALKIN'.

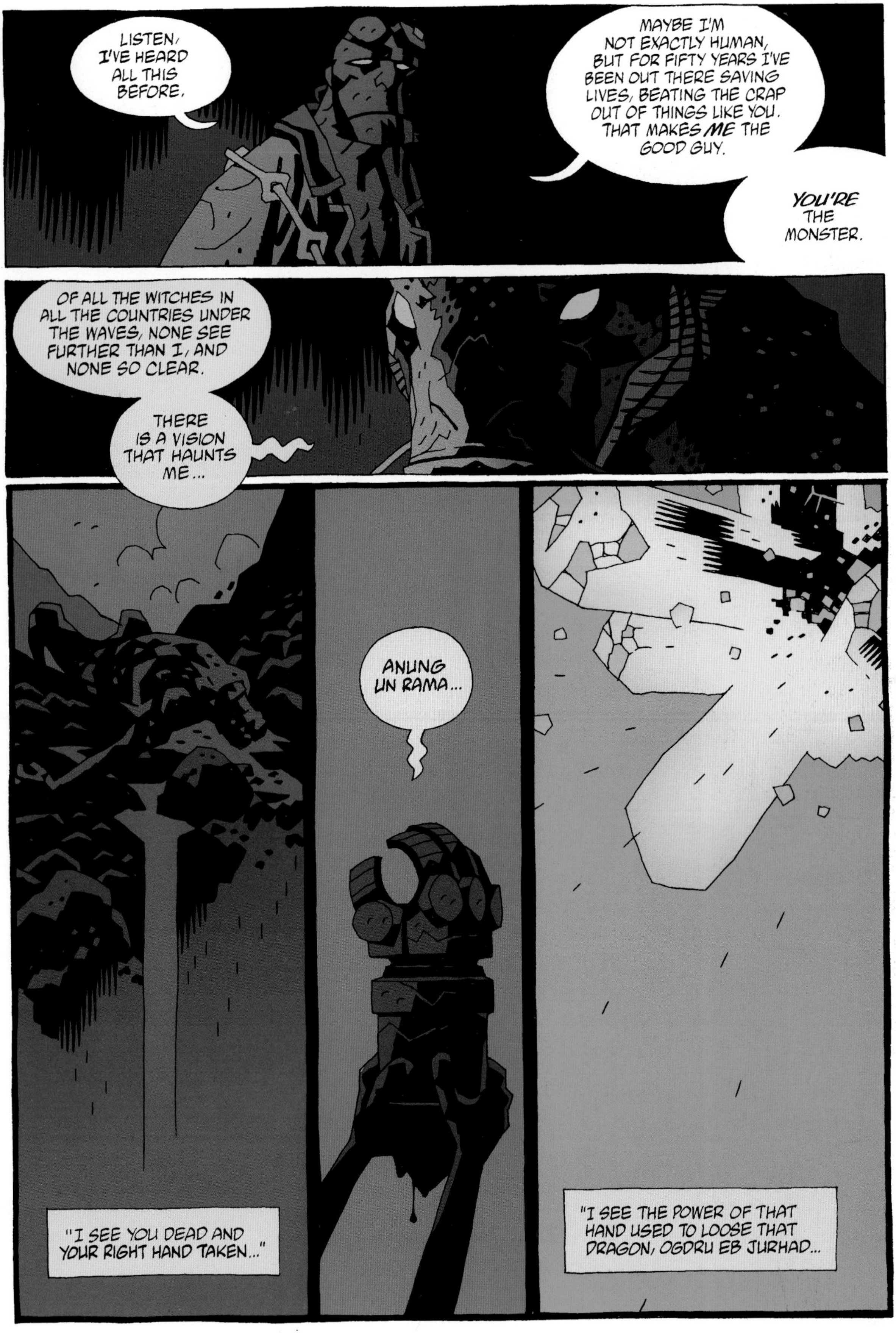
LISTEN, I'VE HEARD ALL THIS BEFORE.
MAYBE I'M NOT EXACTLY HUMAN, BUT FOR FIFTY YEARS I'VE BEEN OUT THERE SAVING LIVES, BEATING THE CRAP OUT OF THINGS LIKE YOU. THAT MAKES *ME* THE GOOD GUY.
YOU'RE THE MONSTER.
OF ALL THE WITCHES IN ALL THE COUNTRIES UNDER THE WAVES, NONE SEE FURTHER THAN I, AND NONE SO CLEAR.
THERE IS A VISION THAT HAUNTS ME...
"I SEE YOU DEAD AND YOUR RIGHT HAND TAKEN..."
ANUNG UN RAMA...
"I SEE THE POWER OF THAT HAND USED TO LOOSE THAT DRAGON, OGDRU EB JURHAD...

"...AND THE WHOLE WORLD LAID WASTE."

SO YOU'VE HAD A *DREAM* THAT WHEN I DIE THE WHOLE WORLD GETS DESTROYED AND YOU'RE GOING TO *PREVENT* THAT-- BY KILLING ME?

YOU'RE A GENIUS.

MORE THAN KILL. YOU MUST BE COMPLETELY UNMADE, CUT INTO PIECES AND SENT TO THE FOUR CORNERS OF THE GLOBE...

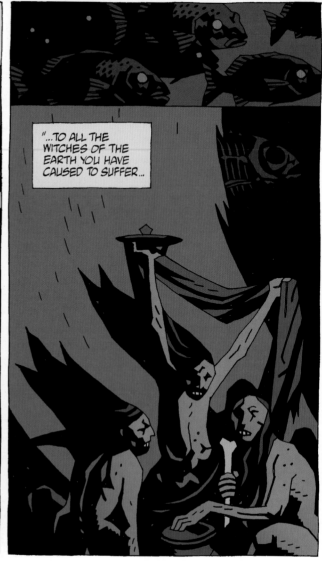

"...TO ALL THE WITCHES OF THE EARTH YOU HAVE CAUSED TO SUFFER..."

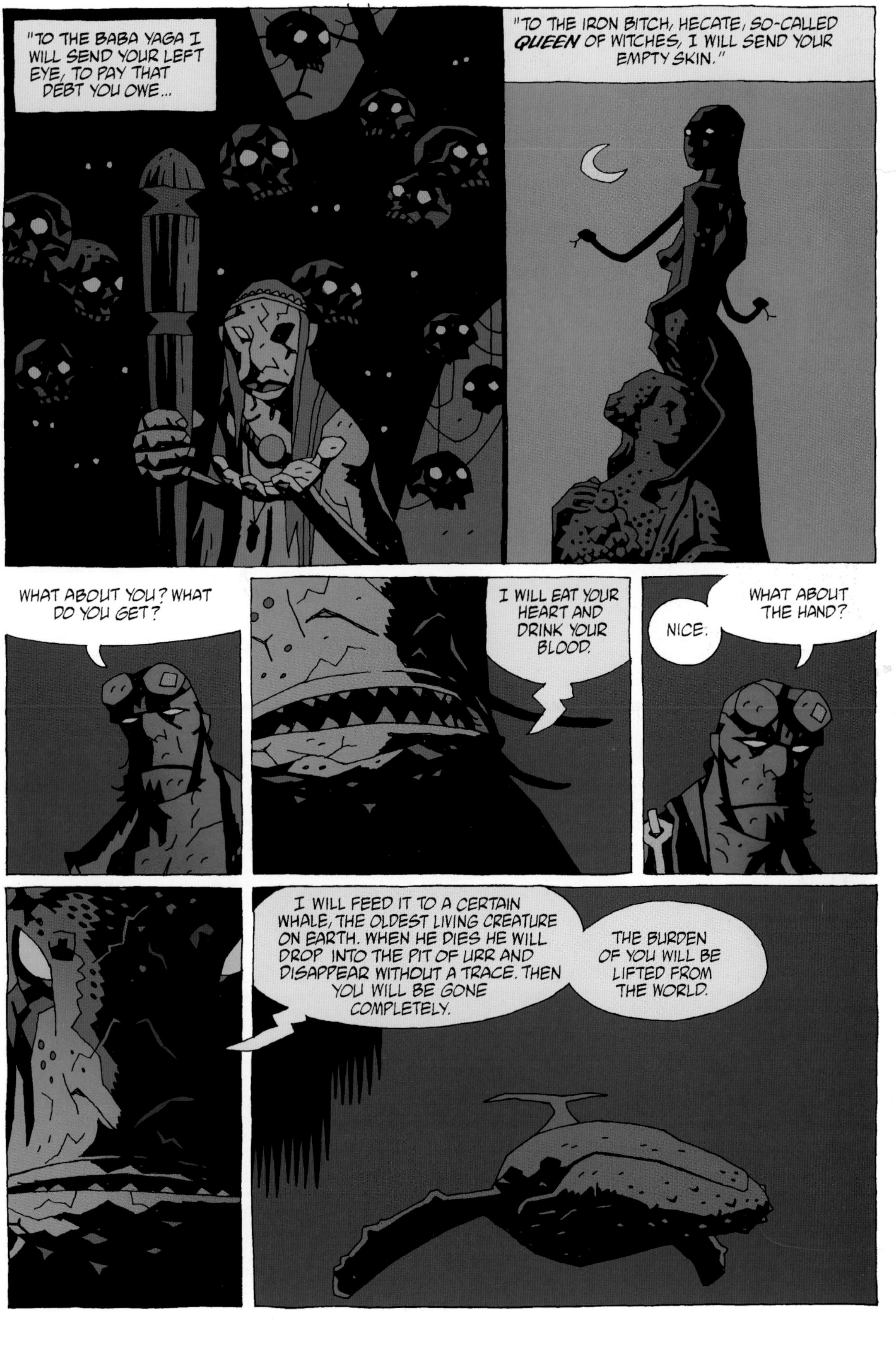
"TO THE BABA YAGA I WILL SEND YOUR LEFT EYE, TO PAY THAT DEBT YOU OWE...
"TO THE IRON BITCH, HECATE, SO-CALLED **QUEEN** OF WITCHES, I WILL SEND YOUR EMPTY SKIN."
WHAT ABOUT YOU? WHAT DO YOU GET?
I WILL EAT YOUR HEART AND DRINK YOUR BLOOD.
NICE.
WHAT ABOUT THE HAND?
I WILL FEED IT TO A CERTAIN WHALE, THE OLDEST LIVING CREATURE ON EARTH. WHEN HE DIES HE WILL DROP INTO THE PIT OF URR AND DISAPPEAR WITHOUT A TRACE. THEN YOU WILL BE GONE COMPLETELY.
THE BURDEN OF YOU WILL BE LIFTED FROM THE WORLD.

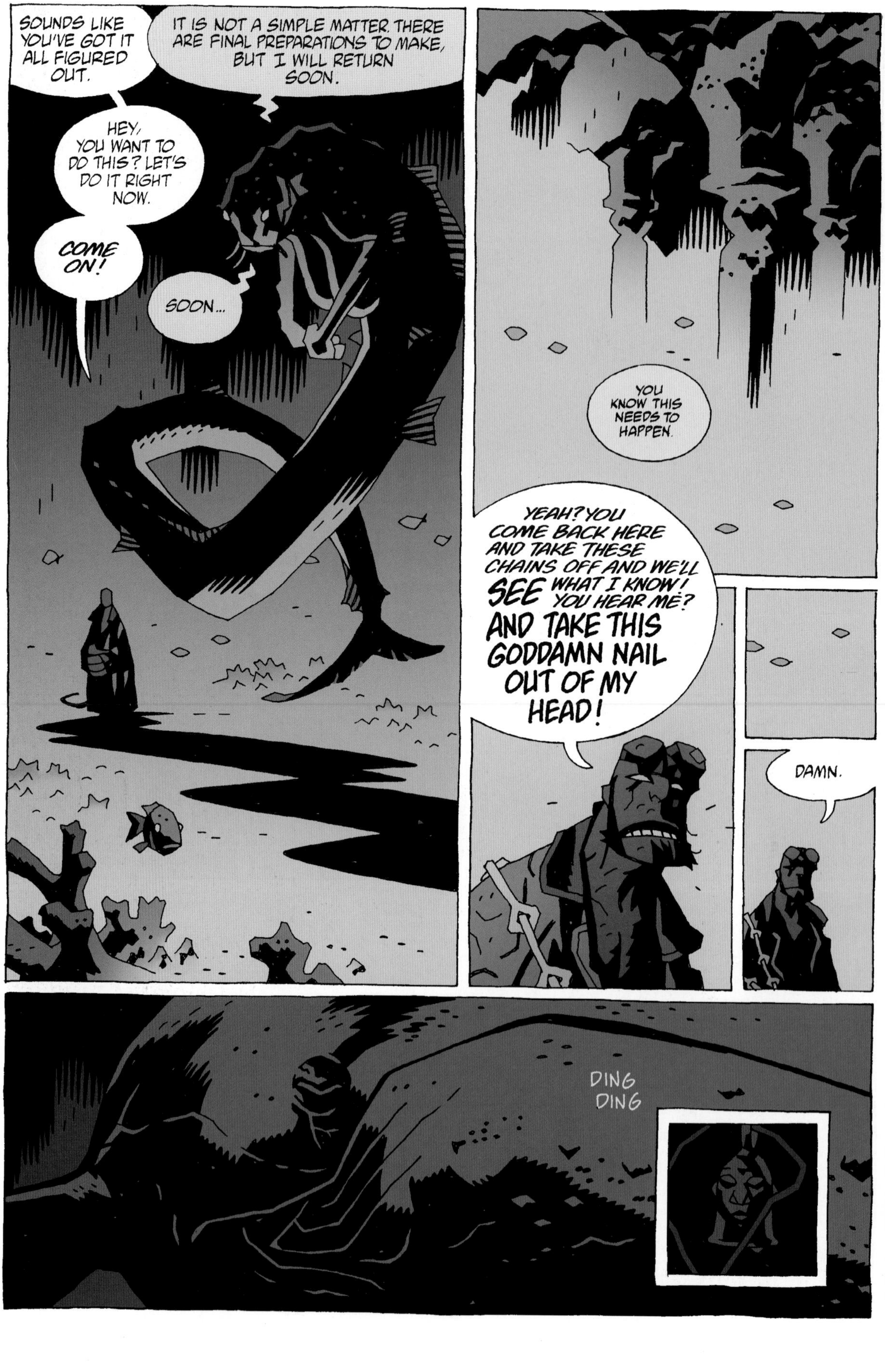

SOUNDS LIKE YOU'VE GOT IT ALL FIGURED OUT.
IT IS NOT A SIMPLE MATTER. THERE ARE FINAL PREPARATIONS TO MAKE, BUT I WILL RETURN SOON.
HEY, YOU WANT TO DO THIS? LET'S DO IT RIGHT NOW.
COME ON!
SOON...
YOU KNOW THIS NEEDS TO HAPPEN.
YEAH? YOU COME BACK HERE AND TAKE THESE CHAINS OFF AND WE'LL SEE WHAT I KNOW! YOU HEAR ME? AND TAKE THIS GODDAMN NAIL OUT OF MY HEAD!
DAMN.
DING DING

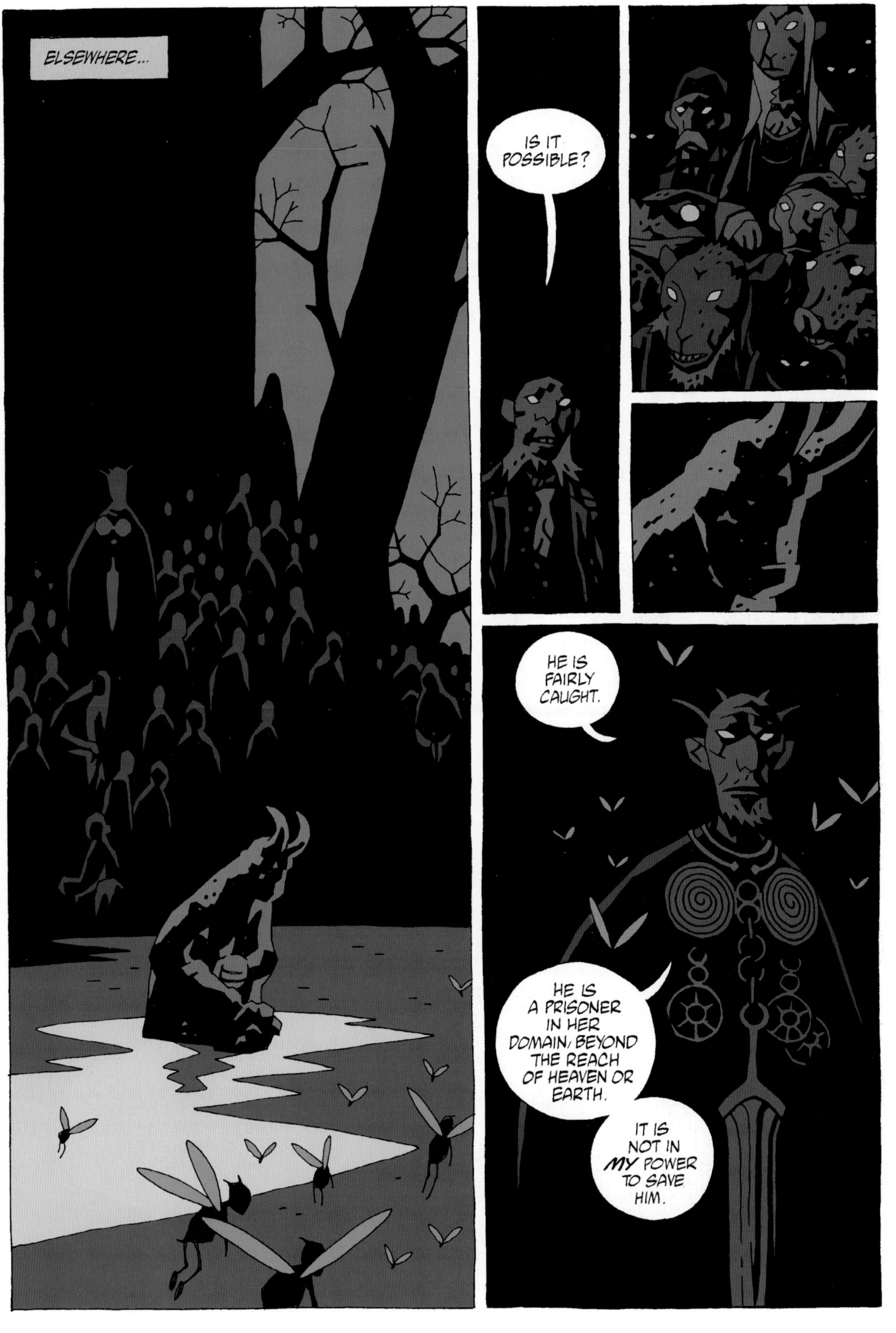
ELSEWHERE...
IS IT POSSIBLE?
HE IS FAIRLY CAUGHT.
HE IS A PRISONER IN HER DOMAIN, BEYOND THE REACH OF HEAVEN OR EARTH.
IT IS NOT IN *MY* POWER TO SAVE HIM.

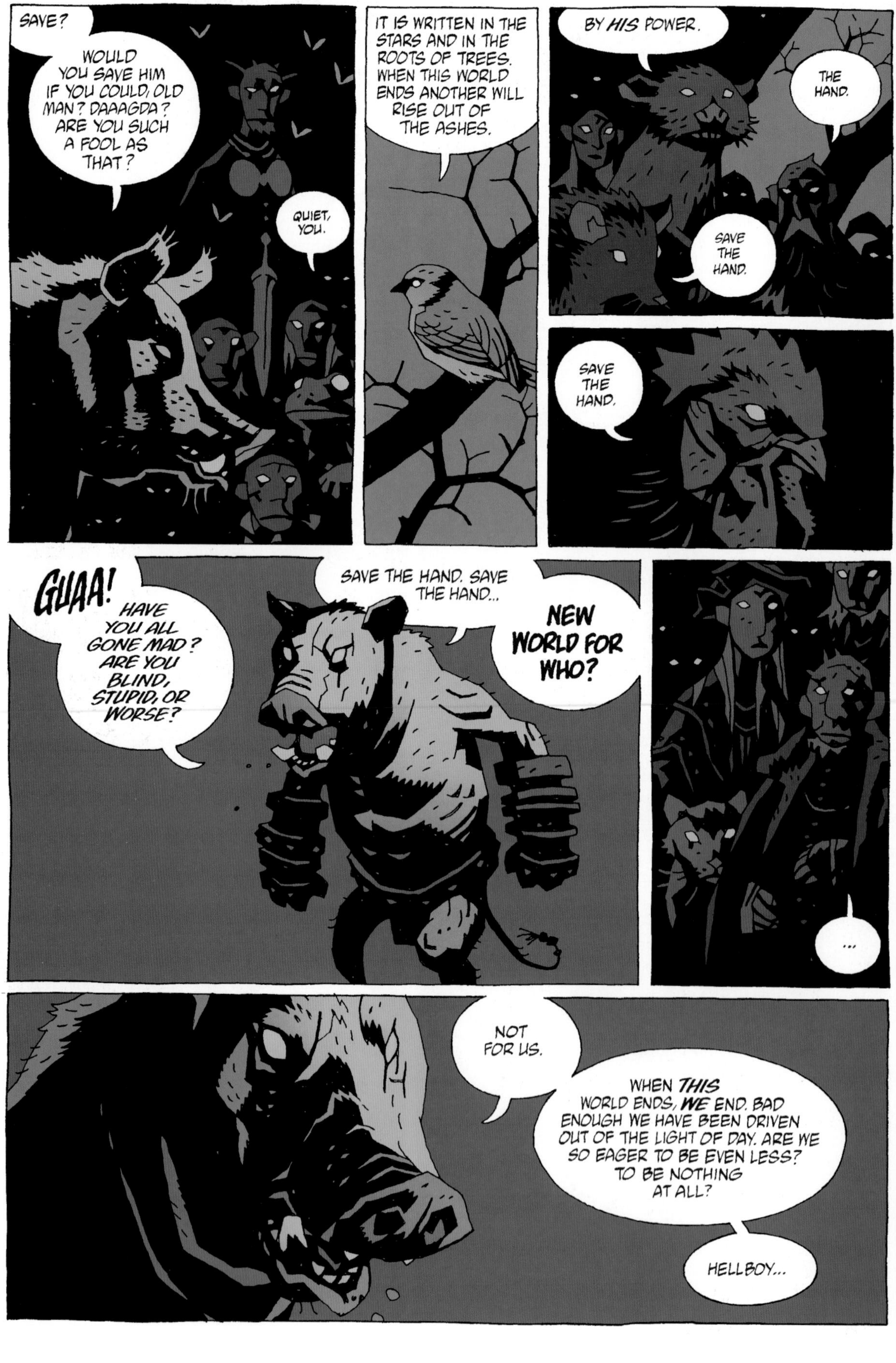

SAVE?
WOULD YOU SAVE HIM IF YOU COULD, OLD MAN? DAAAGDA? ARE YOU SUCH A FOOL AS THAT?
QUIET, YOU.
IT IS WRITTEN IN THE STARS AND IN THE ROOTS OF TREES. WHEN THIS WORLD ENDS ANOTHER WILL RISE OUT OF THE ASHES.
BY HIS POWER.
THE HAND.
SAVE THE HAND.
SAVE THE HAND.
GUAA! HAVE YOU ALL GONE MAD? ARE YOU BLIND, STUPID, OR WORSE?
SAVE THE HAND. SAVE THE HAND...
NEW WORLD FOR WHO?
...
NOT FOR US.
WHEN THIS WORLD ENDS, WE END. BAD ENOUGH WE HAVE BEEN DRIVEN OUT OF THE LIGHT OF DAY. ARE WE SO EAGER TO BE EVEN LESS? TO BE NOTHING AT ALL?
HELLBOY...

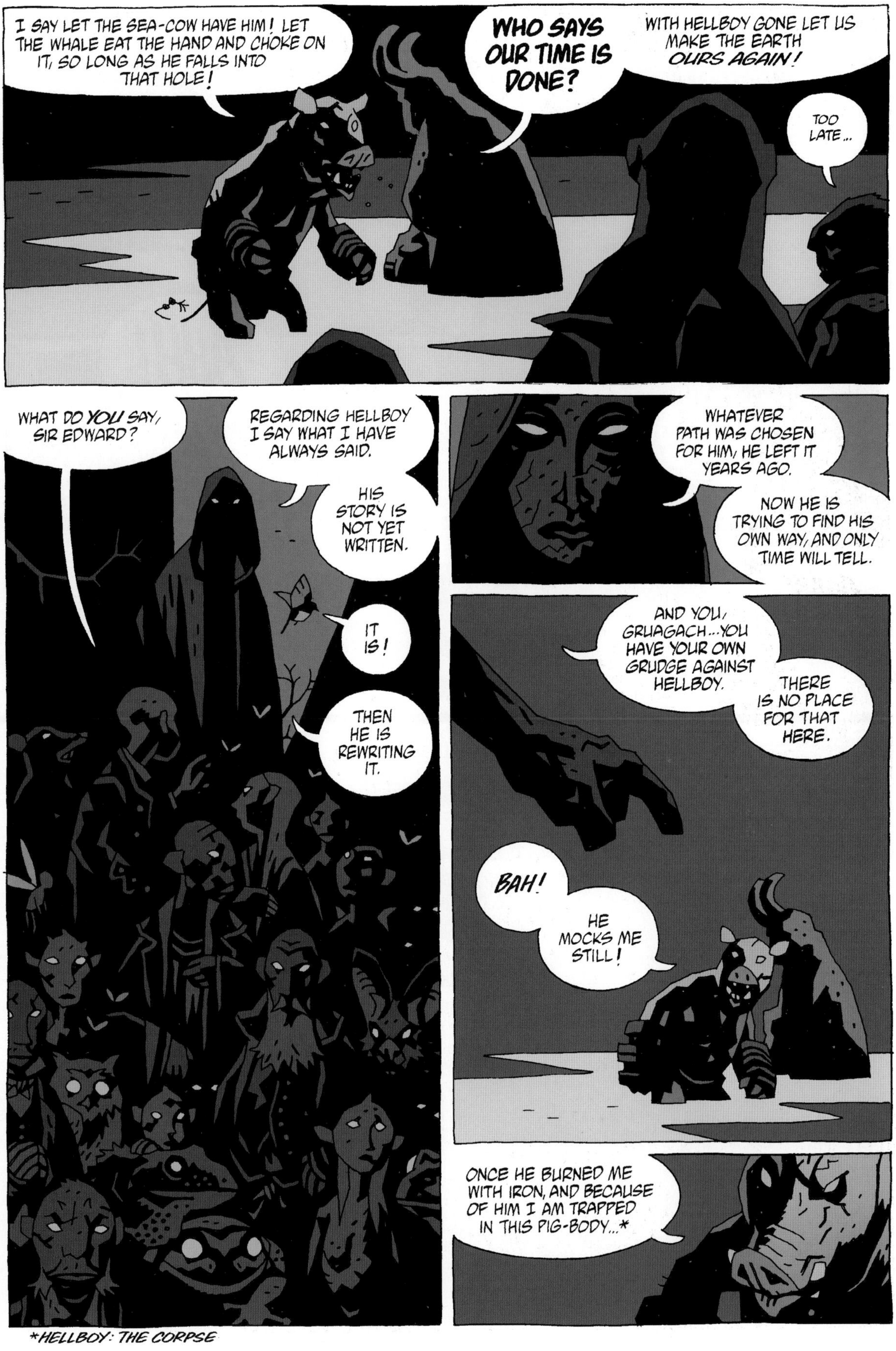
I SAY LET THE SEA-COW HAVE HIM! LET THE WHALE EAT THE HAND AND CHOKE ON IT, SO LONG AS HE FALLS INTO THAT HOLE!
WHO SAYS OUR TIME IS DONE?
WITH HELLBOY GONE LET US MAKE THE EARTH OURS AGAIN!
TOO LATE...
WHAT DO YOU SAY, SIR EDWARD?
REGARDING HELLBOY I SAY WHAT I HAVE ALWAYS SAID.
HIS STORY IS NOT YET WRITTEN.
IT IS!
THEN HE IS REWRITING IT.
WHATEVER PATH WAS CHOSEN FOR HIM, HE LEFT IT YEARS AGO.
NOW HE IS TRYING TO FIND HIS OWN WAY, AND ONLY TIME WILL TELL.
AND YOU, GRUAGACH...YOU HAVE YOUR OWN GRUDGE AGAINST HELLBOY.
THERE IS NO PLACE FOR THAT HERE.
BAH!
HE MOCKS ME STILL!
ONCE HE BURNED ME WITH IRON, AND BECAUSE OF HIM I AM TRAPPED IN THIS PIG-BODY...*

*HELLBOY: THE CORPSE

AND I WILL HAVE MY REVENGE!

AHH!

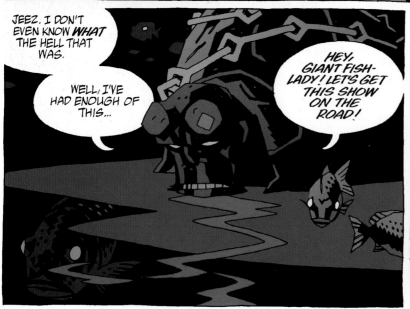

JEEZ. I DON'T EVEN KNOW *WHAT* THE HELL THAT WAS.

WELL, I'VE HAD ENOUGH OF THIS...

HEY, GIANT FISH-LADY! LET'S GET THIS SHOW ON THE ROAD!

COME AND--

SHHH

?

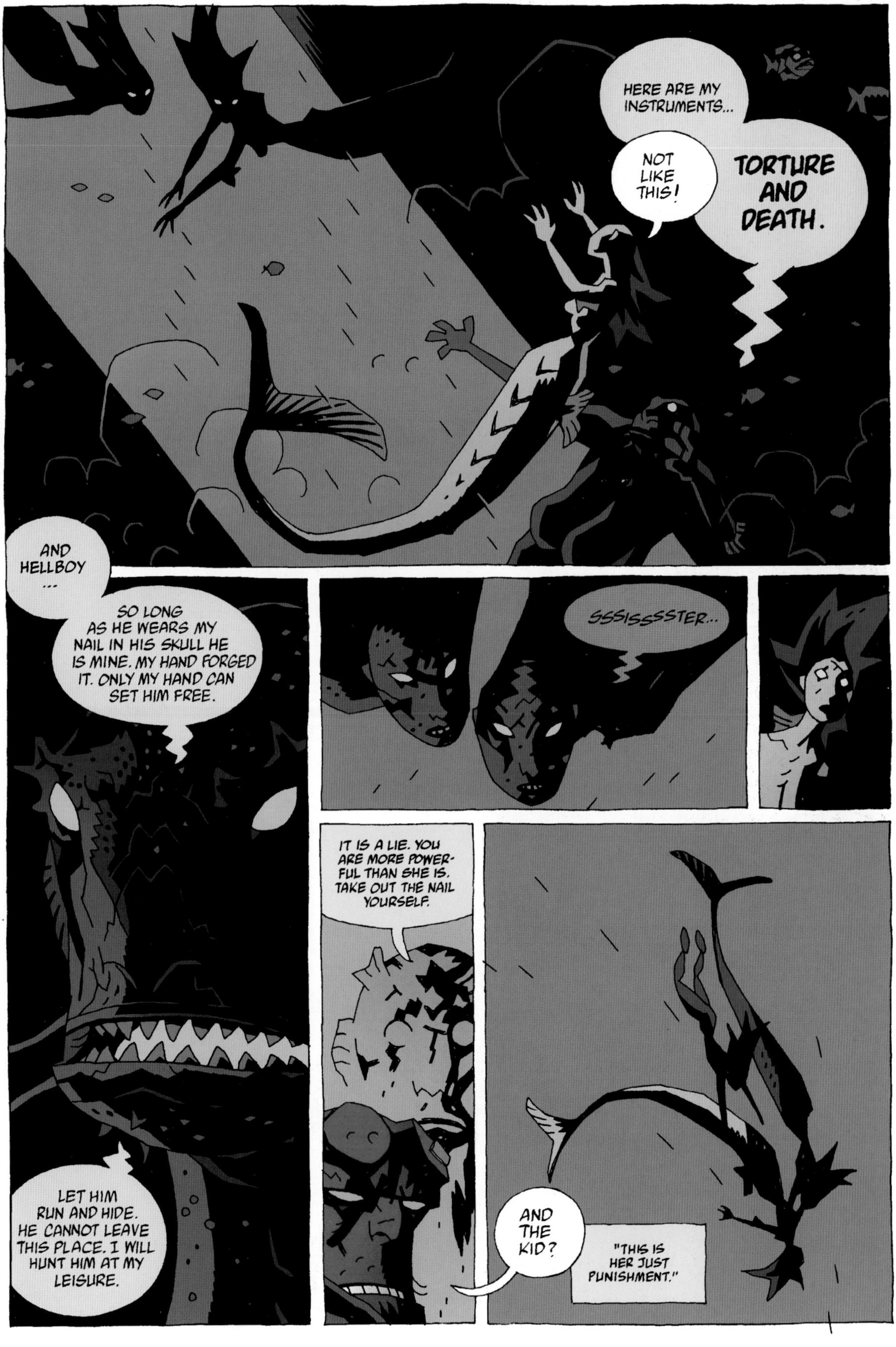

HERE ARE MY INSTRUMENTS...
TORTURE AND DEATH.
NOT LIKE THIS!
AND HELLBOY ...
SO LONG AS HE WEARS MY NAIL IN HIS SKULL HE IS MINE. MY HAND FORGED IT. ONLY MY HAND CAN SET HIM FREE.
LET HIM RUN AND HIDE. HE CANNOT LEAVE THIS PLACE. I WILL HUNT HIM AT MY LEISURE.
SSSISSSSTER...
IT IS A LIE. YOU ARE MORE POWER-FUL THAN SHE IS. TAKE OUT THE NAIL YOURSELF.
AND THE KID?
"THIS IS HER JUST PUNISHMENT."

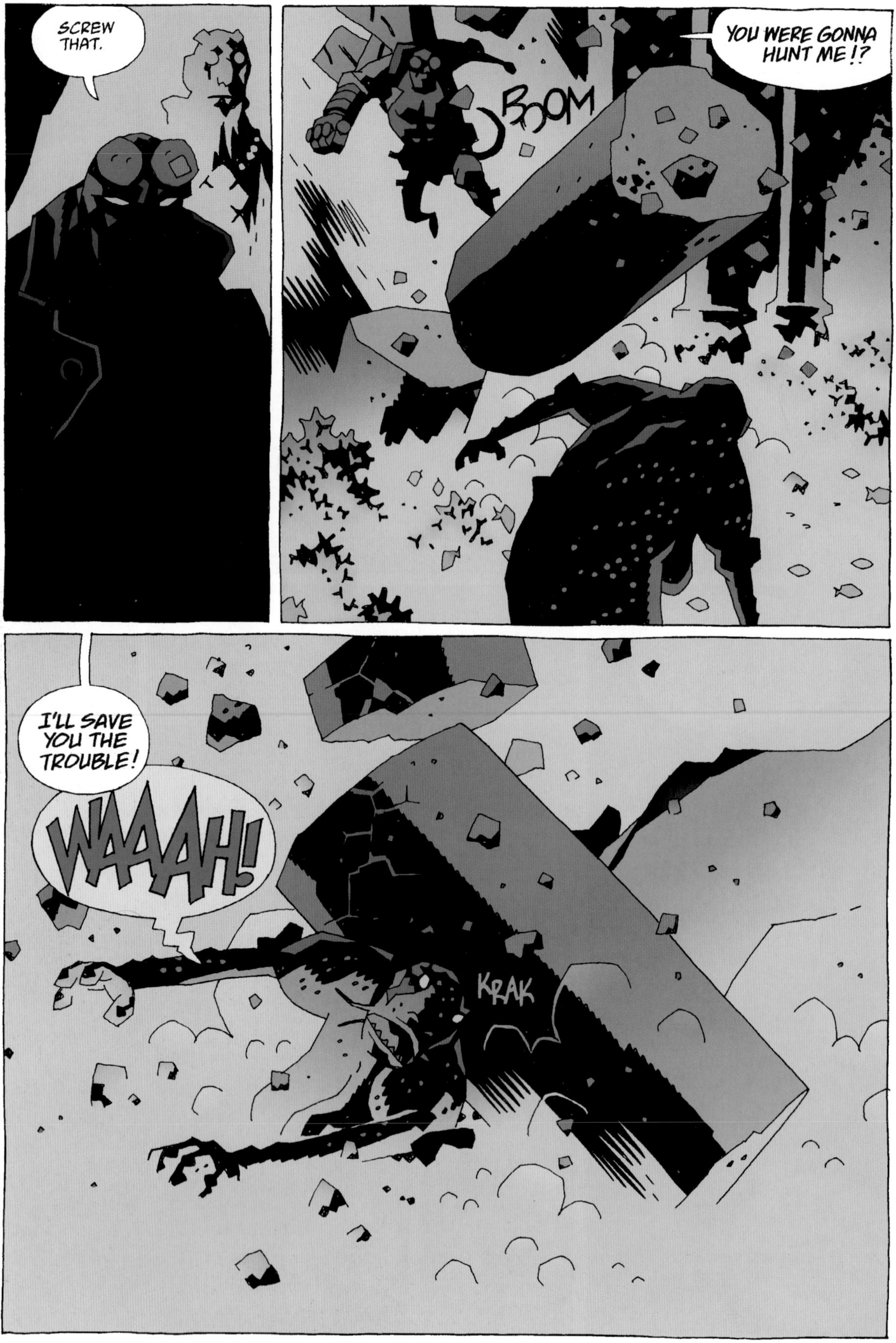
SCREW THAT.
YOU WERE GONNA HUNT ME !?
BOOM
I'LL SAVE YOU THE TROUBLE!
WAAAH!
KRAK

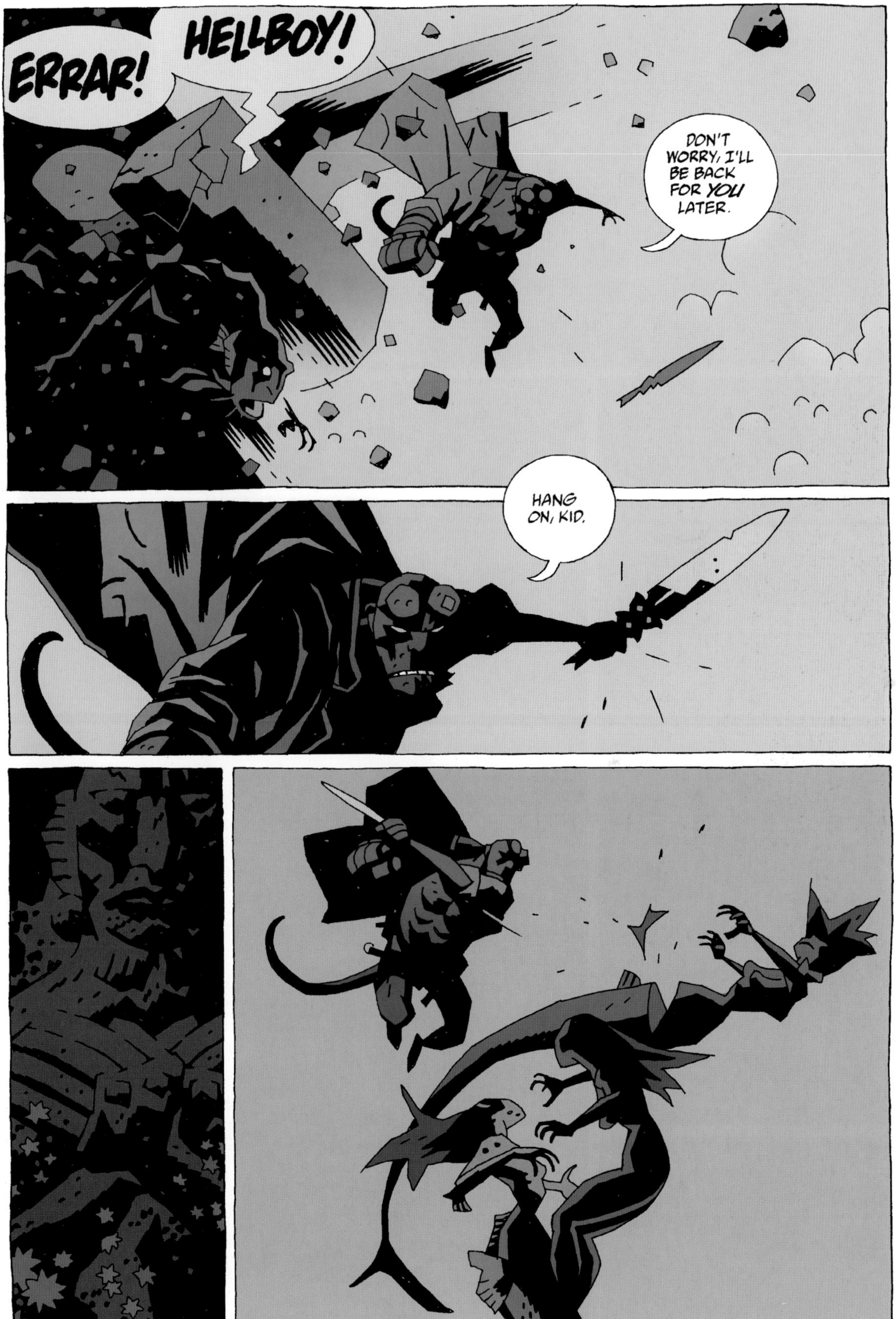
ERRAR!
HELLBOY!
DON'T WORRY, I'LL BE BACK FOR YOU LATER.
HANG ON, KID.

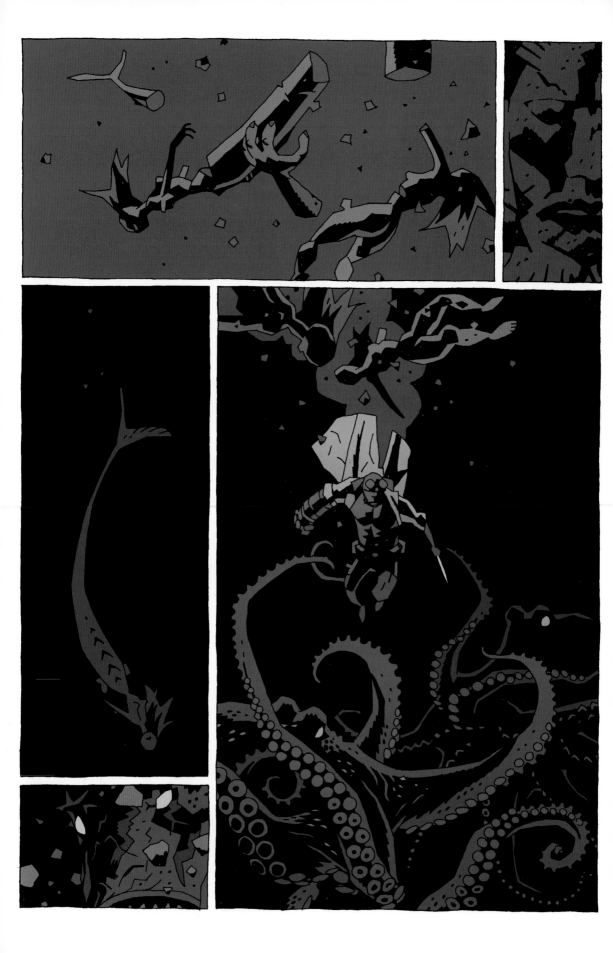

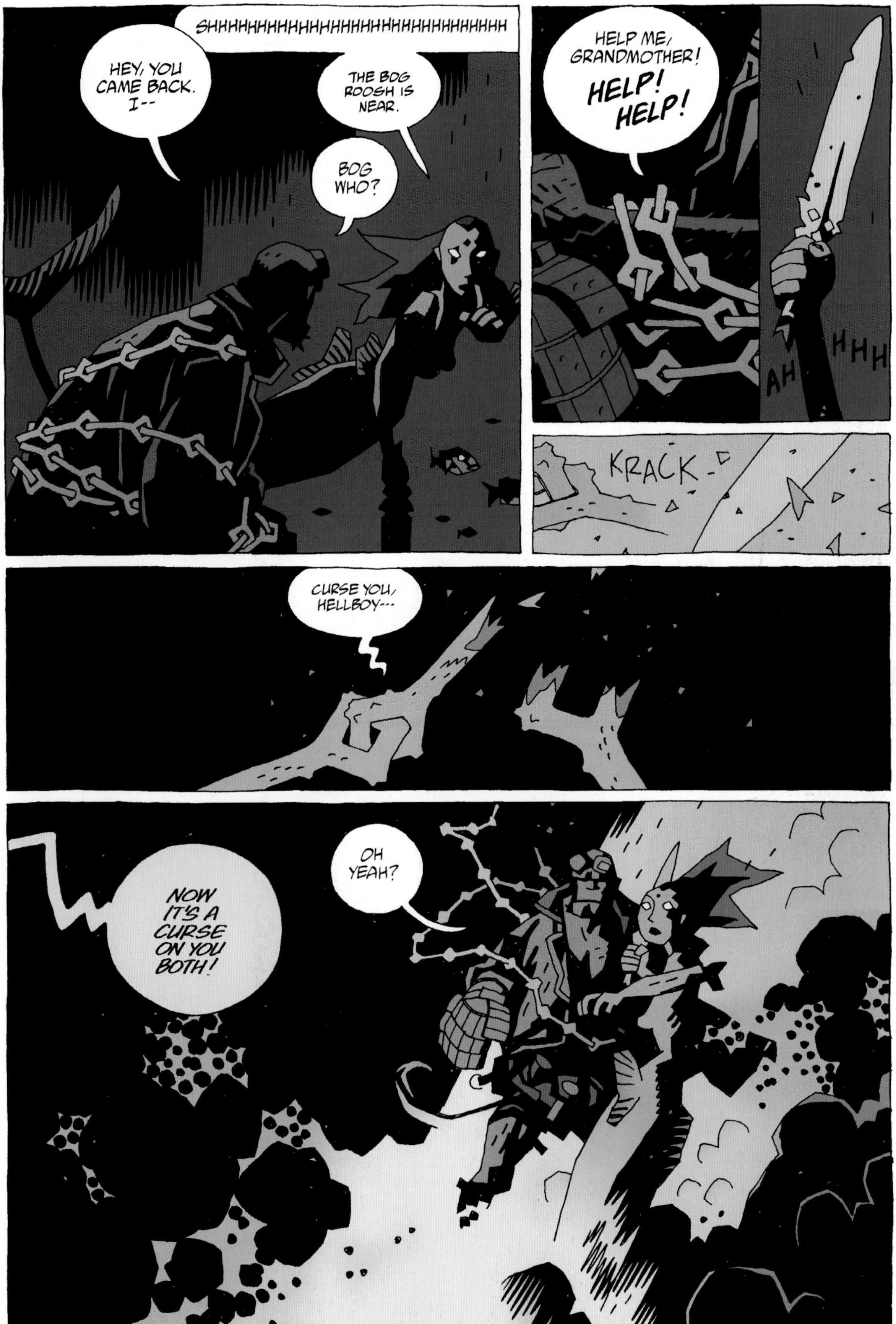
SHHHHHHHHHHHHHHHHHHHHHHHHHHHHHH
HEY, YOU CAME BACK. I--
THE BOG ROOSH IS NEAR.
BOG WHO?
HELP ME, GRANDMOTHER! HELP! HELP!
AHHHH
KRACK
CURSE YOU, HELLBOY---
NOW IT'S A CURSE ON YOU BOTH!
OH YEAH?

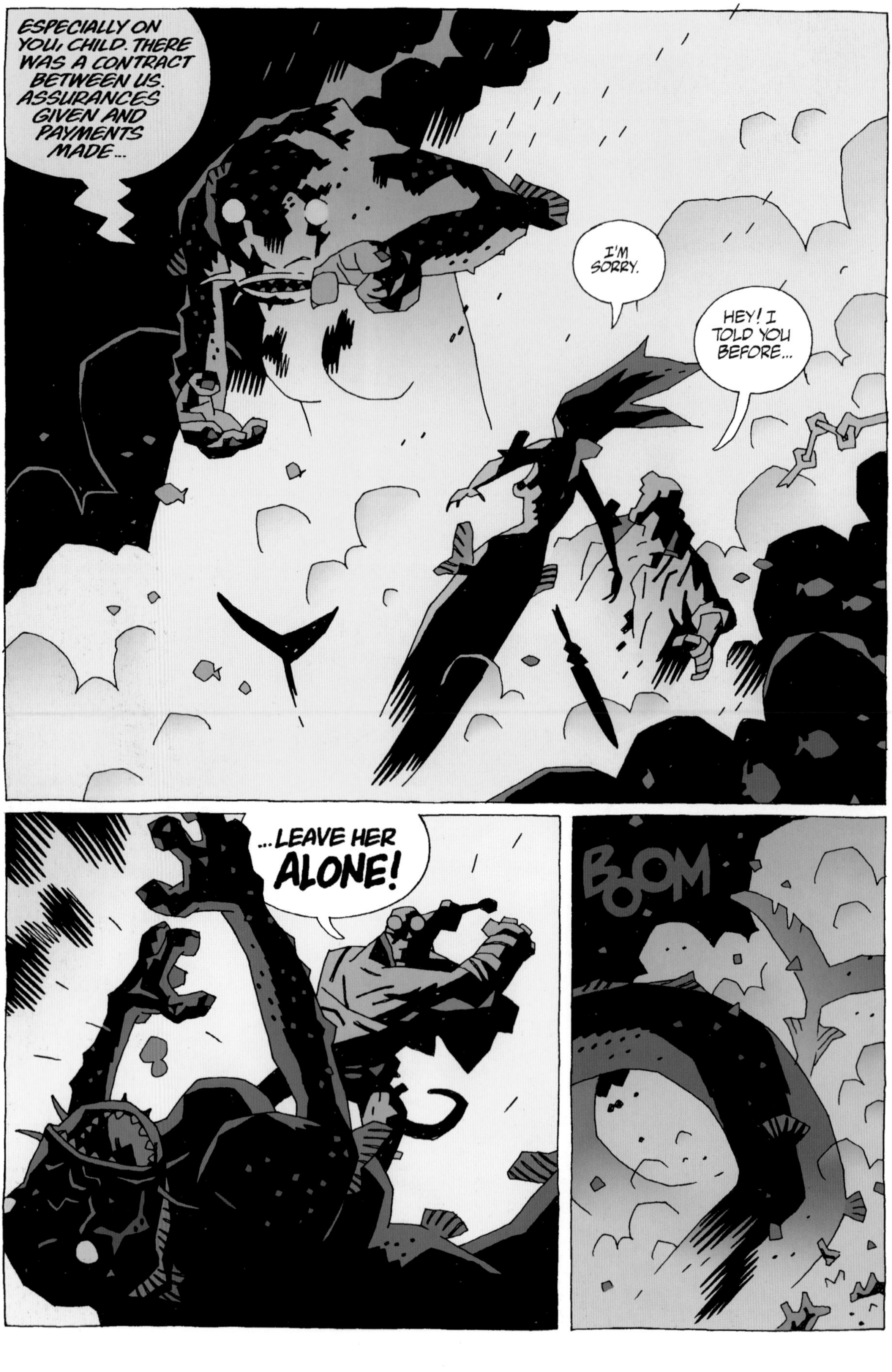
ESPECIALLY ON YOU, CHILD. THERE WAS A CONTRACT BETWEEN US. ASSURANCES GIVEN AND PAYMENTS MADE...
I'M SORRY.
HEY! I TOLD YOU BEFORE...
...LEAVE HER ALONE!
BOOM

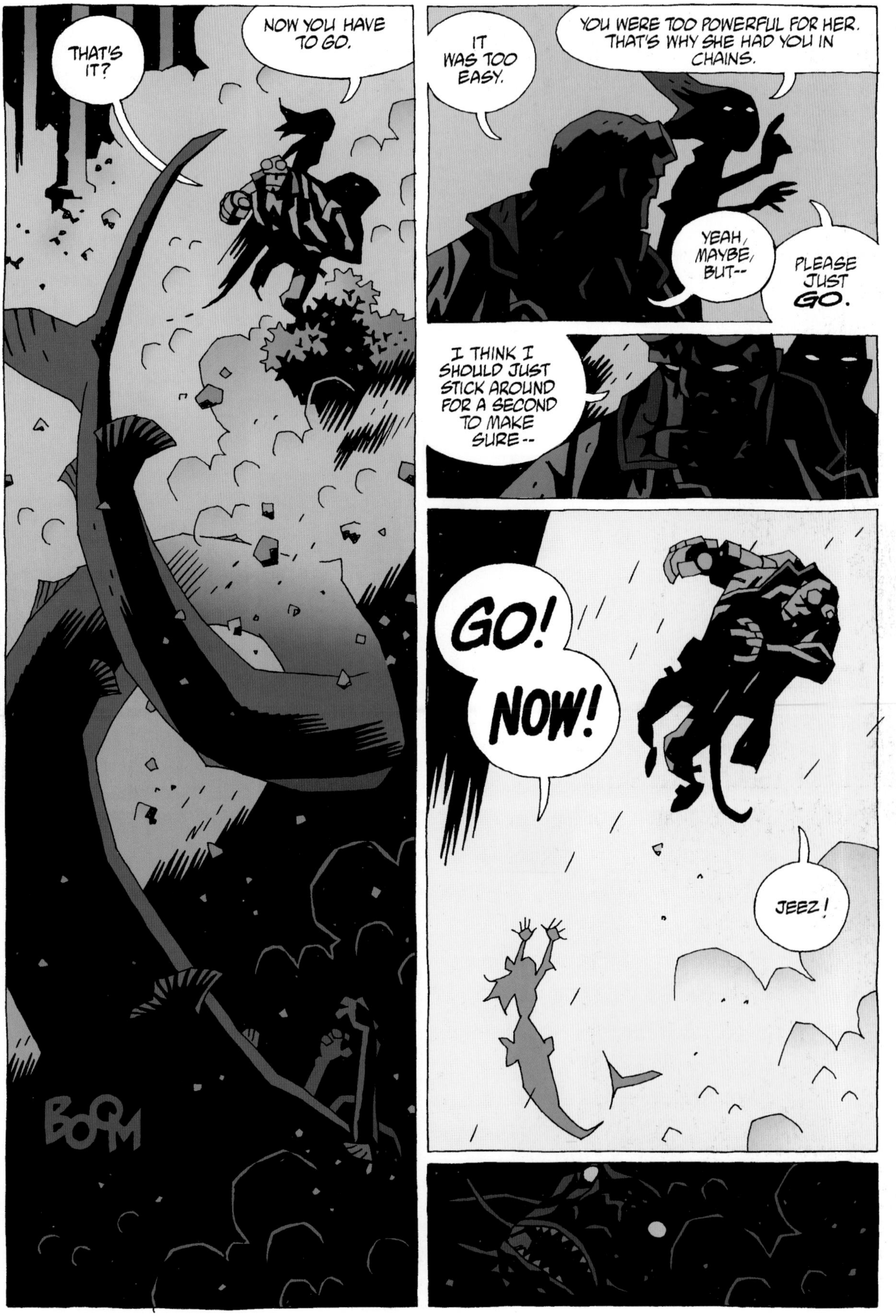
THAT'S IT?
NOW YOU HAVE TO GO.
BOOM
IT WAS TOO EASY.
YOU WERE TOO POWERFUL FOR HER. THAT'S WHY SHE HAD YOU IN CHAINS.
YEAH, MAYBE, BUT--
PLEASE JUST GO.
I THINK I SHOULD JUST STICK AROUND FOR A SECOND TO MAKE SURE--
GO!
NOW!
JEEZ!

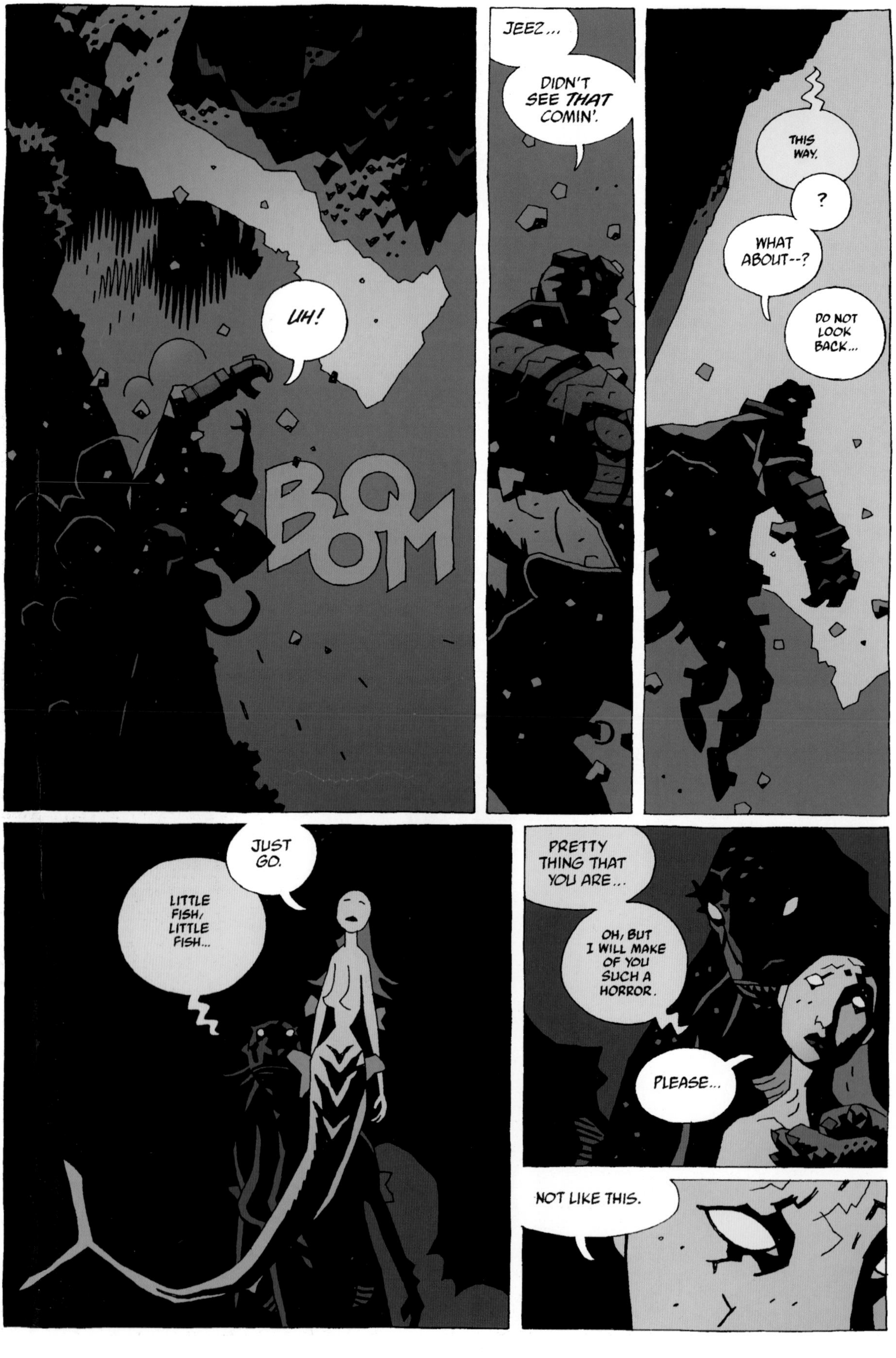
UH!
BOOM
JEEZ...
DIDN'T SEE *THAT* COMIN'.
THIS WAY.
?
WHAT ABOUT--?
DO NOT LOOK BACK...
JUST GO.
LITTLE FISH, LITTLE FISH...
PRETTY THING THAT YOU ARE...
OH, BUT I WILL MAKE OF YOU SUCH A HORROR.
PLEASE...
NOT LIKE THIS.

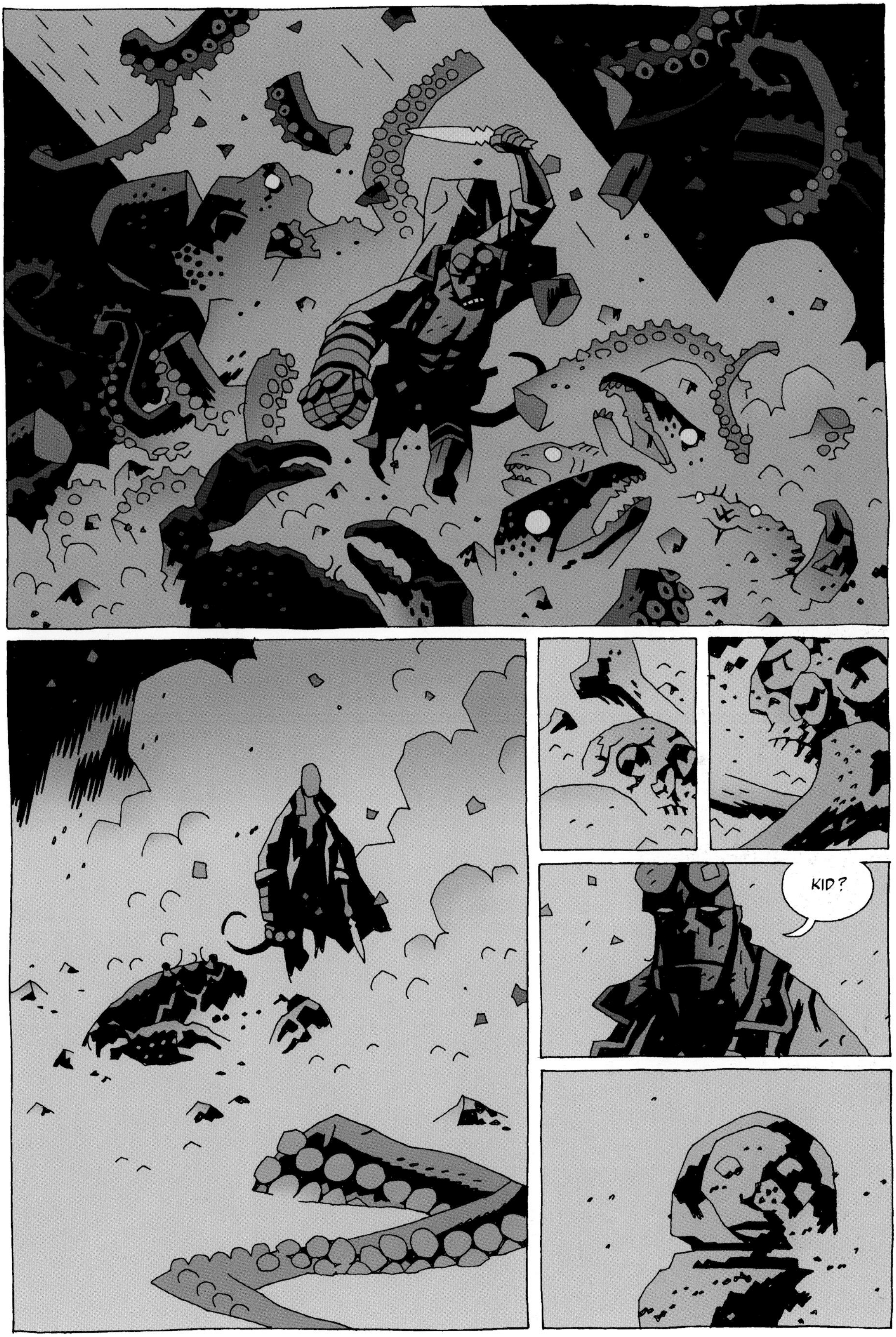
KID?

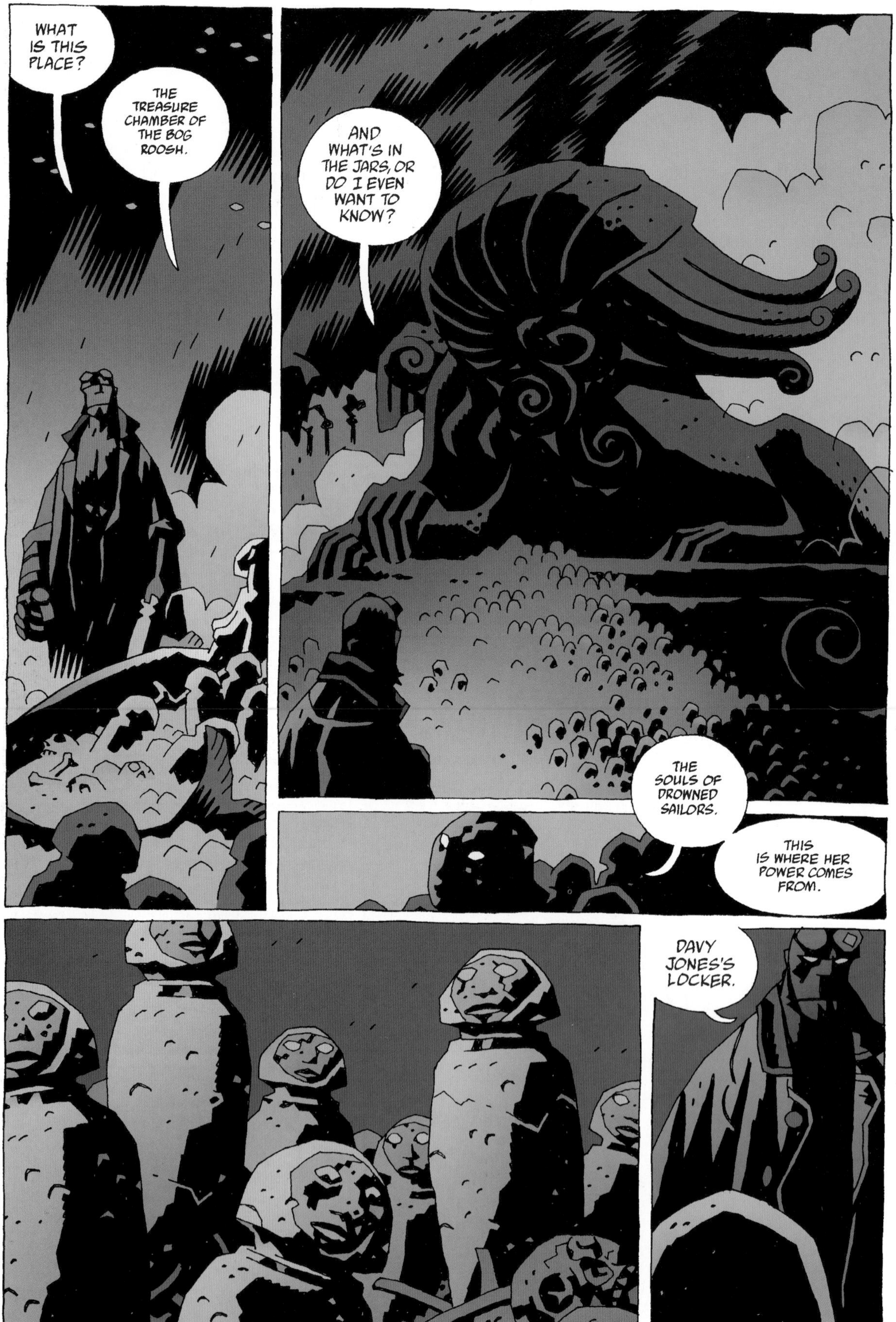
WHAT IS THIS PLACE?
THE TREASURE CHAMBER OF THE BOG ROOSH.
AND WHAT'S IN THE JARS, OR DO I EVEN WANT TO KNOW?
THE SOULS OF DROWNED SAILORS.
THIS IS WHERE HER POWER COMES FROM.
DAVY JONES'S LOCKER.

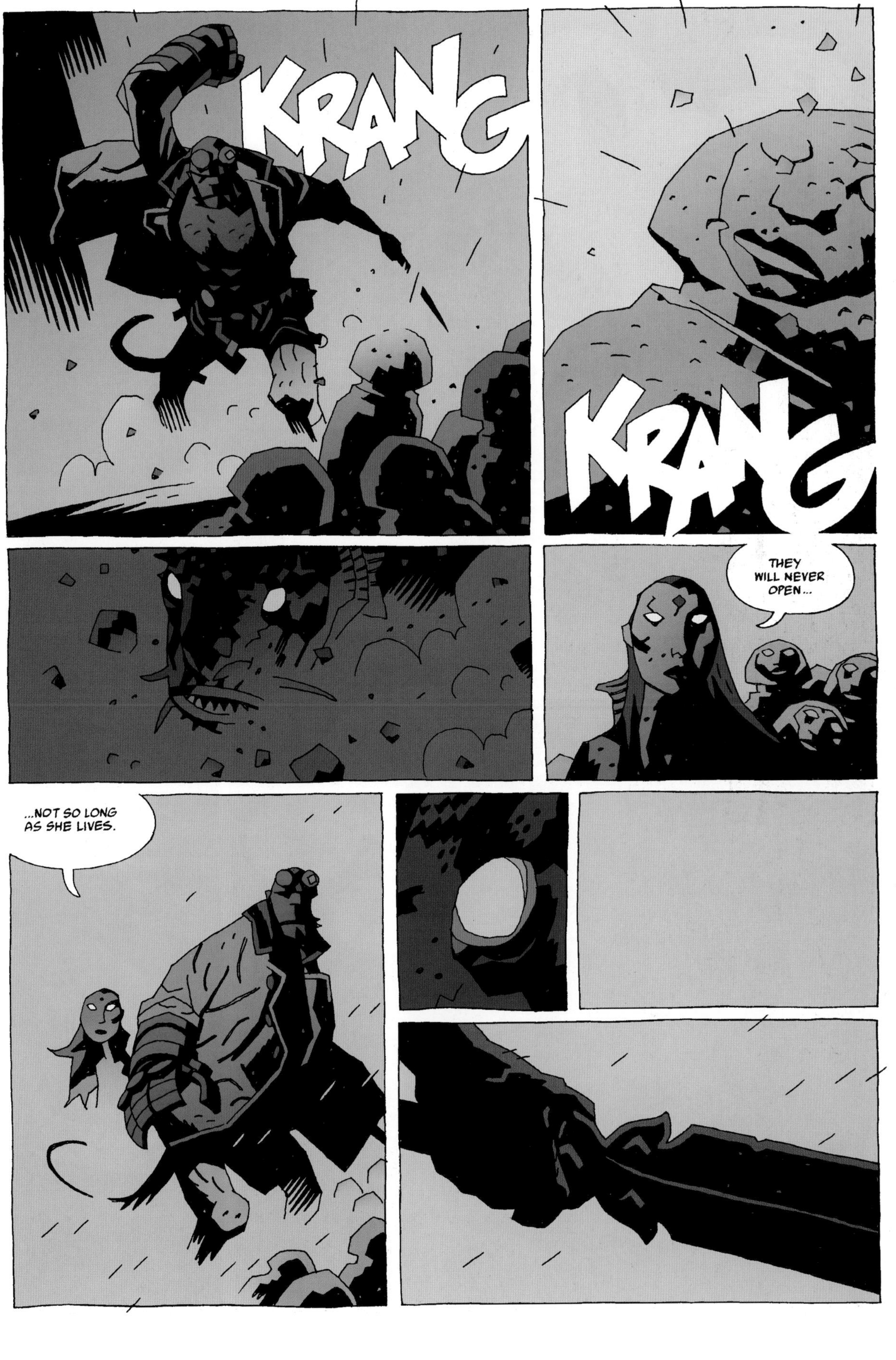
KRANG
KRANG
THEY WILL NEVER OPEN...
...NOT SO LONG AS SHE LIVES.

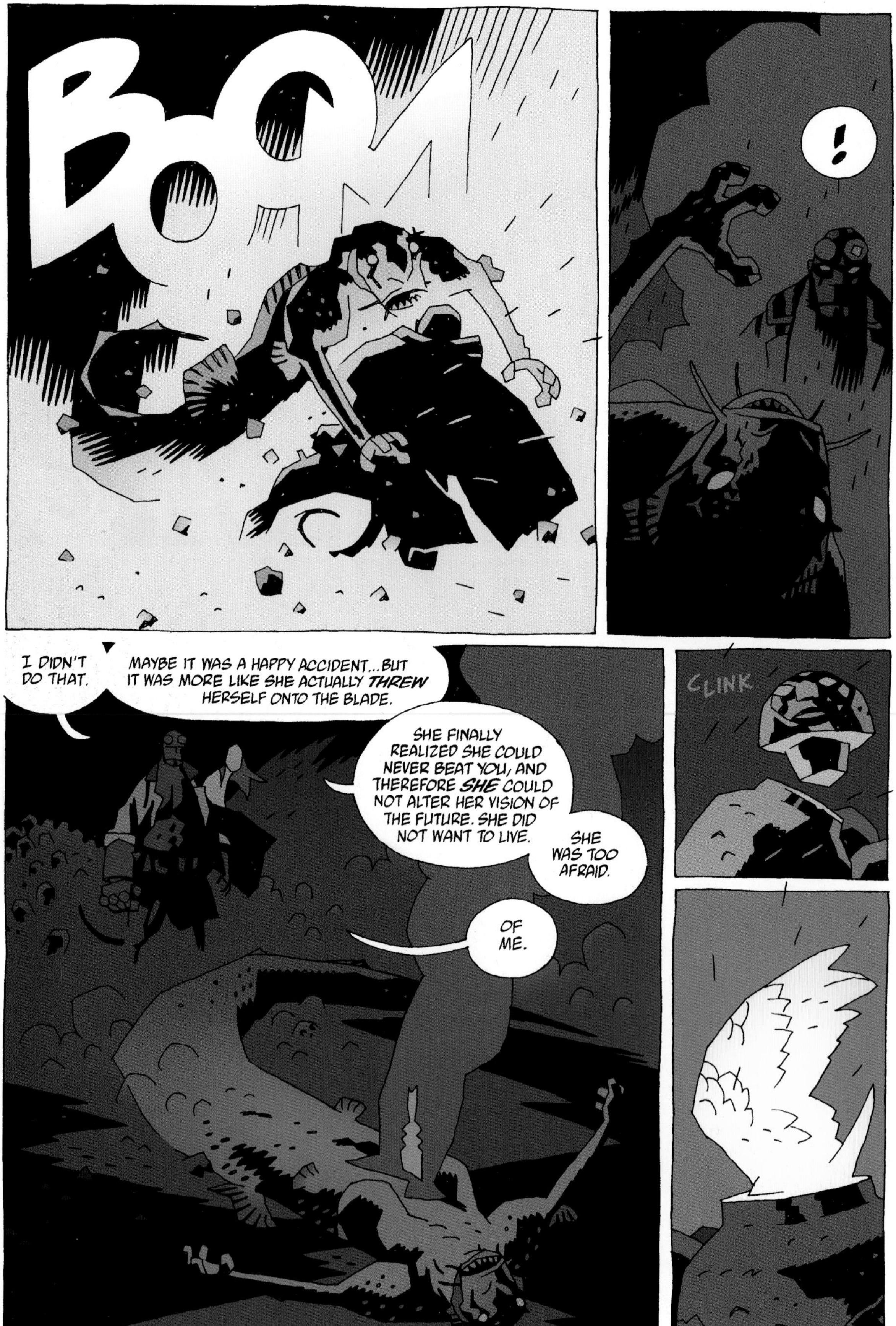
BOOM
!
I DIDN'T DO THAT.
MAYBE IT WAS A HAPPY ACCIDENT...BUT IT WAS MORE LIKE SHE ACTUALLY *THREW* HERSELF ONTO THE BLADE.
CLINK
SHE FINALLY REALIZED SHE COULD NEVER BEAT YOU, AND THEREFORE *SHE* COULD NOT ALTER HER VISION OF THE FUTURE. SHE DID NOT WANT TO LIVE.
SHE WAS TOO AFRAID.
OF ME.

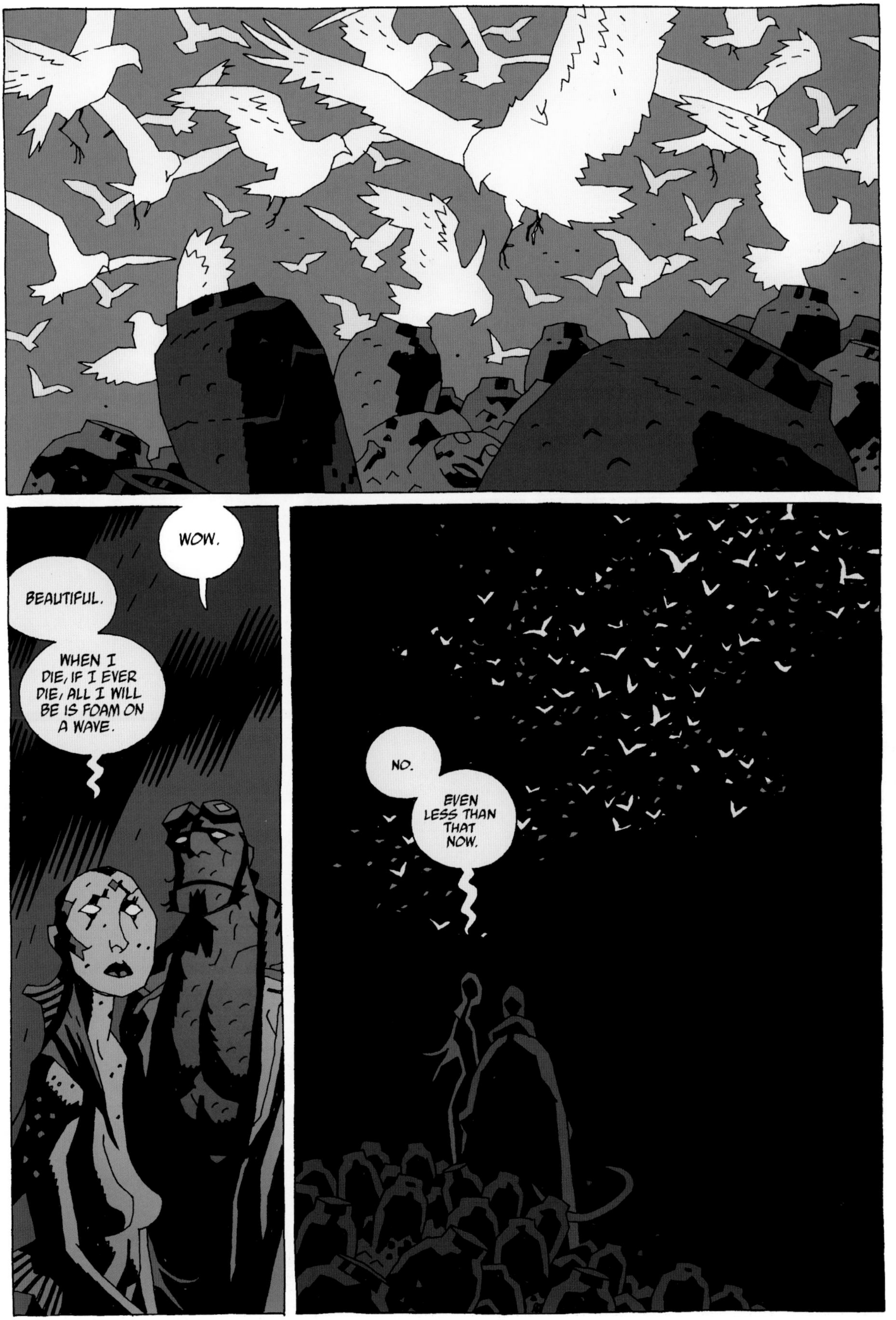
WOW.
BEAUTIFUL.
WHEN I DIE, IF I EVER DIE, ALL I WILL BE IS FOAM ON A WAVE.
NO.
EVEN LESS THAN THAT NOW.

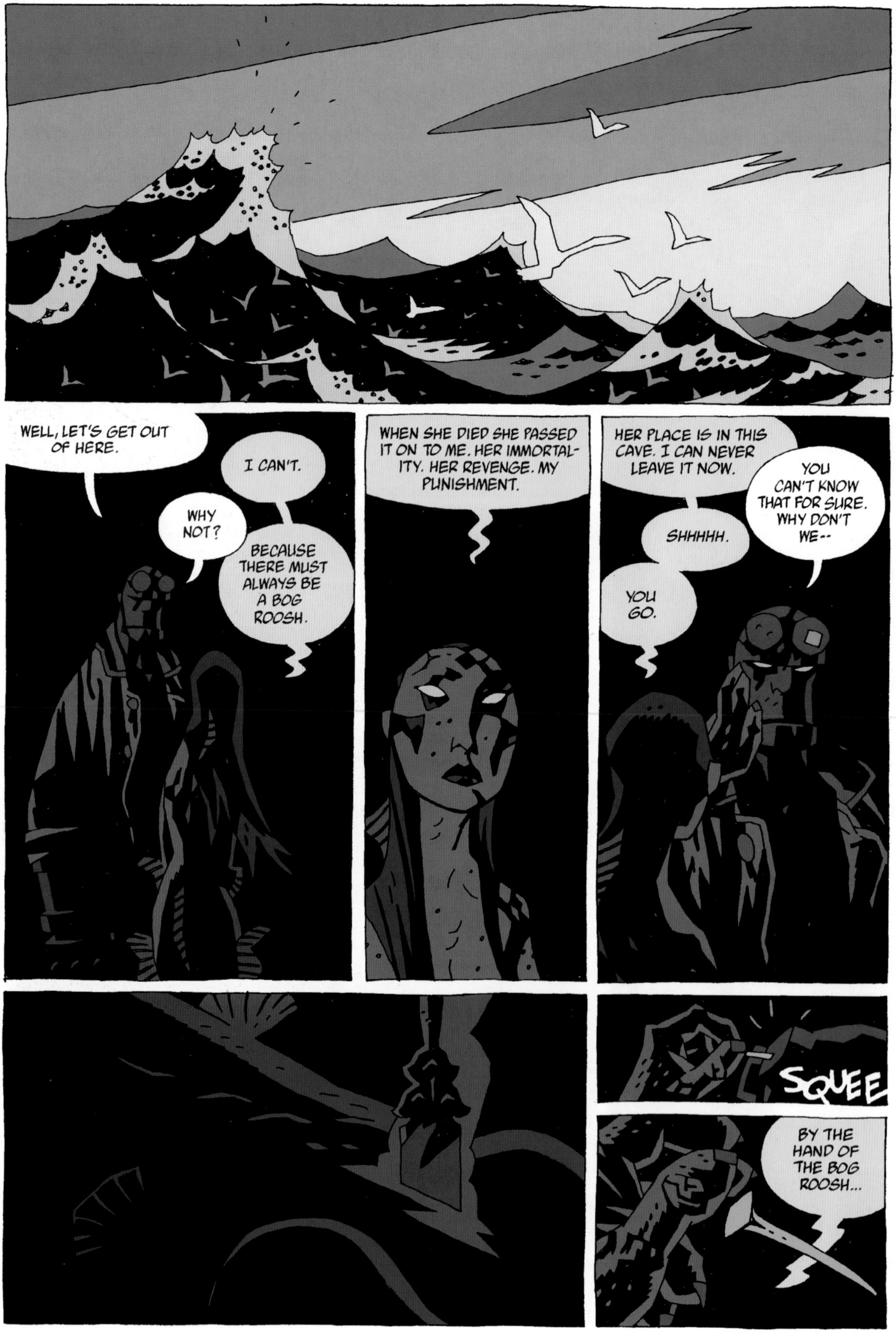
WELL, LET'S GET OUT OF HERE.
I CAN'T.
WHY NOT?
BECAUSE THERE MUST ALWAYS BE A BOG ROOSH.
WHEN SHE DIED SHE PASSED IT ON TO ME. HER IMMORTALITY. HER REVENGE. MY PUNISHMENT.
HER PLACE IS IN THIS CAVE. I CAN NEVER LEAVE IT NOW.
YOU CAN'T KNOW THAT FOR SURE. WHY DON'T WE--
SHHHHH.
YOU GO.
SQUEE
BY THE HAND OF THE BOG ROOSH...

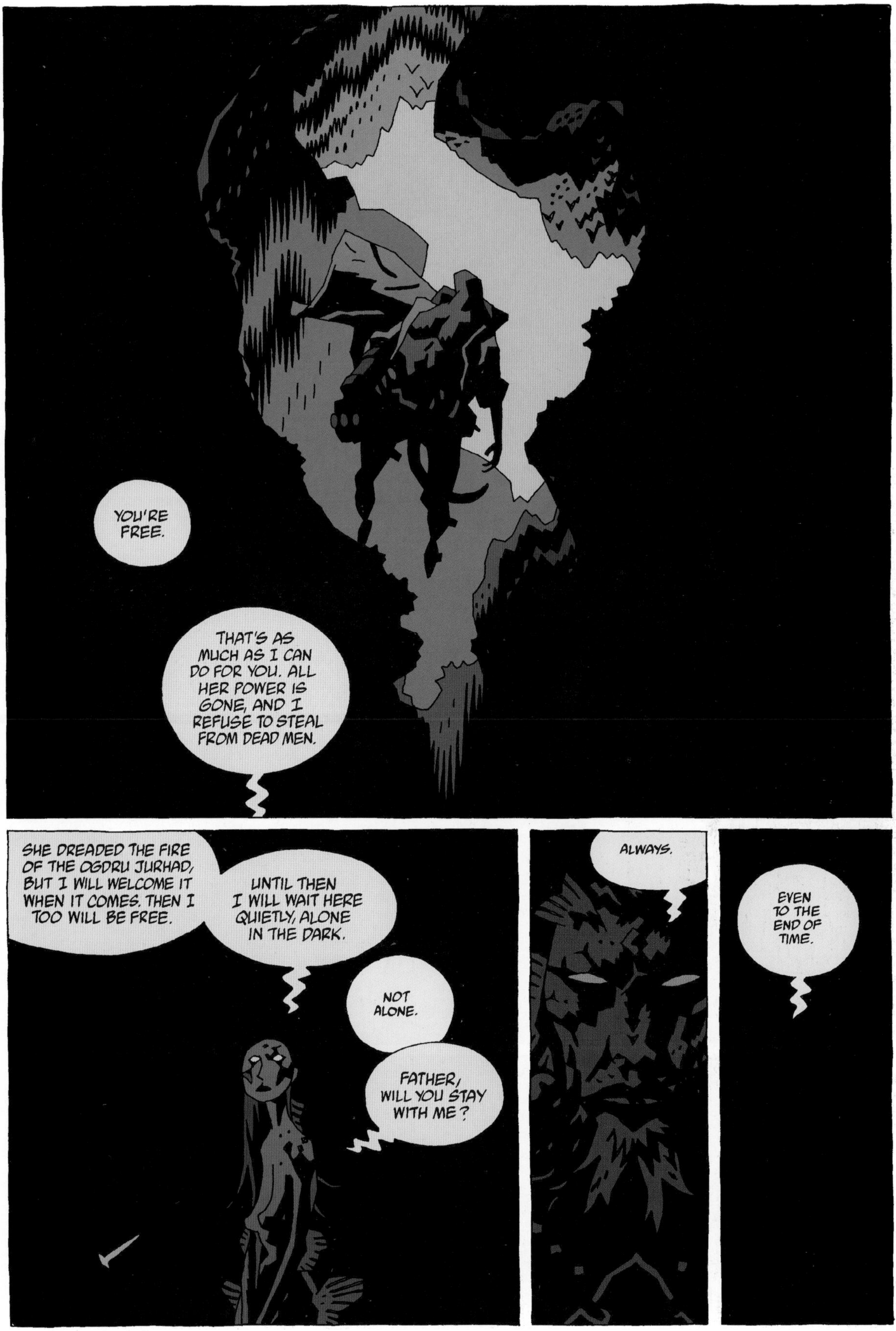
YOU'RE FREE.
THAT'S AS MUCH AS I CAN DO FOR YOU. ALL HER POWER IS GONE, AND I REFUSE TO STEAL FROM DEAD MEN.
SHE DREADED THE FIRE OF THE OGDRU JURHAD, BUT I WILL WELCOME IT WHEN IT COMES. THEN I TOO WILL BE FREE.
UNTIL THEN I WILL WAIT HERE QUIETLY, ALONE IN THE DARK.
NOT ALONE.
FATHER, WILL YOU STAY WITH ME?
ALWAYS.
EVEN TO THE END OF TIME.

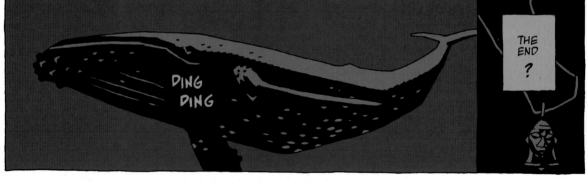

DING
DING

THE
END
?

THE ISLAND

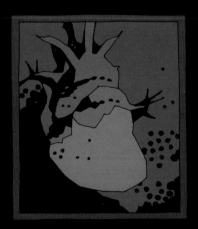

THIS WAS A ROUGH ONE.

My original idea was a story inspired by the Sargasso Sea stories of William Hope Hodgson (1877-1917) and his novel, *The Boats of the Glen Carrig*—a graveyard of ships and a strange island overrun with weird fungus and monsters. Simple enough. Fun. I plotted a two-issue miniseries and drew the first eight pages. No problem. Then I had to stop work for a while, go to Prague, and watch final filming of the *Hellboy* movie. Cool. Except that I got hit with a nasty Eastern European flu and was ordered to stay in my hotel room for a week. Solitary confinement in a foreign country. With nothing to do but sit and think, I became convinced that my story was crap and I would need to start over.

When I got back to New York I replotted *The Island*. Now it was a three-issue miniseries. It still had the ships and the fungus, but now there was also this strange mansion with an old man and his servant. This time I drew nineteen pages and then sort of . . . ran out of gas. Not sure what happened. I really like that story, and plan to do it one of these days, but right then it just wasn't working. I scrapped the idea of the fungus people (though I dearly love fungus people), tried replotting it as one issue, bumped it back up to two issues, and, finally, that's the story you have here.

I created Hellboy way back in 1993. Since then I've figured a lot of stuff out about his world, its history, and how it all works. The question has always been how much do you tell people and when do you tell them? I've been keeping a lot of secrets. Then along comes this Hellboy movie, and suddenly we have the Ogdru Jahad popping out of their prisons and waggling their tentacles at the cameras. Hell, if you were going to see them, I figured I should show the *real* version of them in the comic first. And I'll do one better. I'll give their origin. And, while I'm at it, I might as well throw in the creation of the world, the rise and fall of angels, and the origin of mankind. After all, the audience has, by now, been waiting a long time for a new Hellboy comic. I better give them something big.

The Island was published as a two-issue miniseries in 2005, and is the end of the first chapter of Hellboy's life. The Epilogue, published here for the first time, gives us a first look at where things are going— stranger places.

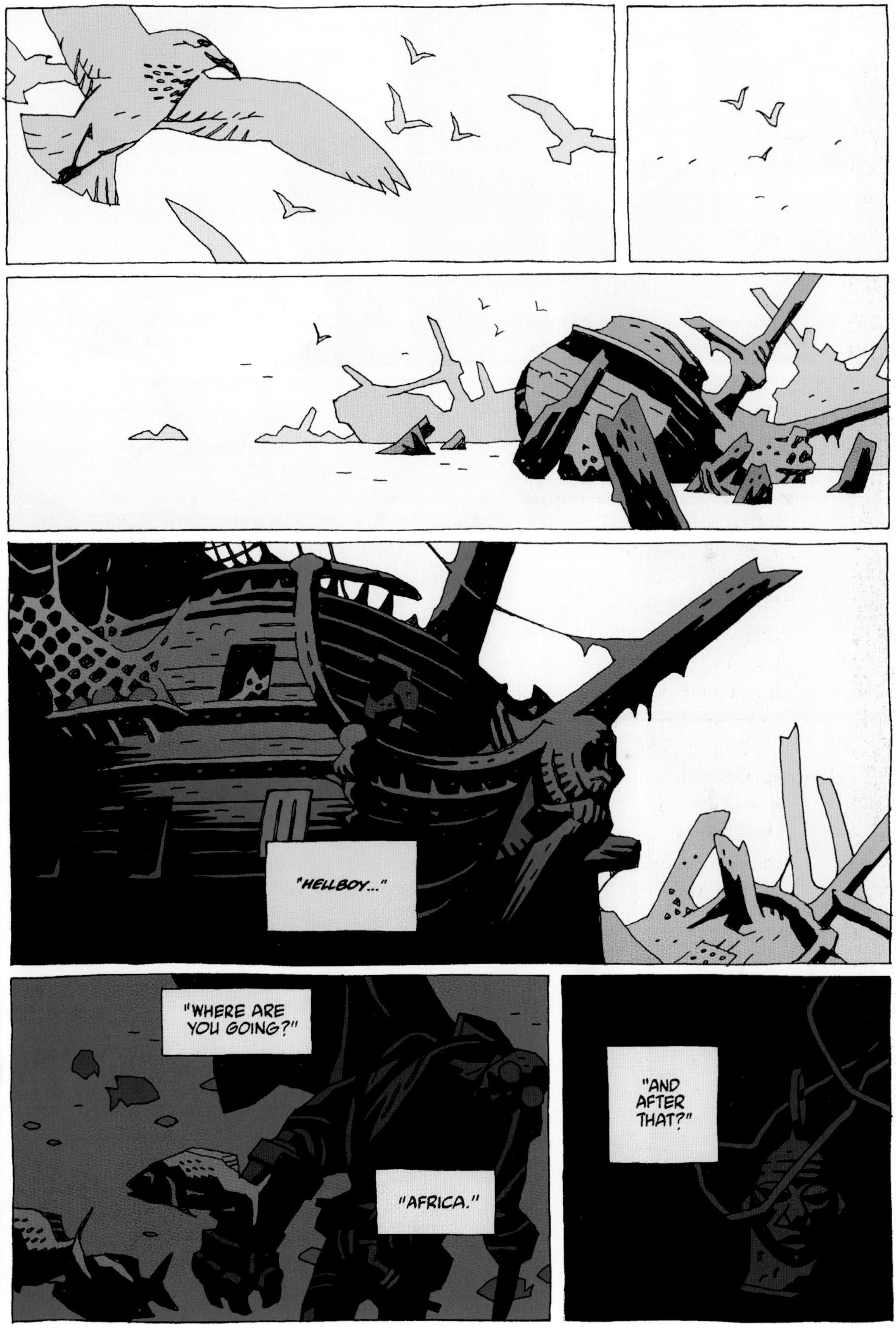
"HELLBOY..."
"WHERE ARE YOU GOING?"
"AFRICA."
"AND AFTER THAT?"

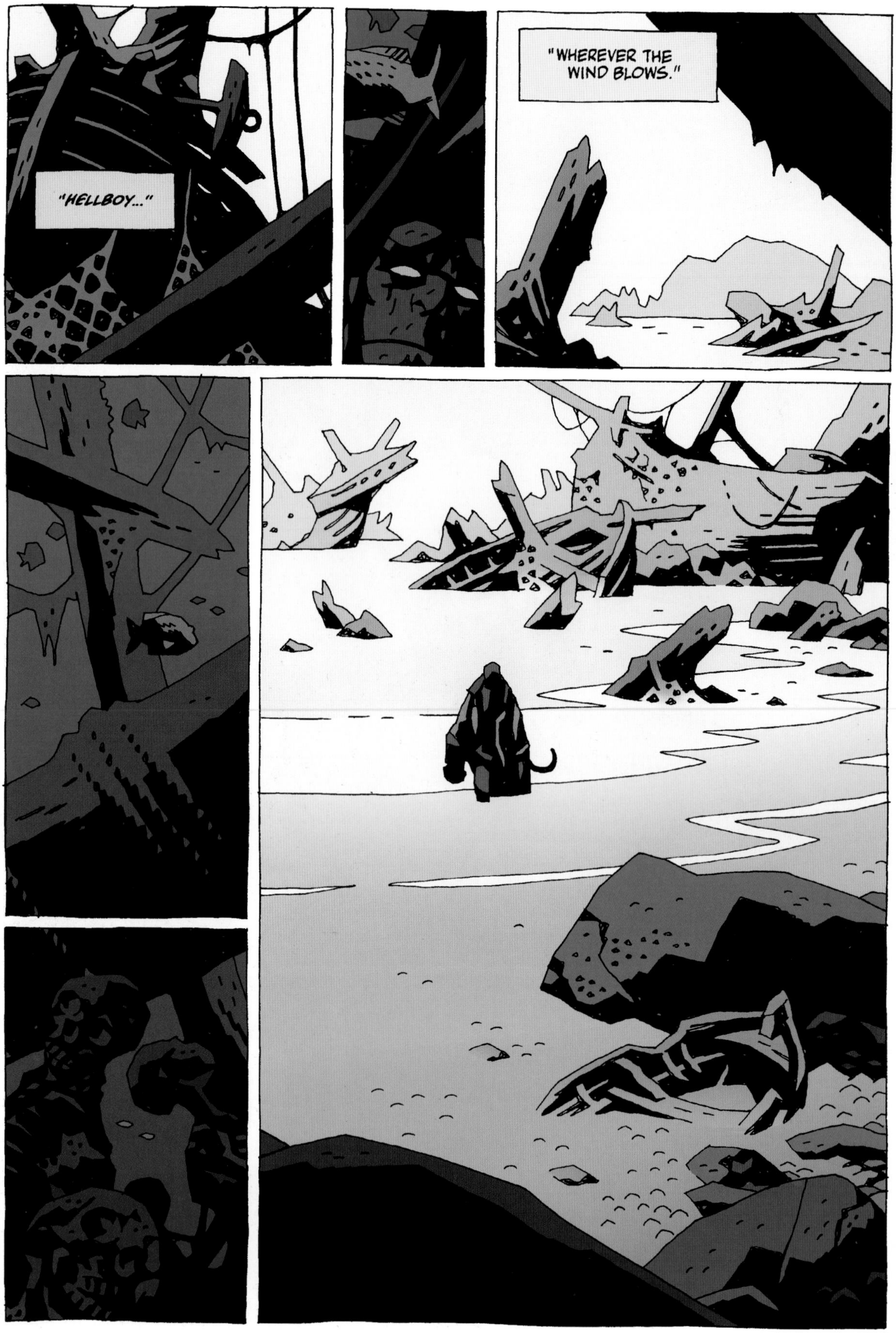
"HELLBOY..."
"WHEREVER THE WIND BLOWS."

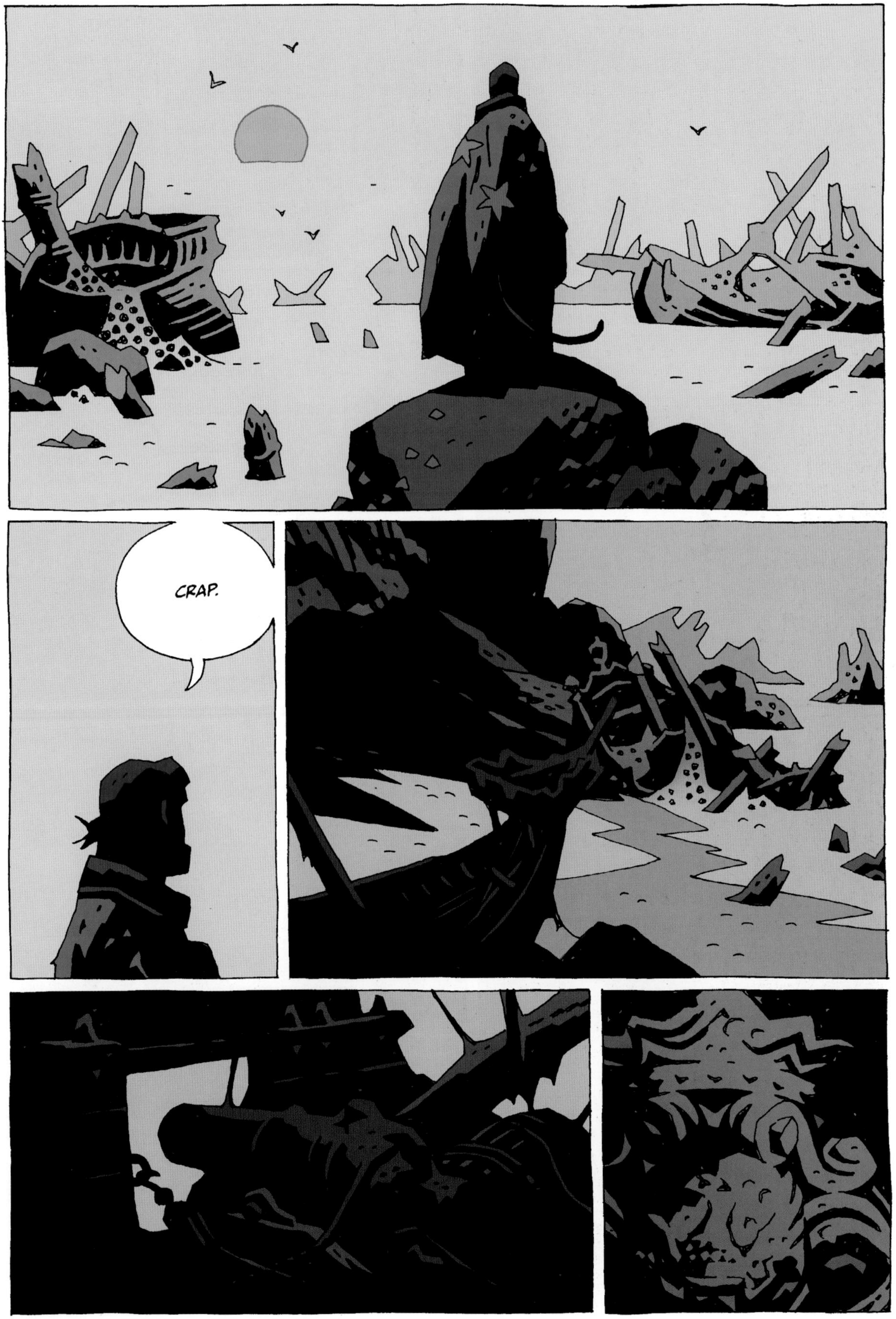
CRAP.

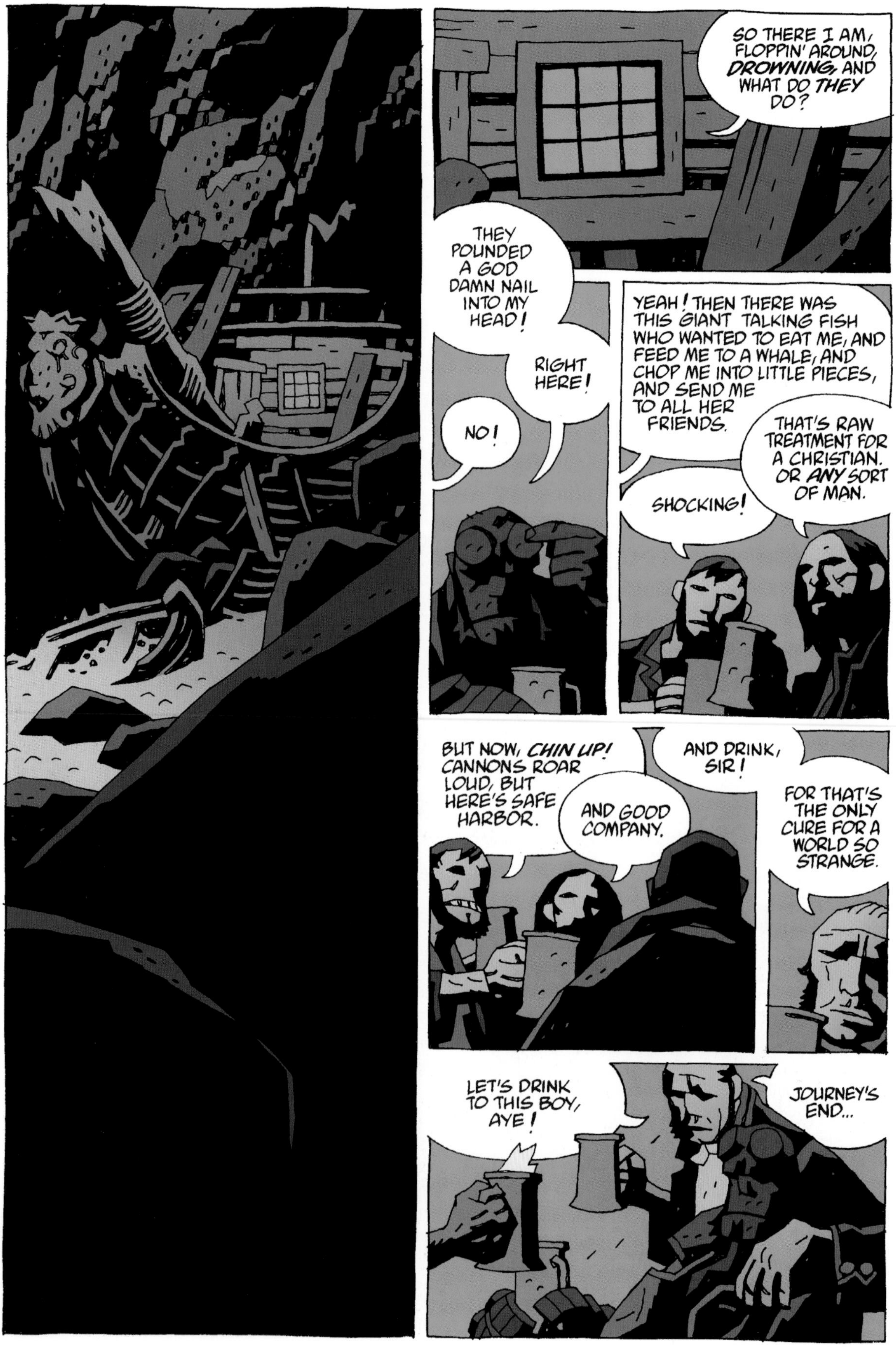
SO THERE I AM, FLOPPIN' AROUND, DROWNING, AND WHAT DO THEY DO?
THEY POUNDED A GOD DAMN NAIL INTO MY HEAD!
RIGHT HERE!
NO!
YEAH! THEN THERE WAS THIS GIANT TALKING FISH WHO WANTED TO EAT ME, AND FEED ME TO A WHALE, AND CHOP ME INTO LITTLE PIECES, AND SEND ME TO ALL HER FRIENDS.
SHOCKING!
THAT'S RAW TREATMENT FOR A CHRISTIAN. OR ANY SORT OF MAN.
BUT NOW, CHIN UP! CANNONS ROAR LOUD, BUT HERE'S SAFE HARBOR.
AND GOOD COMPANY.
AND DRINK, SIR!
FOR THAT'S THE ONLY CURE FOR A WORLD SO STRANGE.
LET'S DRINK TO THIS BOY, AYE!
JOURNEY'S END...

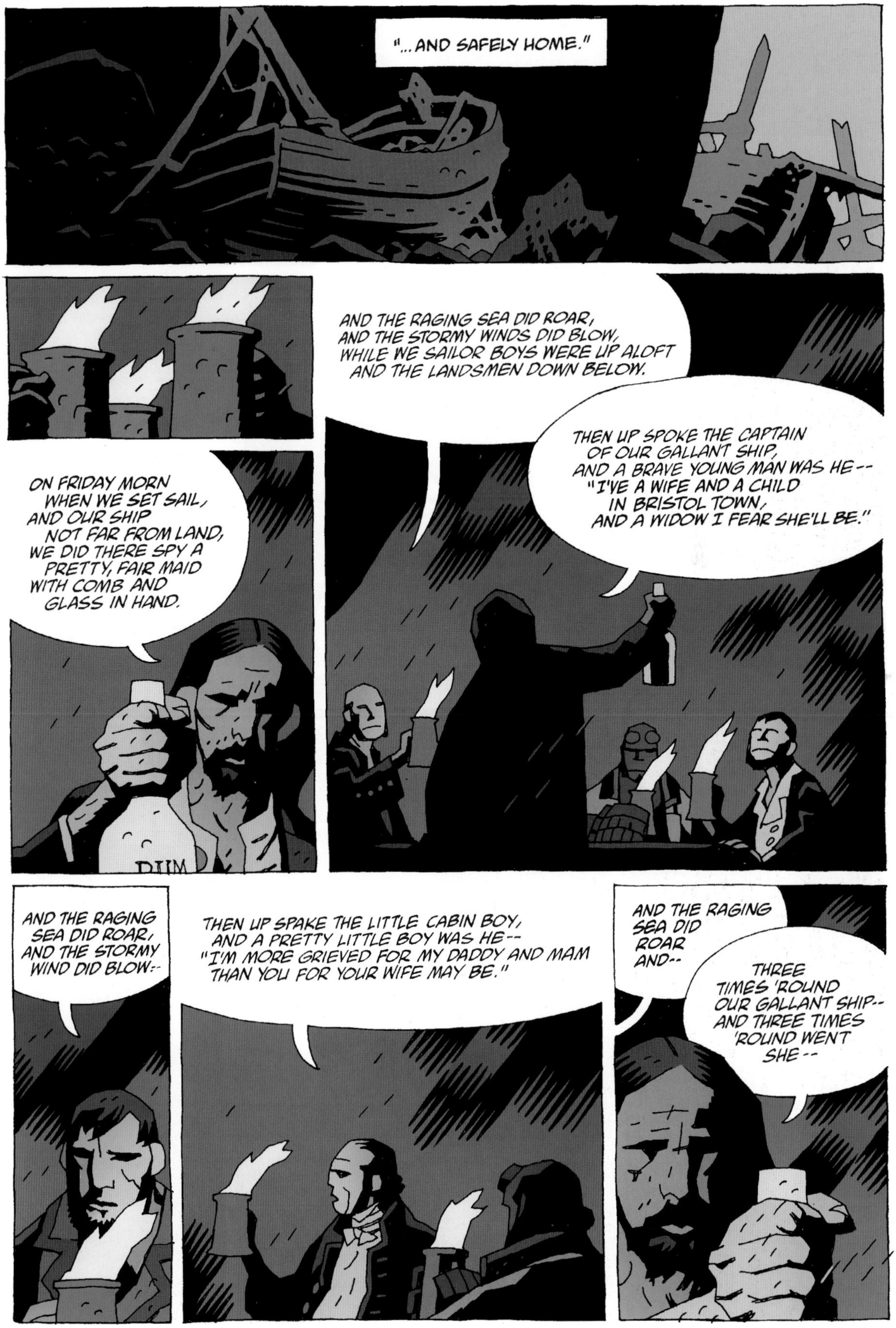
"...AND SAFELY HOME."
AND THE RAGING SEA DID ROAR, AND THE STORMY WINDS DID BLOW, WHILE WE SAILOR BOYS WERE UP ALOFT AND THE LANDSMEN DOWN BELOW.
ON FRIDAY MORN WHEN WE SET SAIL, AND OUR SHIP NOT FAR FROM LAND, WE DID THERE SPY A PRETTY, FAIR MAID WITH COMB AND GLASS IN HAND.
THEN UP SPOKE THE CAPTAIN OF OUR GALLANT SHIP, AND A BRAVE YOUNG MAN WAS HE-- "I'VE A WIFE AND A CHILD IN BRISTOL TOWN, AND A WIDOW I FEAR SHE'LL BE."
AND THE RAGING SEA DID ROAR, AND THE STORMY WIND DID BLOW:-
THEN UP SPAKE THE LITTLE CABIN BOY, AND A PRETTY LITTLE BOY WAS HE-- "I'M MORE GRIEVED FOR MY DADDY AND MAM THAN YOU FOR YOUR WIFE MAY BE."
AND THE RAGING SEA DID ROAR AND--
THREE TIMES 'ROUND OUR GALLANT SHIP-- AND THREE TIMES 'ROUND WENT SHE--

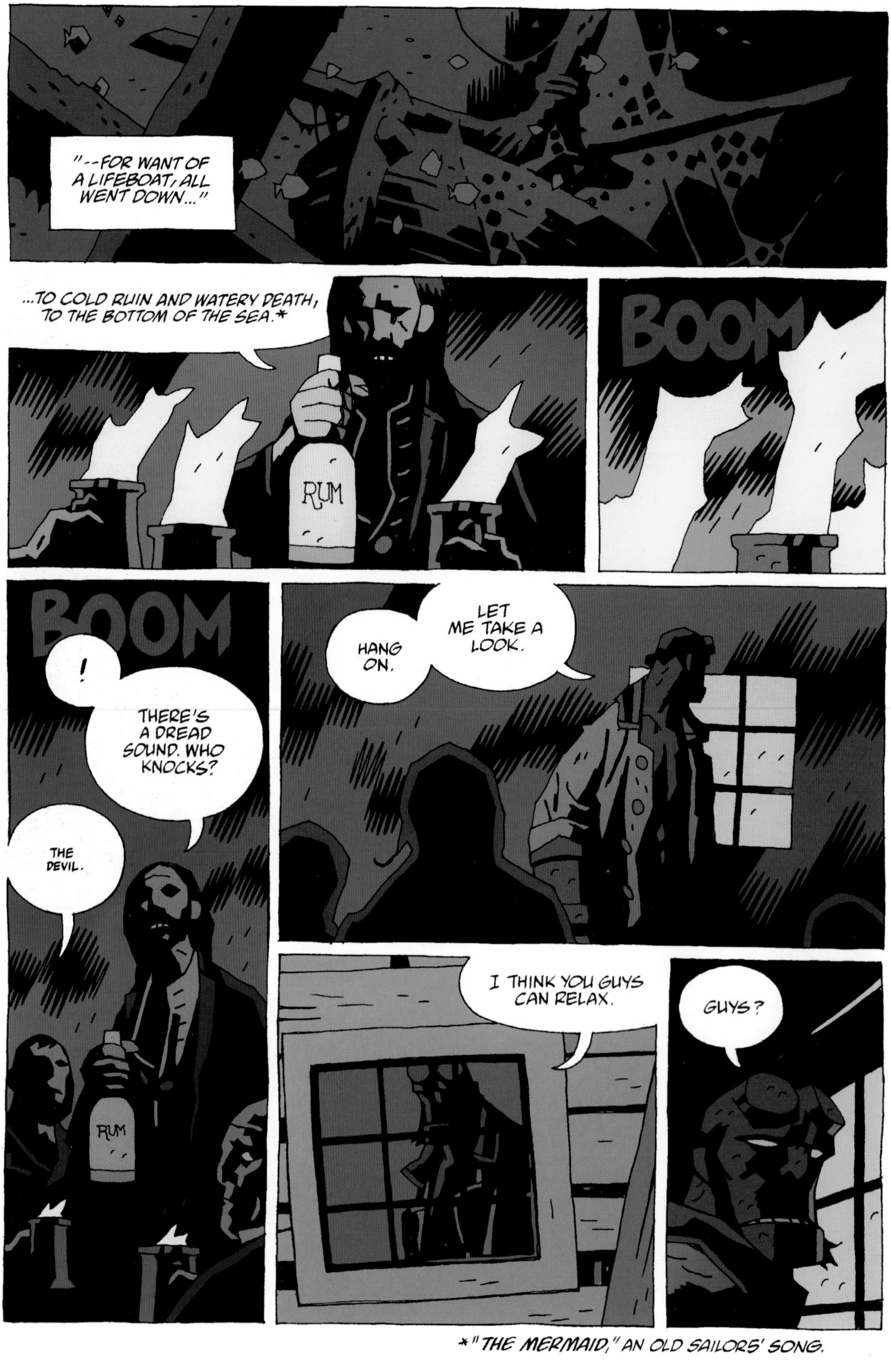
"--FOR WANT OF A LIFEBOAT, ALL WENT DOWN..."
...TO COLD RUIN AND WATERY DEATH, TO THE BOTTOM OF THE SEA.*
RUM
BOOM
BOOM
!
THERE'S A DREAD SOUND. WHO KNOCKS?
THE DEVIL.
RUM
HANG ON.
LET ME TAKE A LOOK.
I THINK YOU GUYS CAN RELAX.
GUYS?

*"*THE MERMAID*," AN OLD SAILORS' SONG.

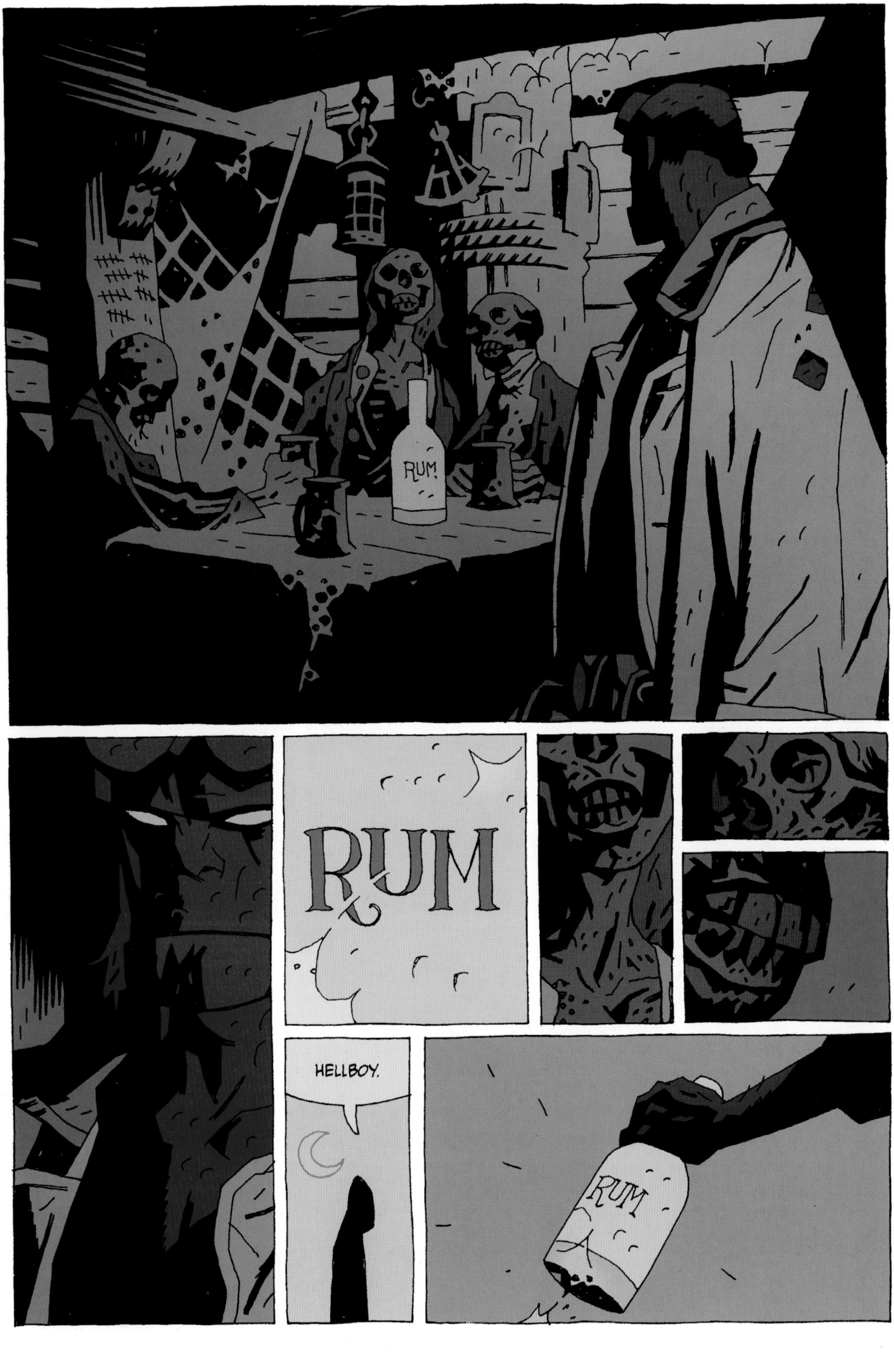
RUM
RUM
HELLBOY.
RUM

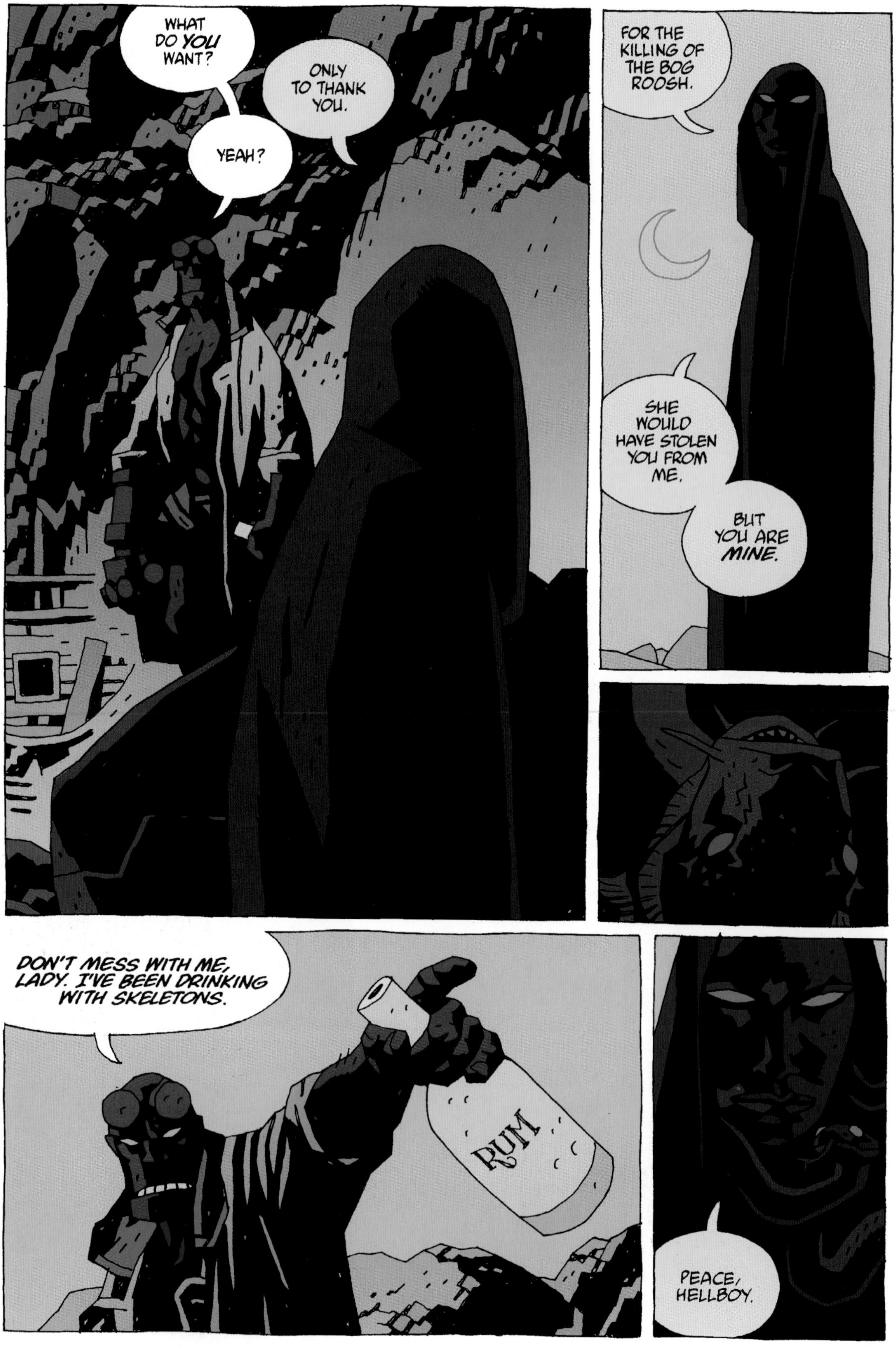
WHAT DO YOU WANT?
ONLY TO THANK YOU.
YEAH?
FOR THE KILLING OF THE BOG ROOSH.
SHE WOULD HAVE STOLEN YOU FROM ME.
BUT YOU ARE MINE.
DON'T MESS WITH ME, LADY. I'VE BEEN DRINKING WITH SKELETONS.
RUM
PEACE, HELLBOY.

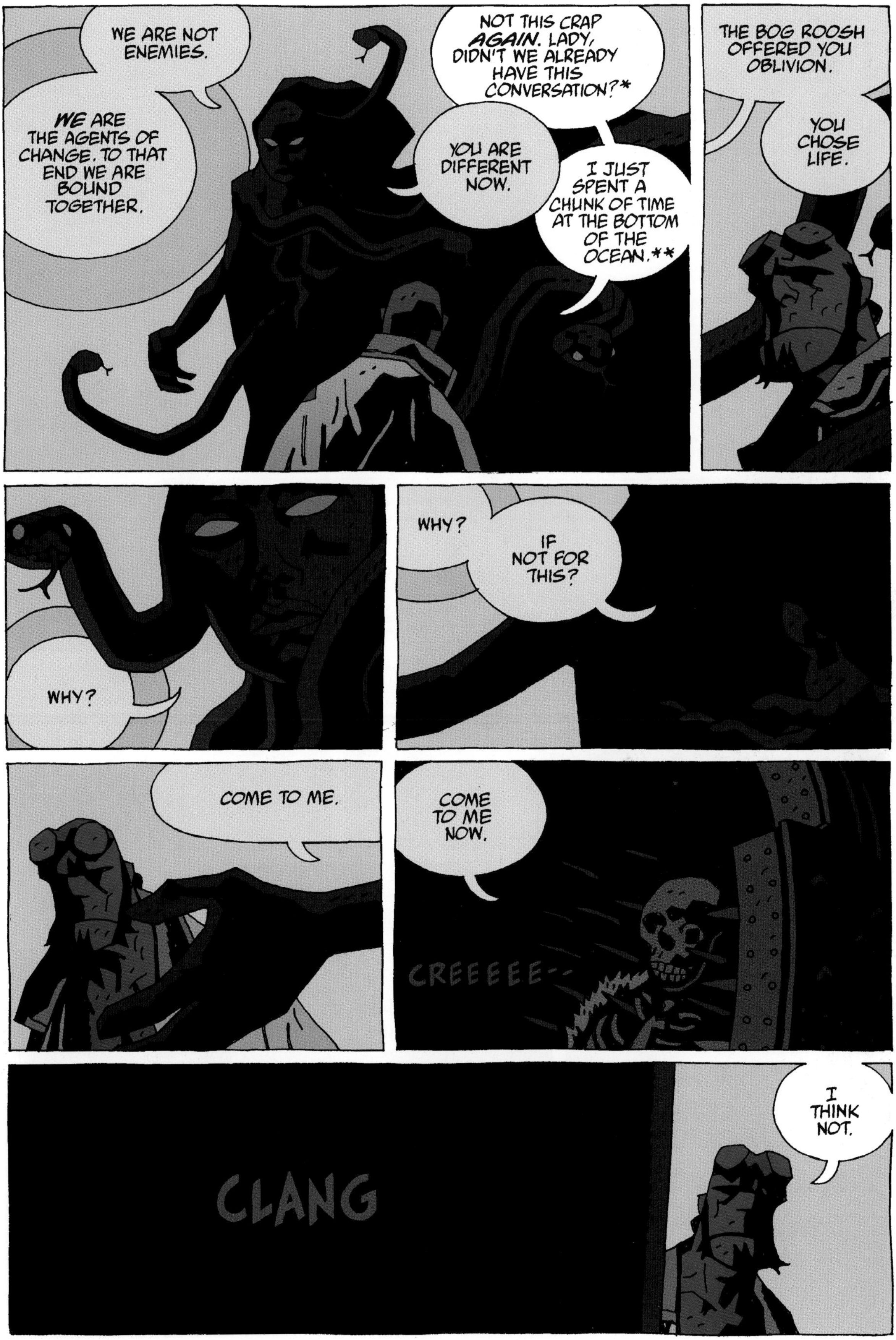
WE ARE NOT ENEMIES.
WE ARE THE AGENTS OF CHANGE. TO THAT END WE ARE BOUND TOGETHER.
NOT THIS CRAP AGAIN. LADY, DIDN'T WE ALREADY HAVE THIS CONVERSATION?*
YOU ARE DIFFERENT NOW.
I JUST SPENT A CHUNK OF TIME AT THE BOTTOM OF THE OCEAN.**
THE BOG ROOSH OFFERED YOU OBLIVION.
YOU CHOSE LIFE.
WHY?
WHY?
IF NOT FOR THIS?
COME TO ME.
COME TO ME NOW.
CREEEEE--
CLANG
I THINK NOT.

***HELLBOY:** WAKE THE DEVIL

**OVER TWO YEARS

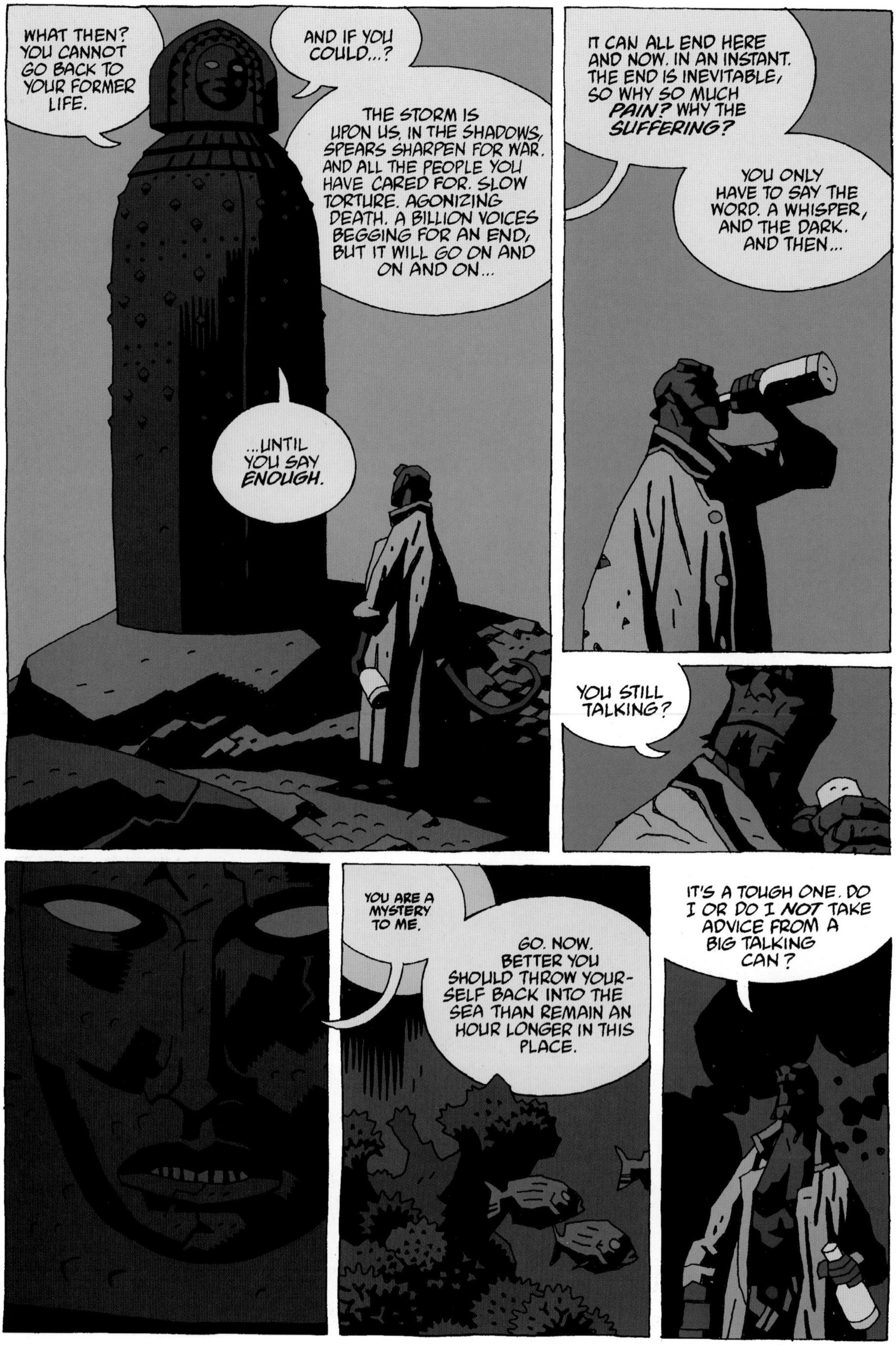
WHAT THEN? YOU CANNOT GO BACK TO YOUR FORMER LIFE.
AND IF YOU COULD...?
THE STORM IS UPON US. IN THE SHADOWS, SPEARS SHARPEN FOR WAR. AND ALL THE PEOPLE YOU HAVE CARED FOR. SLOW TORTURE. AGONIZING DEATH. A BILLION VOICES BEGGING FOR AN END, BUT IT WILL GO ON AND ON AND ON...
...UNTIL YOU SAY ENOUGH.
IT CAN ALL END HERE AND NOW. IN AN INSTANT. THE END IS INEVITABLE, SO WHY SO MUCH PAIN? WHY THE SUFFERING?
YOU ONLY HAVE TO SAY THE WORD. A WHISPER, AND THE DARK. AND THEN...
YOU STILL TALKING?
YOU ARE A MYSTERY TO ME.
GO. NOW. BETTER YOU SHOULD THROW YOURSELF BACK INTO THE SEA THAN REMAIN AN HOUR LONGER IN THIS PLACE.
IT'S A TOUGH ONE. DO I OR DO I NOT TAKE ADVICE FROM A BIG TALKING CAN?

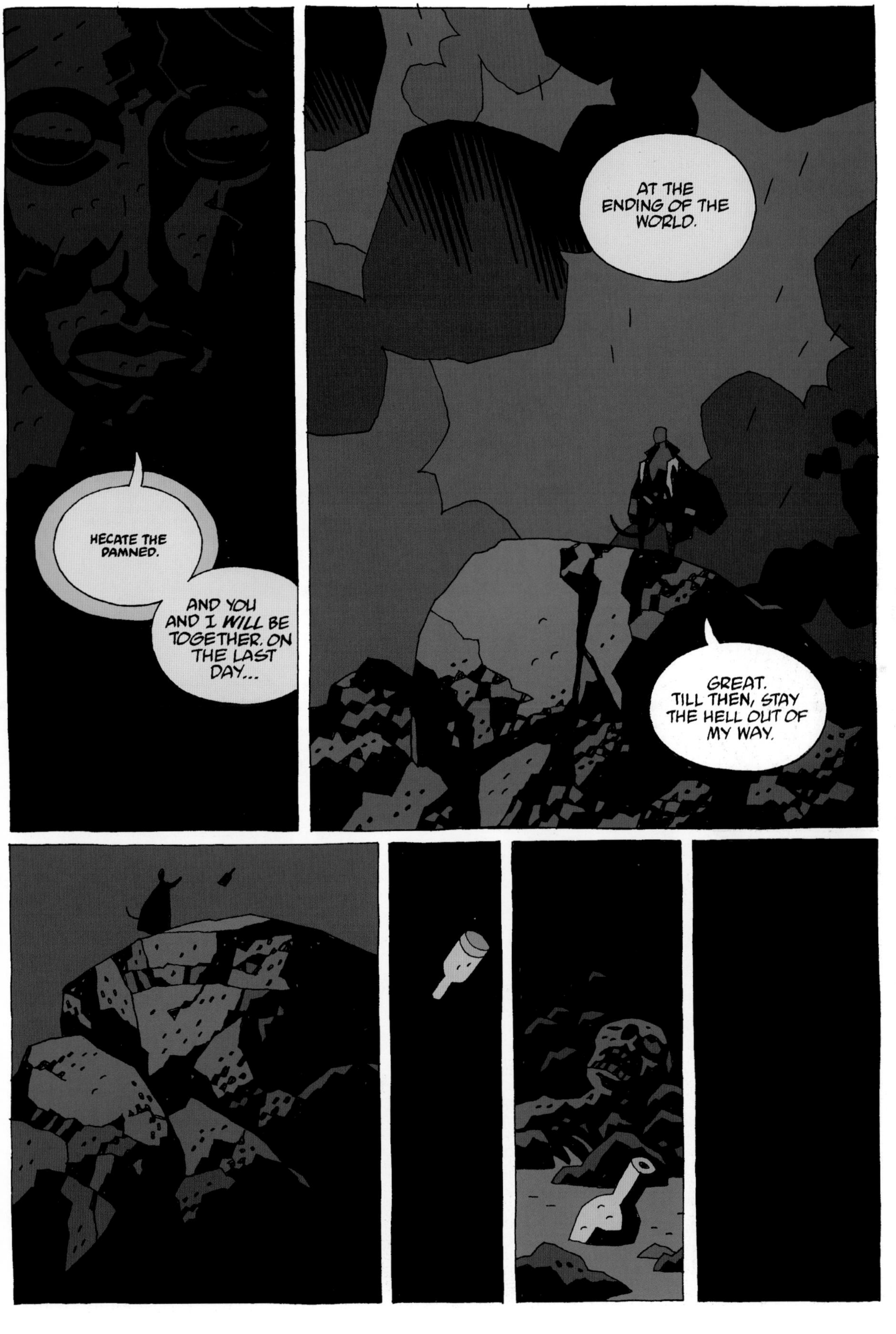
HECATE THE DAMNED.
AND YOU AND I WILL BE TOGETHER, ON THE LAST DAY...
AT THE ENDING OF THE WORLD.
GREAT. TILL THEN, STAY THE HELL OUT OF MY WAY.

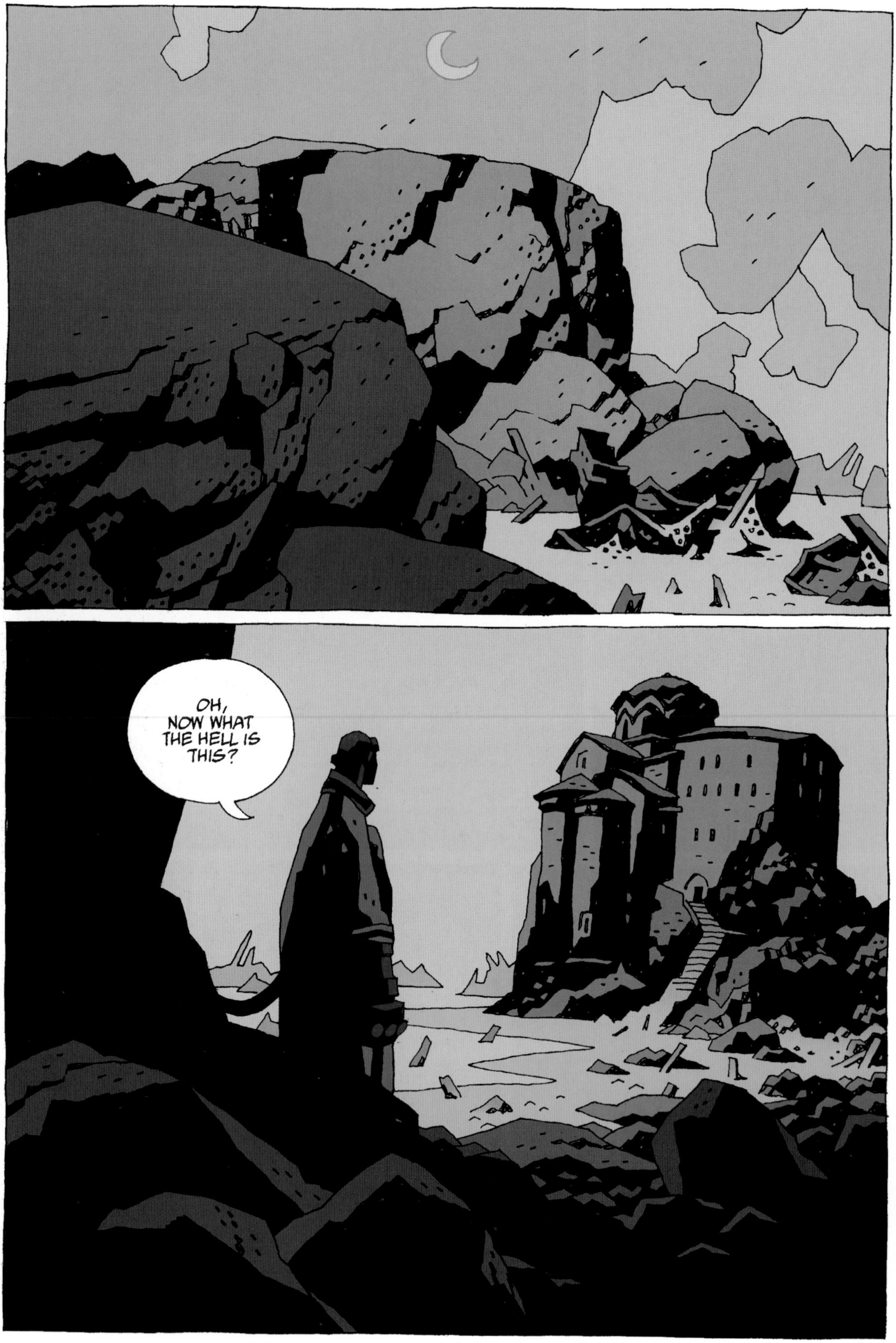
OH, NOW WHAT THE HELL IS THIS?

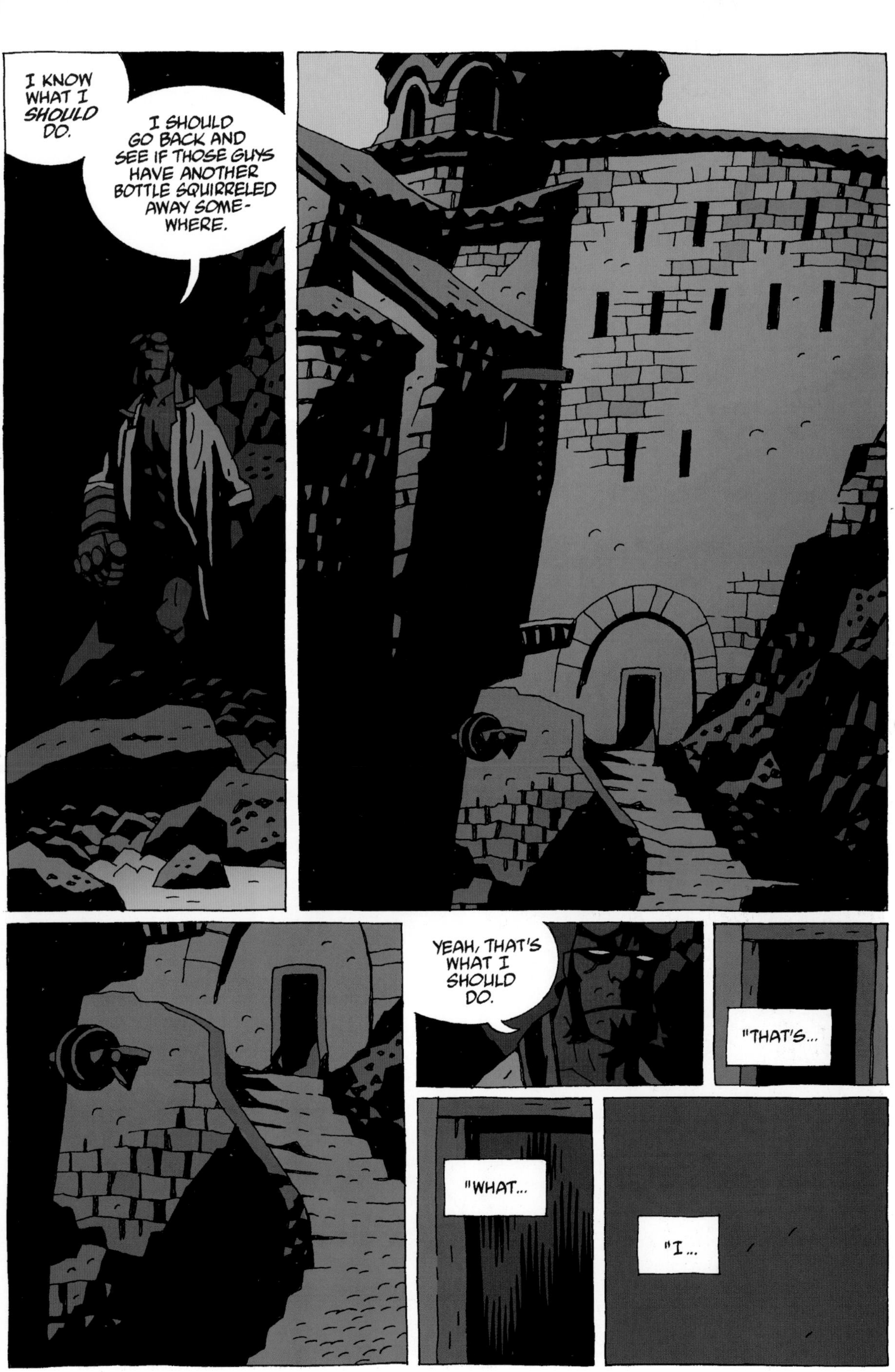
I KNOW WHAT I *SHOULD* DO.
I SHOULD GO BACK AND SEE IF THOSE GUYS HAVE ANOTHER BOTTLE SQUIRRELED AWAY SOME-WHERE.
YEAH, THAT'S WHAT I SHOULD DO.
"THAT'S...
"WHAT...
"I...

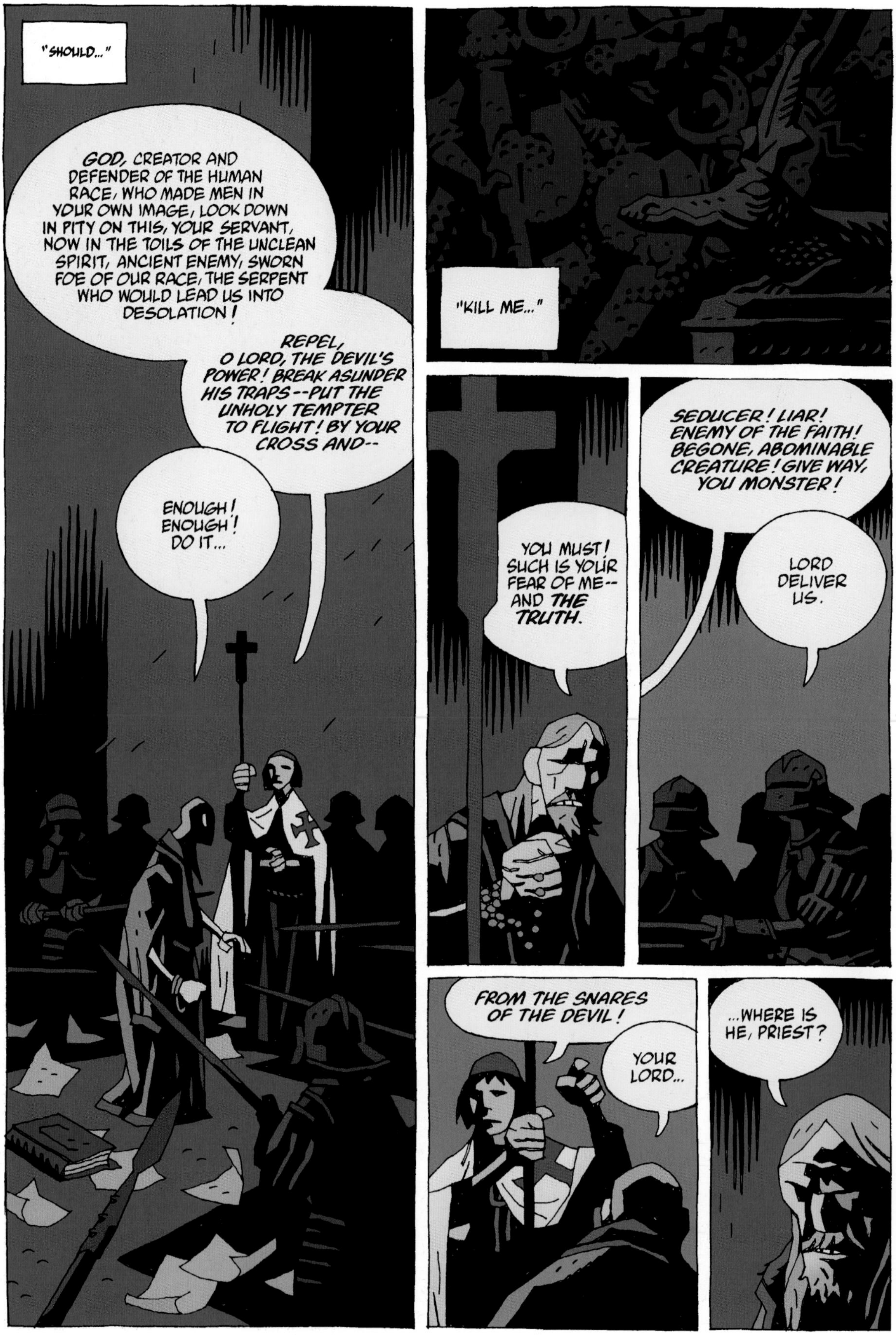
"SHOULD..."
GOD, CREATOR AND DEFENDER OF THE HUMAN RACE, WHO MADE MEN IN YOUR OWN IMAGE, LOOK DOWN IN PITY ON THIS, YOUR SERVANT, NOW IN THE TOILS OF THE UNCLEAN SPIRIT, ANCIENT ENEMY, SWORN FOE OF OUR RACE, THE SERPENT WHO WOULD LEAD US INTO DESOLATION!
REPEL, O LORD, THE DEVIL'S POWER! BREAK ASUNDER HIS TRAPS--PUT THE UNHOLY TEMPTER TO FLIGHT! BY YOUR CROSS AND--
ENOUGH! ENOUGH! DO IT...
"KILL ME..."
YOU MUST! SUCH IS YOUR FEAR OF ME--AND THE TRUTH.
SEDUCER! LIAR! ENEMY OF THE FAITH! BEGONE, ABOMINABLE CREATURE! GIVE WAY, YOU MONSTER!
LORD DELIVER US.
FROM THE SNARES OF THE DEVIL!
YOUR LORD...
...WHERE IS HE, PRIEST?

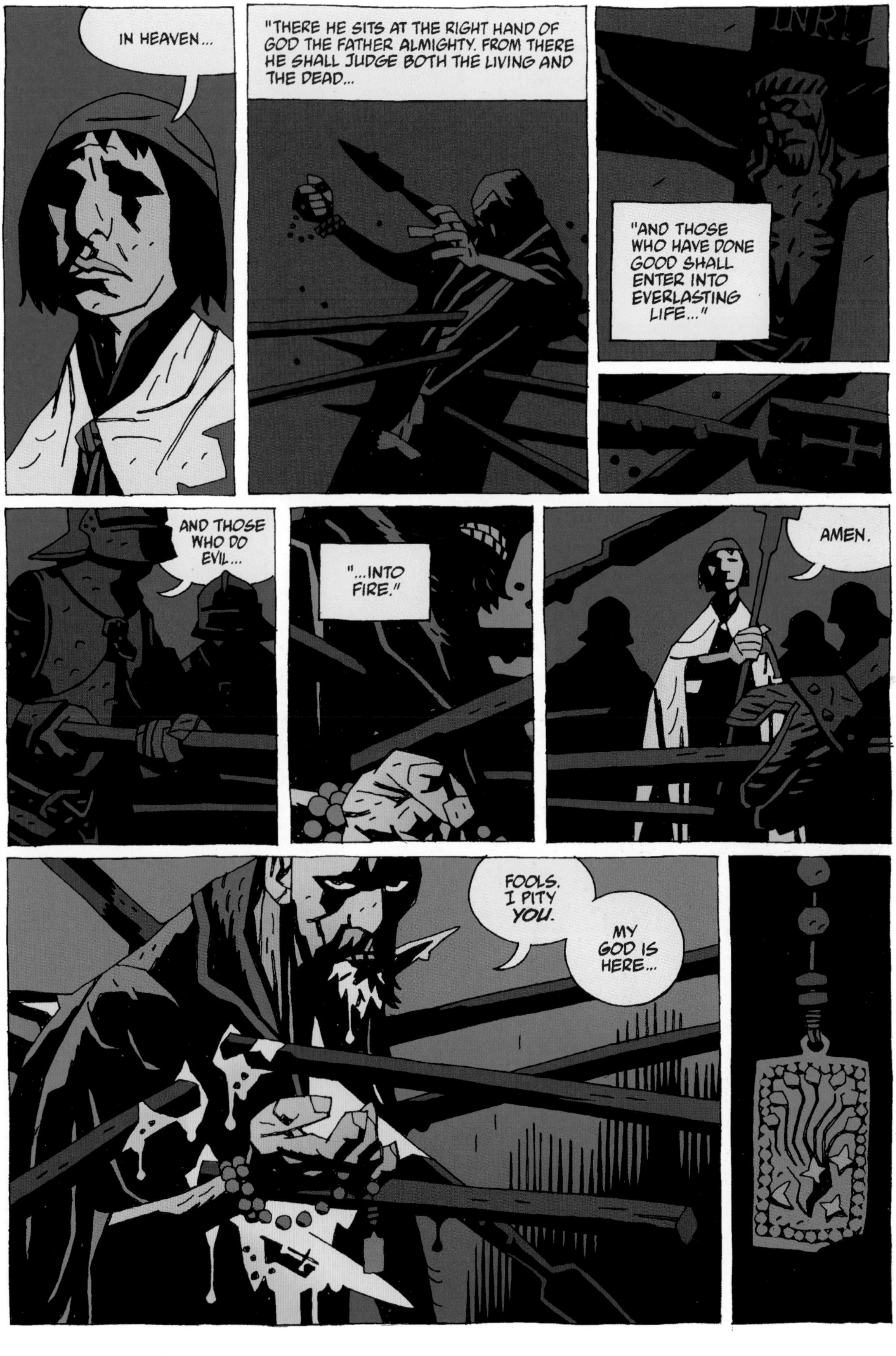
IN HEAVEN...
"THERE HE SITS AT THE RIGHT HAND OF GOD THE FATHER ALMIGHTY. FROM THERE HE SHALL JUDGE BOTH THE LIVING AND THE DEAD...
INRI
"AND THOSE WHO HAVE DONE GOOD SHALL ENTER INTO EVERLASTING LIFE..."
AND THOSE WHO DO EVIL...
"...INTO FIRE."
AMEN.
FOOLS. I PITY *YOU*.
MY GOD IS HERE...

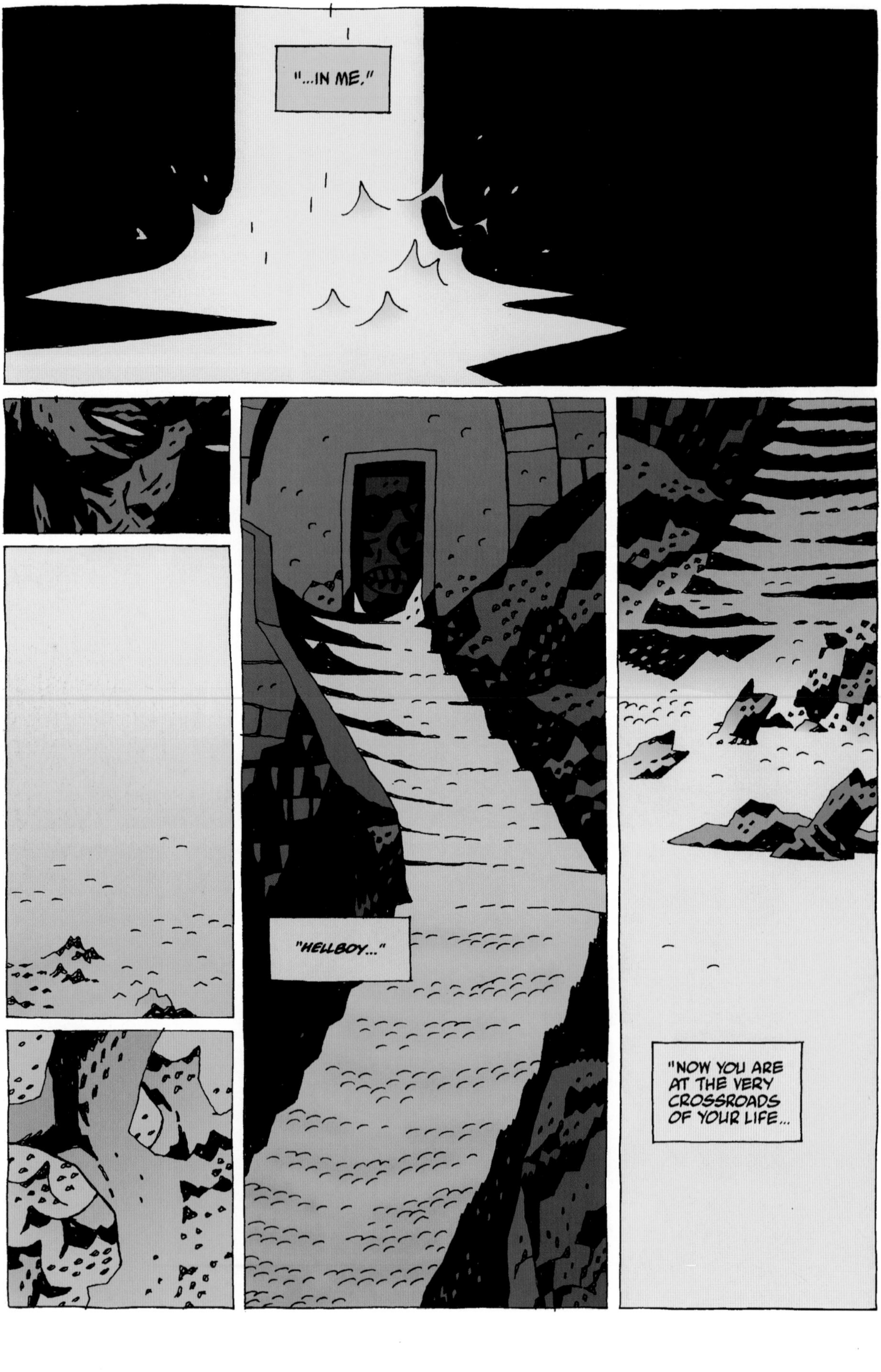
"...IN ME."
"HELLBOY..."
"NOW YOU ARE AT THE VERY CROSSROADS OF YOUR LIFE...

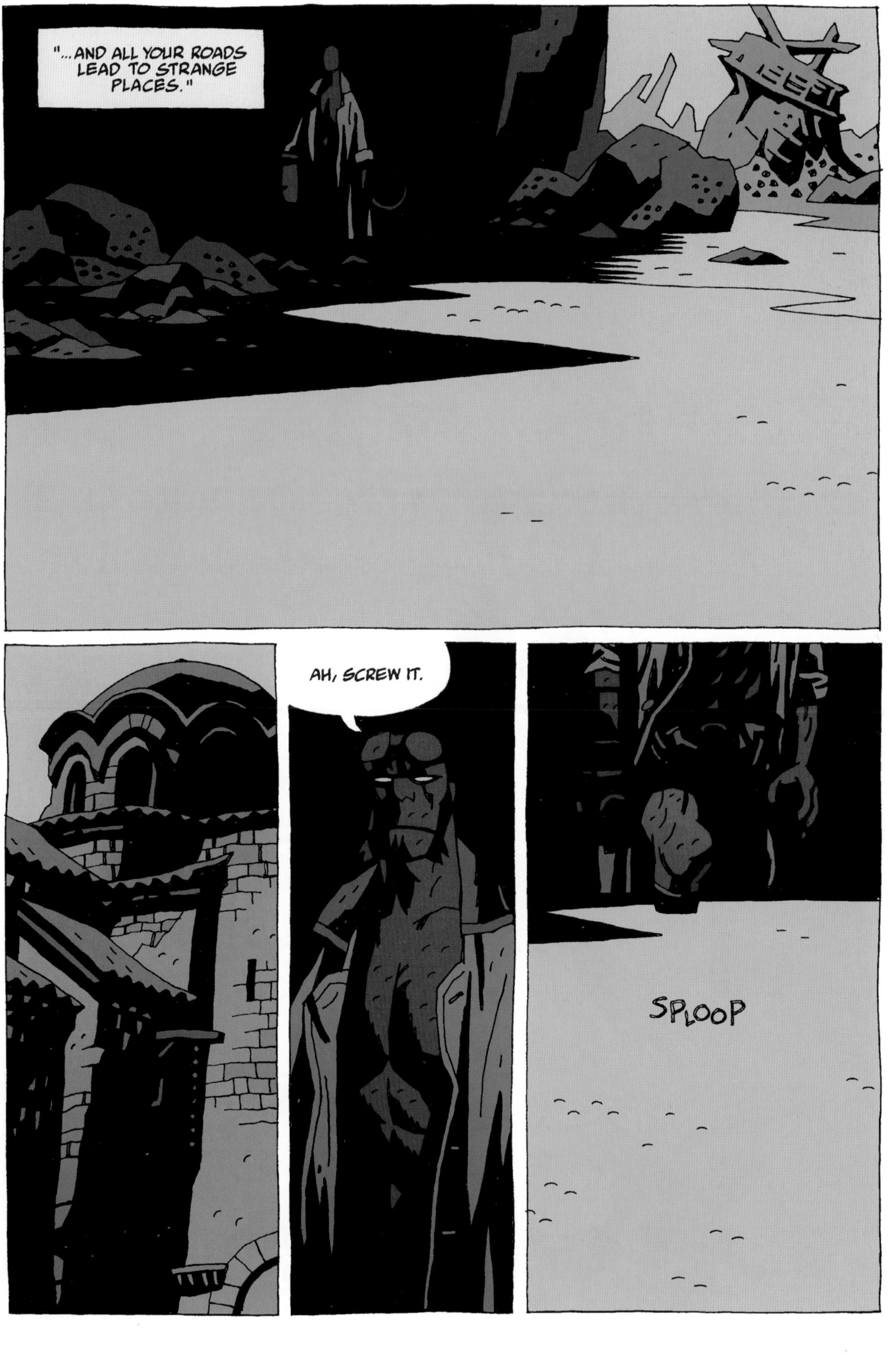
"...AND ALL YOUR ROADS LEAD TO STRANGE PLACES."
AH, SCREW IT.
SPLOOP

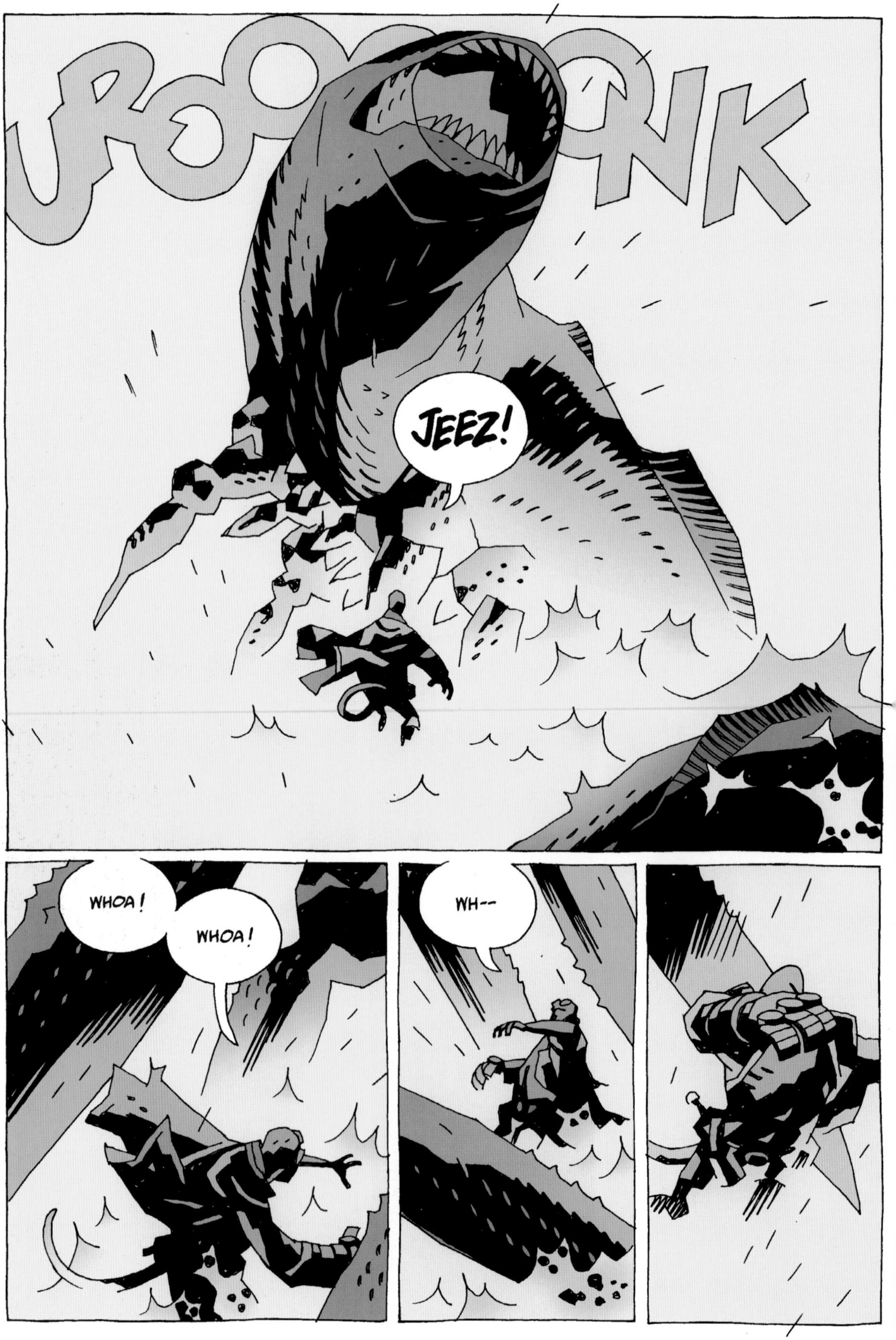

UROOOONK
JEEZ!
WHOA!
WHOA!
WH--

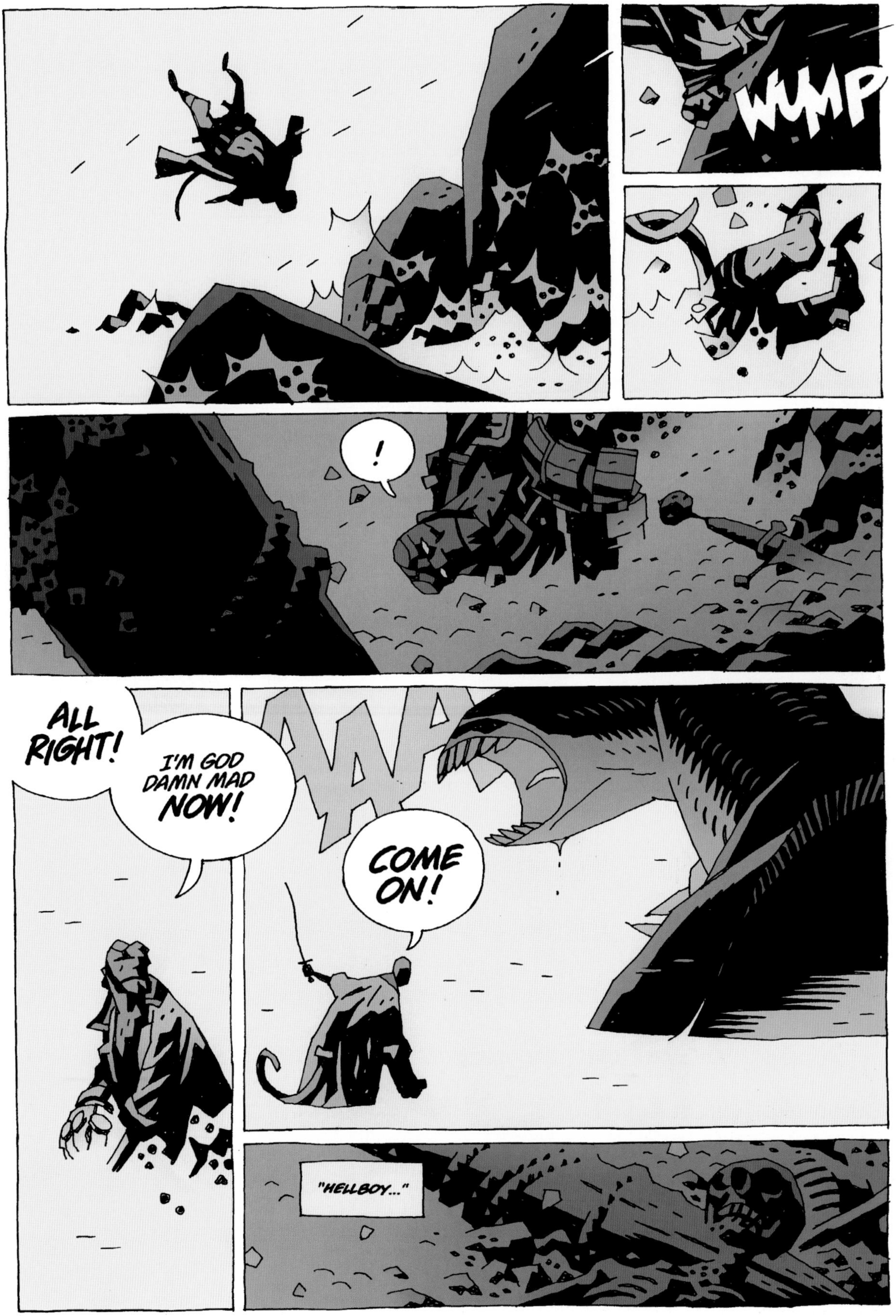
WUMP
!
ALL RIGHT!
I'M GOD DAMN MAD NOW!
COME ON!
"HELLBOY..."

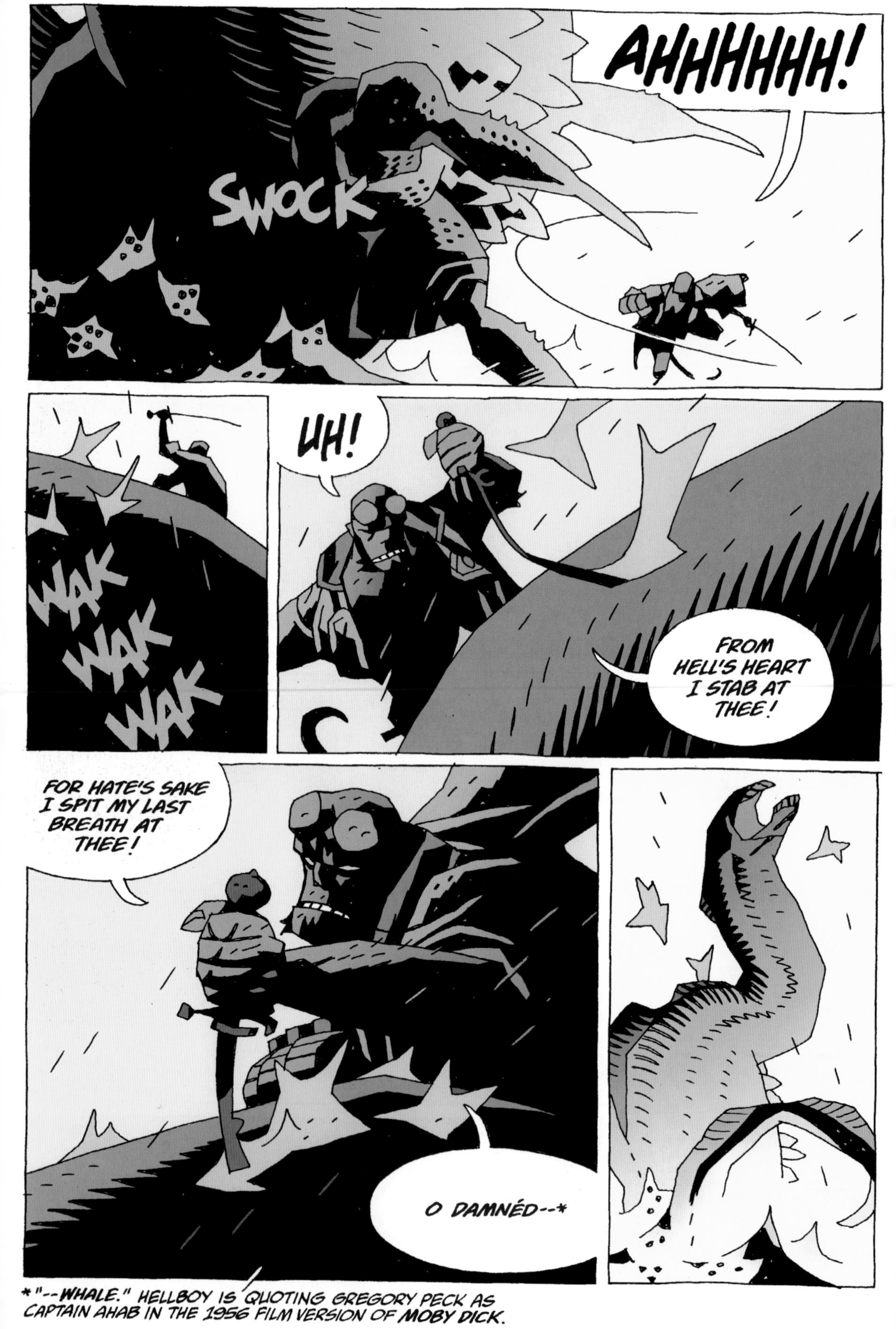
AHHHHHH!
SWOCK
WAK
WAK
WAK
UH!
FROM HELL'S HEART I STAB AT THEE!
FOR HATE'S SAKE I SPIT MY LAST BREATH AT THEE!
O DAMNÉD--*

*"--**WHALE.**" HELLBOY IS QUOTING GREGORY PECK AS CAPTAIN AHAB IN THE 1956 FILM VERSION OF **MOBY DICK**.

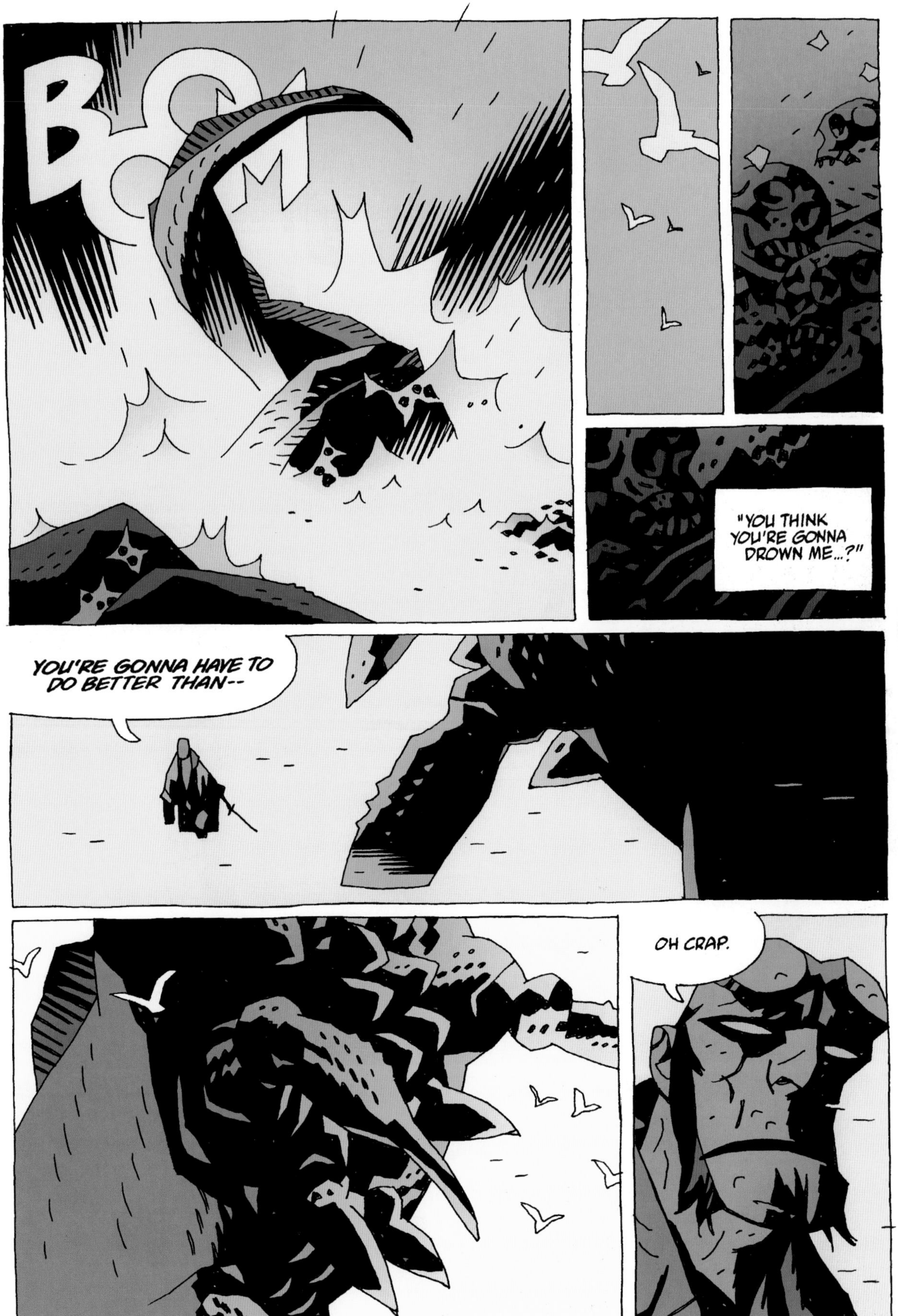
BOOM
"YOU THINK YOU'RE GONNA DROWN ME...?"
YOU'RE GONNA HAVE TO DO BETTER THAN--
OH CRAP.

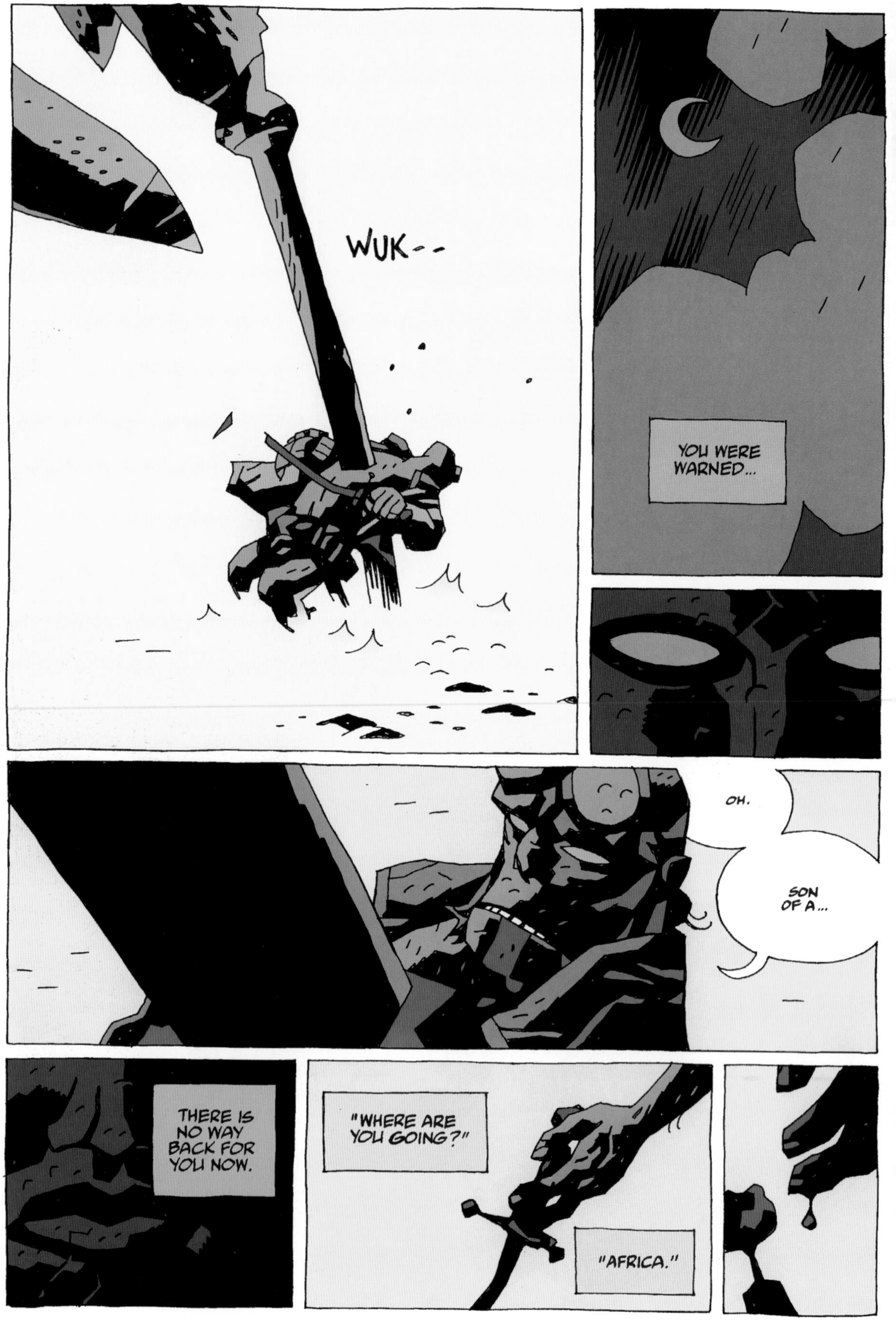
WUK--
YOU WERE WARNED...
OH.
SON OF A...
THERE IS NO WAY BACK FOR YOU NOW.
"WHERE ARE YOU GOING?"
"AFRICA."

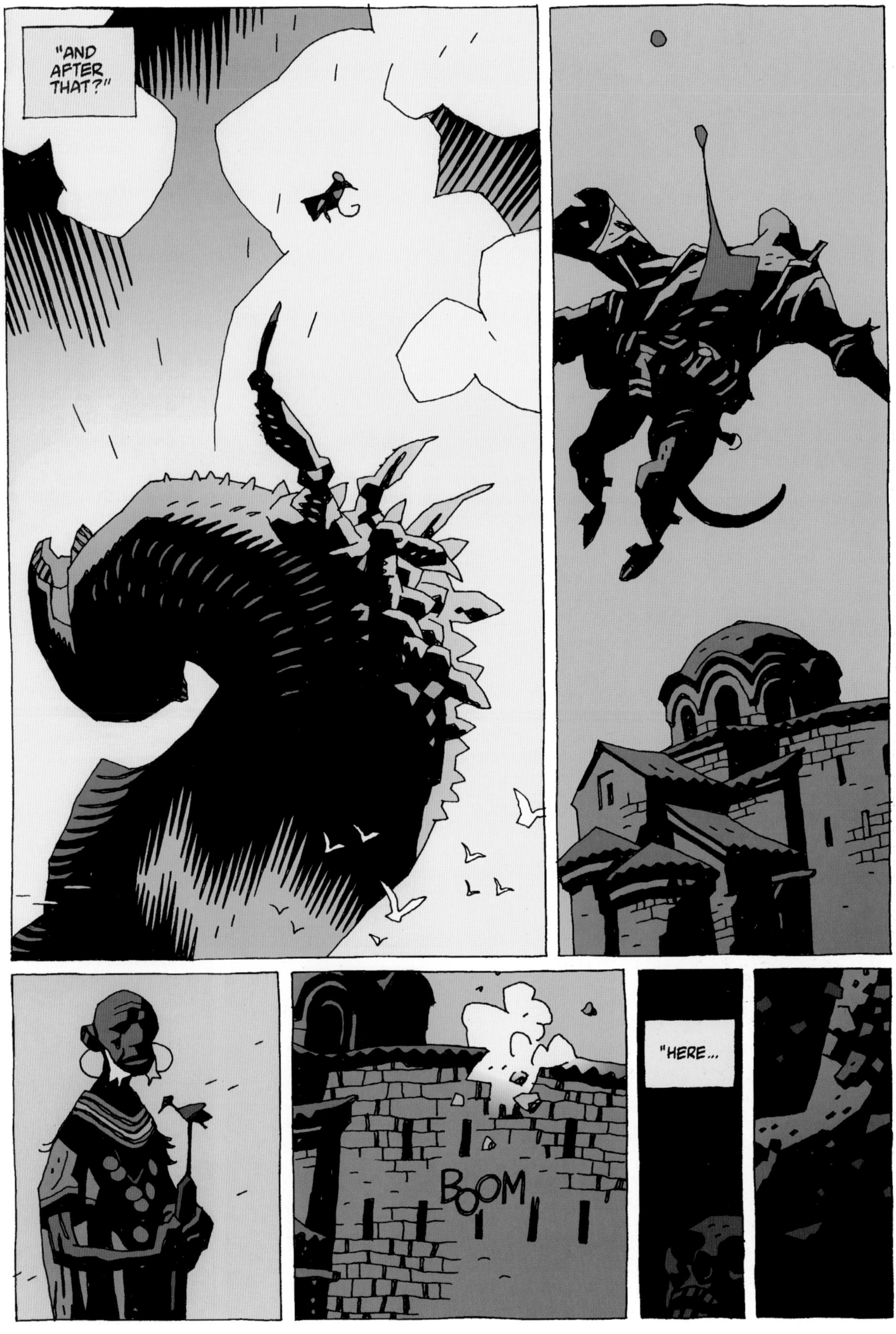
"AND AFTER THAT?"
BOOM
"HERE...

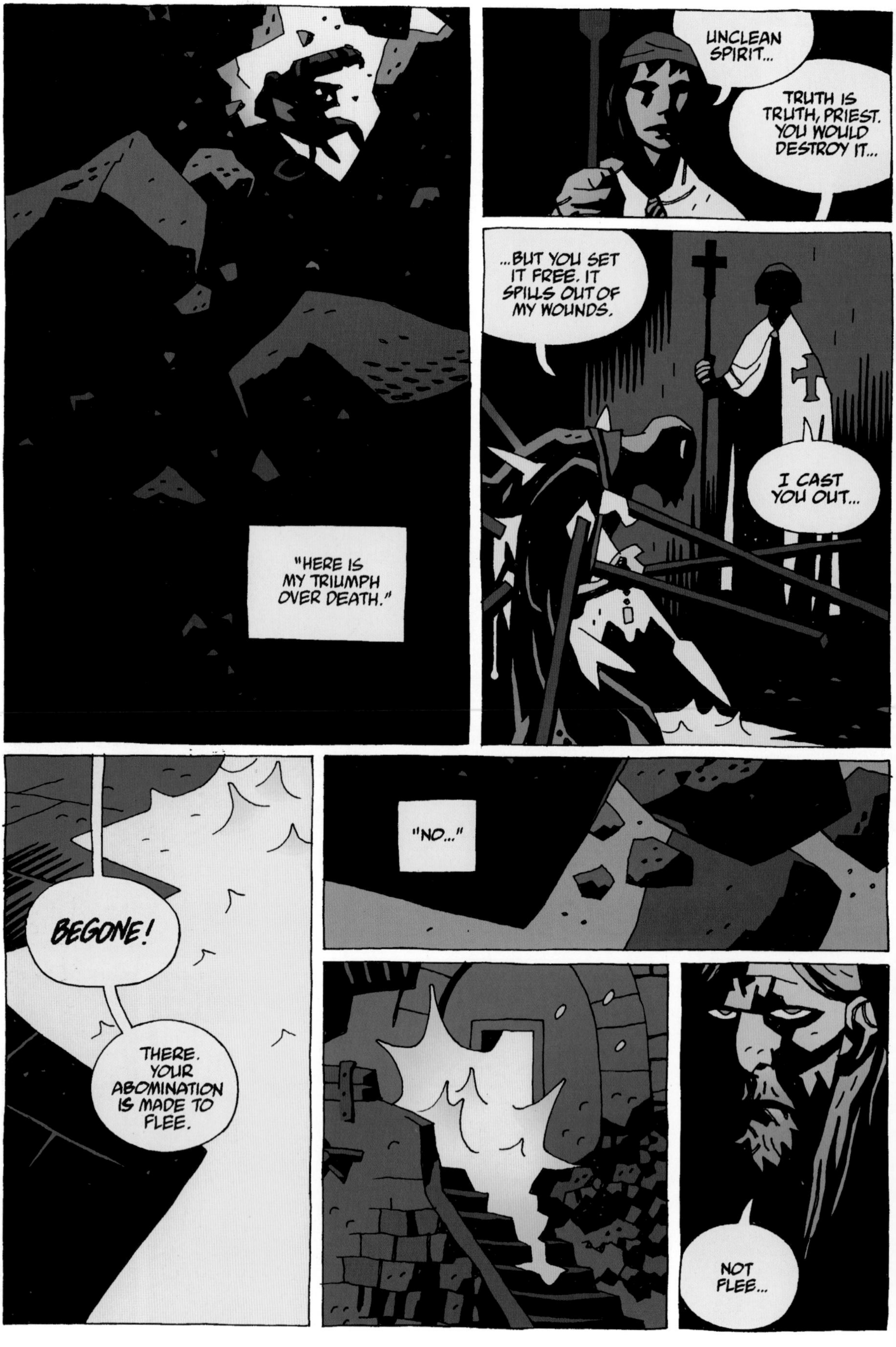

"HERE IS MY TRIUMPH OVER DEATH."
UNCLEAN SPIRIT...
TRUTH IS TRUTH, PRIEST. YOU WOULD DESTROY IT...
...BUT YOU SET IT FREE. IT SPILLS OUT OF MY WOUNDS.
I CAST YOU OUT...
BEGONE!
THERE. YOUR ABOMINATION IS MADE TO FLEE.
"NO..."
NOT FLEE...

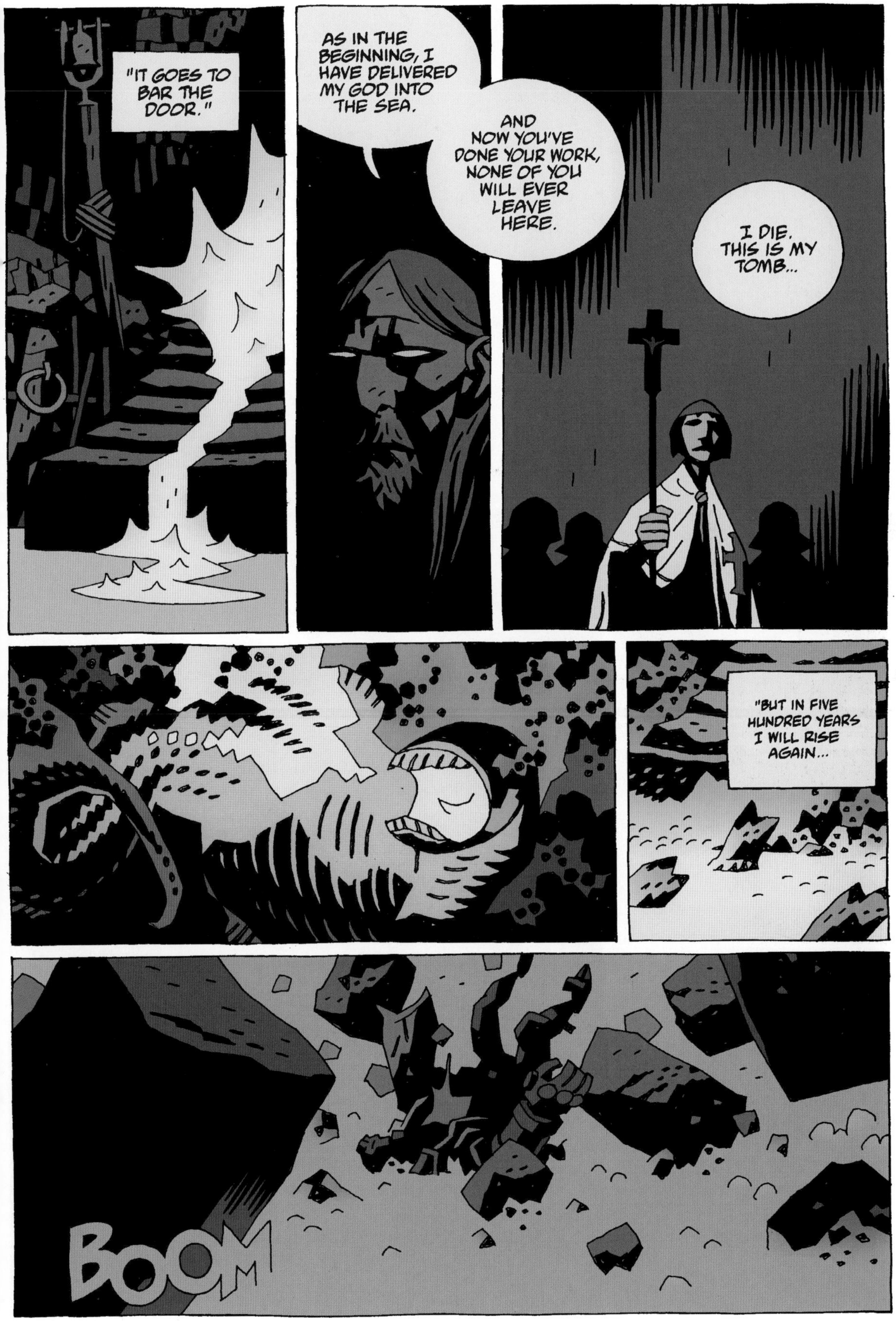
"IT GOES TO BAR THE DOOR."
AS IN THE BEGINNING, I HAVE DELIVERED MY GOD INTO THE SEA.
AND NOW YOU'VE DONE YOUR WORK, NONE OF YOU WILL EVER LEAVE HERE.
I DIE. THIS IS MY TOMB...
"BUT IN FIVE HUNDRED YEARS I WILL RISE AGAIN...
BOOM

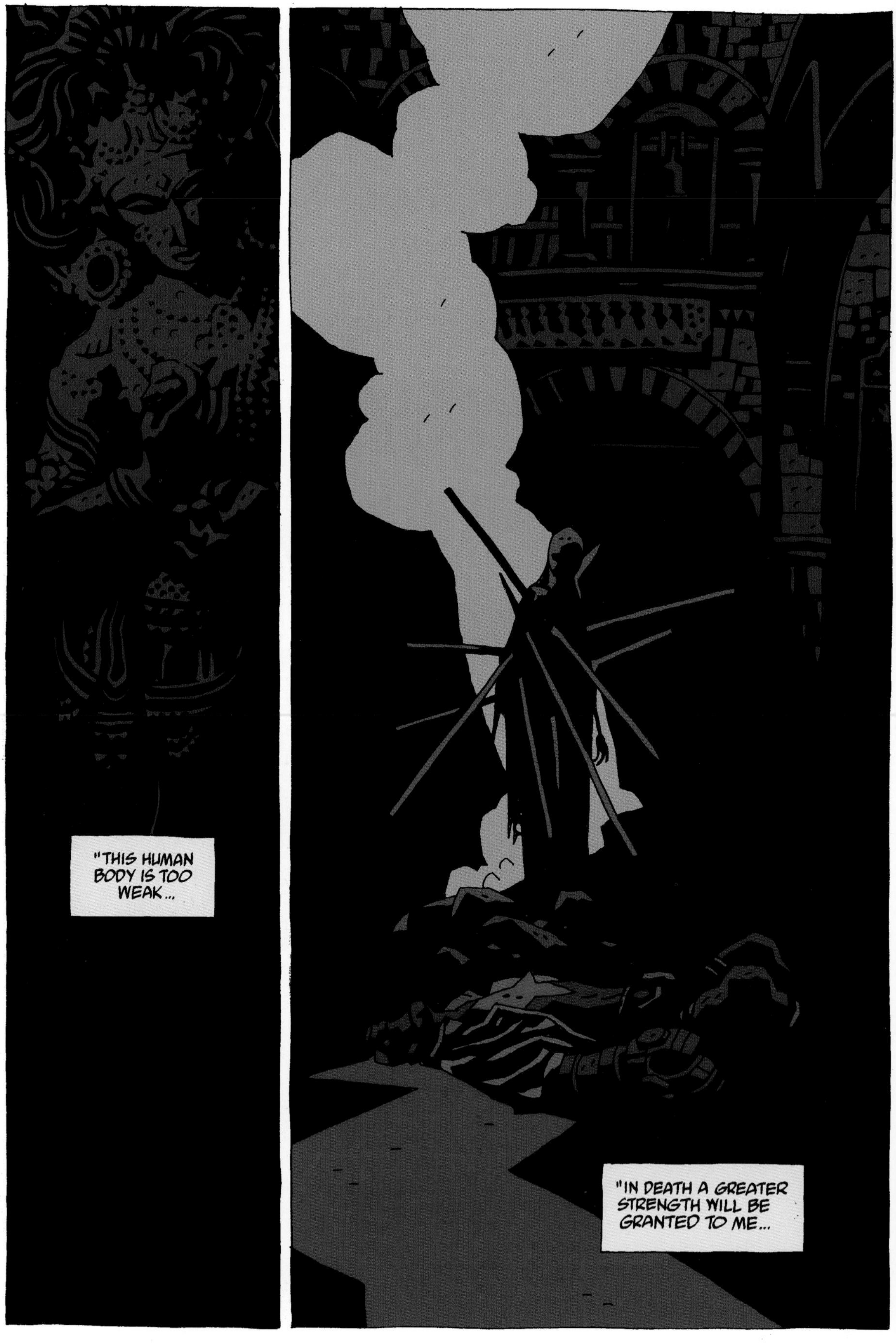
"THIS HUMAN BODY IS TOO WEAK...
"IN DEATH A GREATER STRENGTH WILL BE GRANTED TO ME...

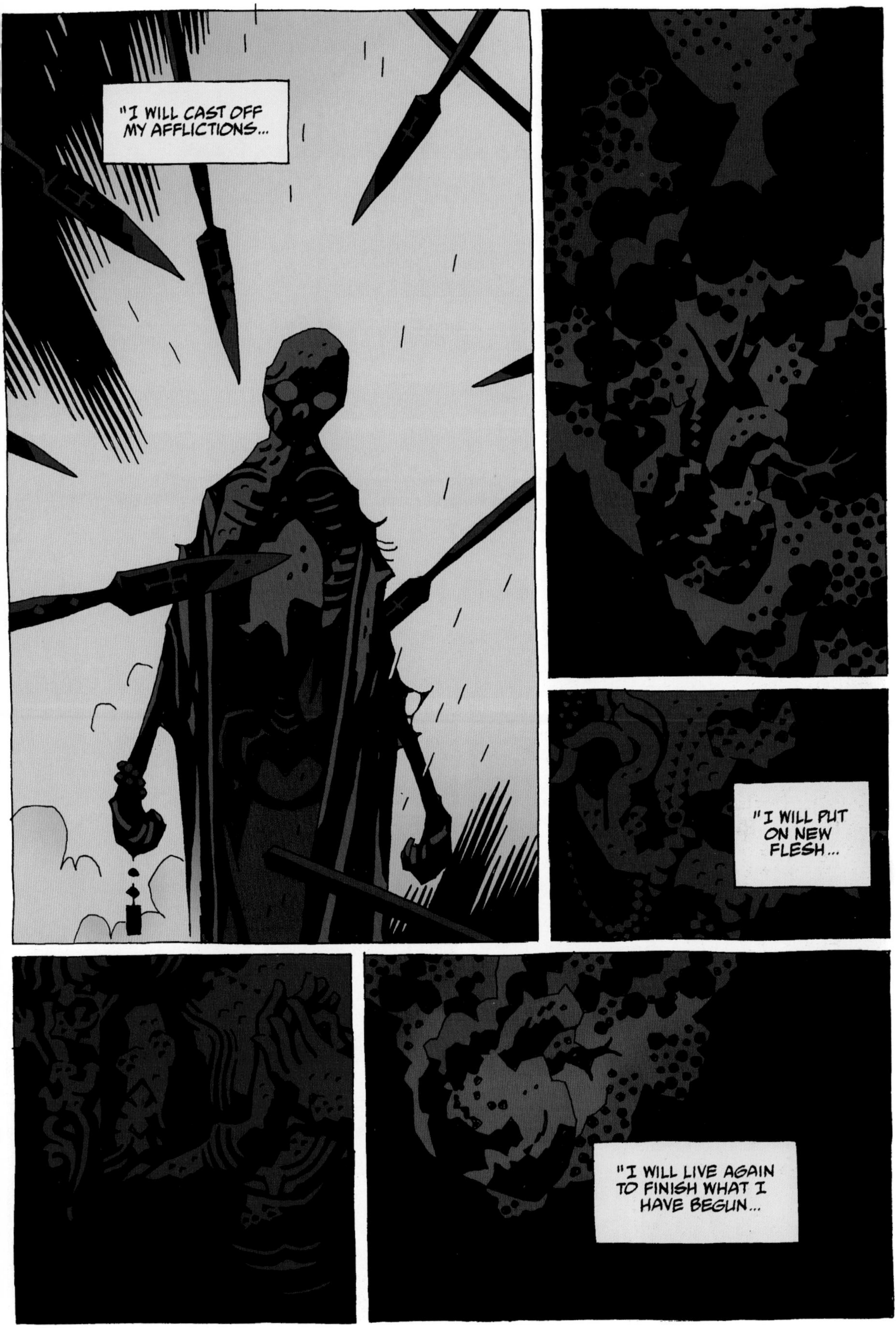
"I WILL CAST OFF MY AFFLICTIONS...
"I WILL PUT ON NEW FLESH...
"I WILL LIVE AGAIN TO FINISH WHAT I HAVE BEGUN...

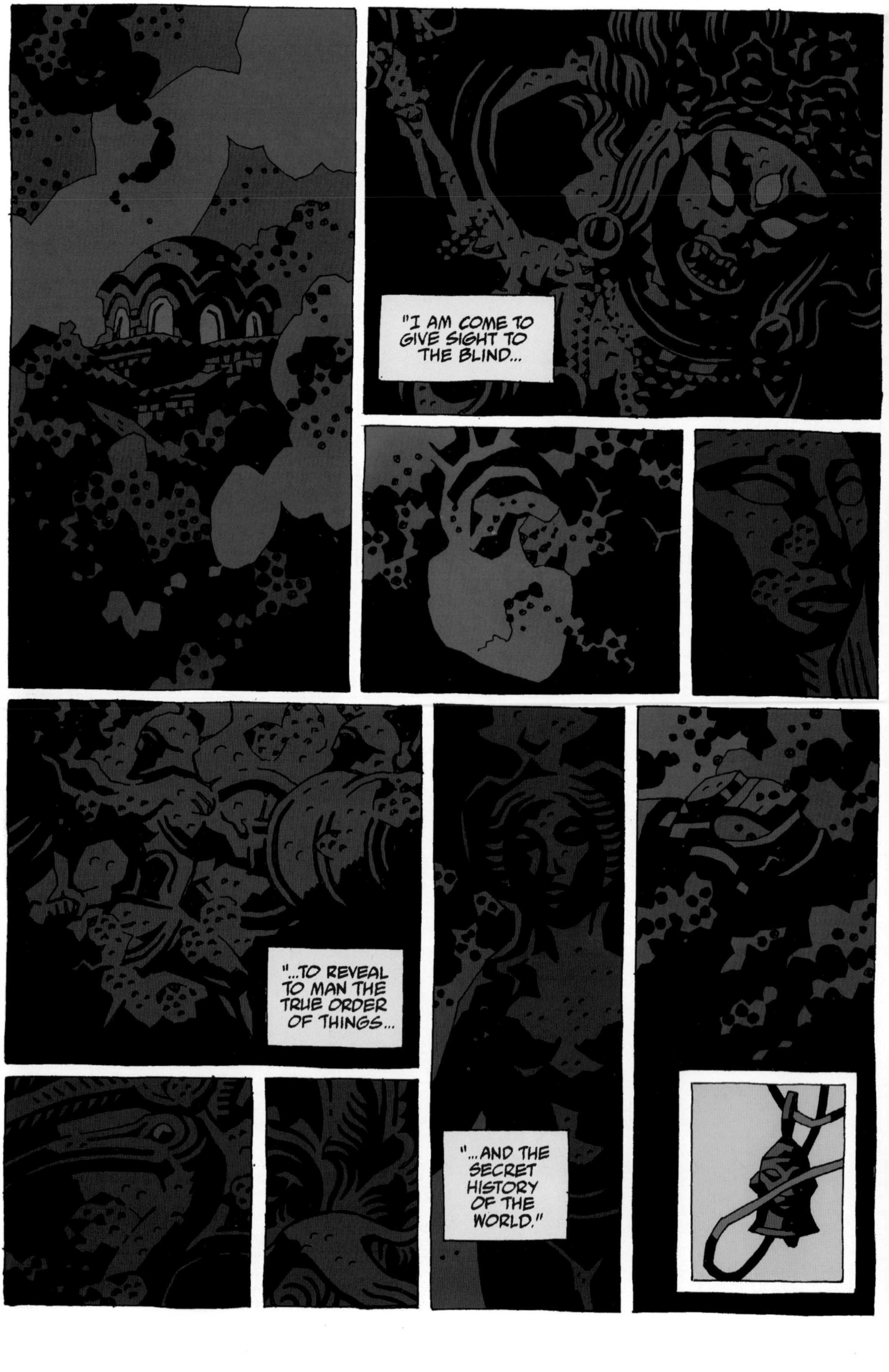
"I AM COME TO GIVE SIGHT TO THE BLIND...
"...TO REVEAL TO MAN THE TRUE ORDER OF THINGS...
"...AND THE SECRET HISTORY OF THE WORLD."

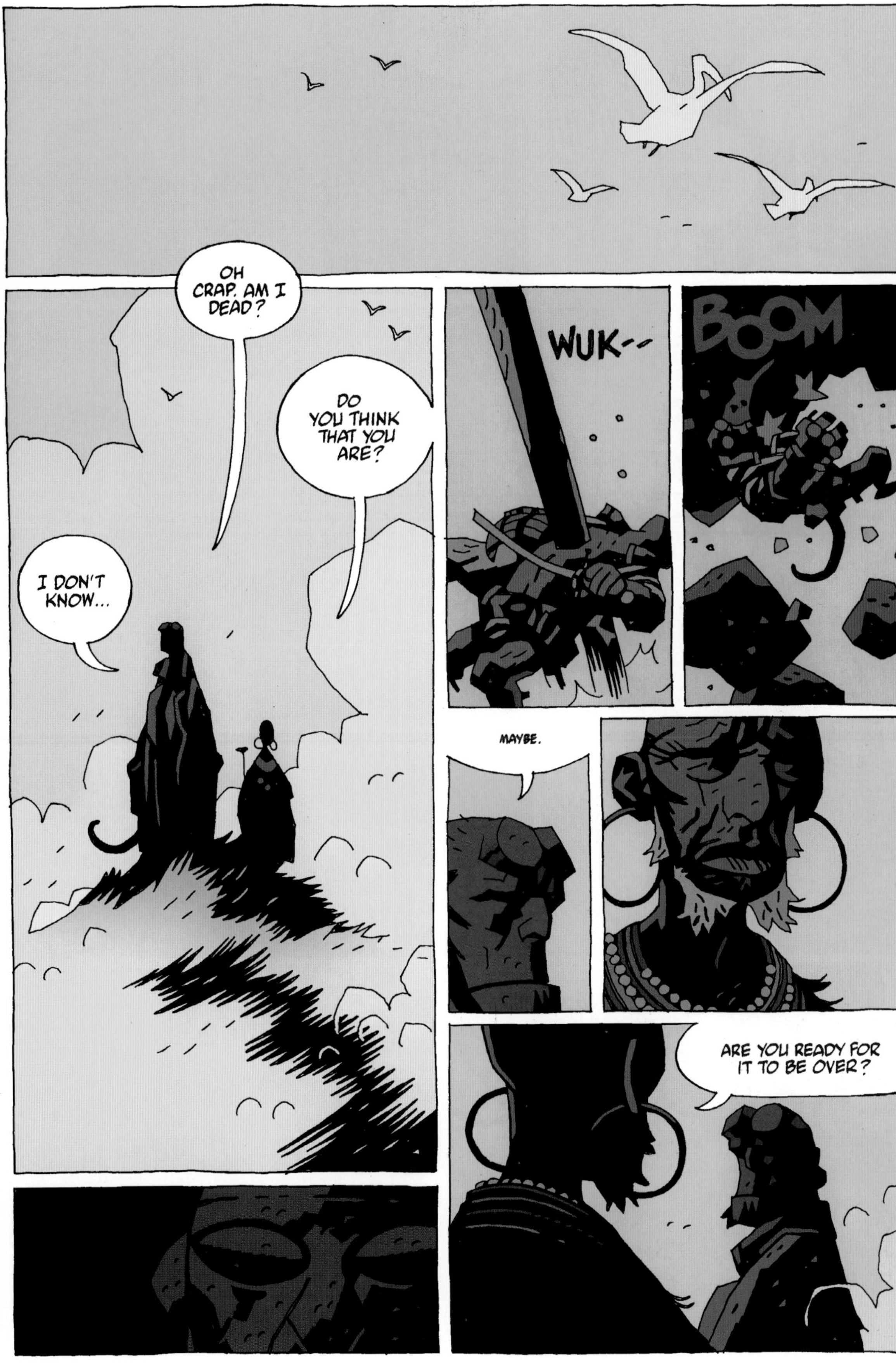
OH CRAP. AM I DEAD?
DO YOU THINK THAT YOU ARE?
I DON'T KNOW...
WUK--
BOOM
MAYBE.
ARE YOU READY FOR IT TO BE OVER?

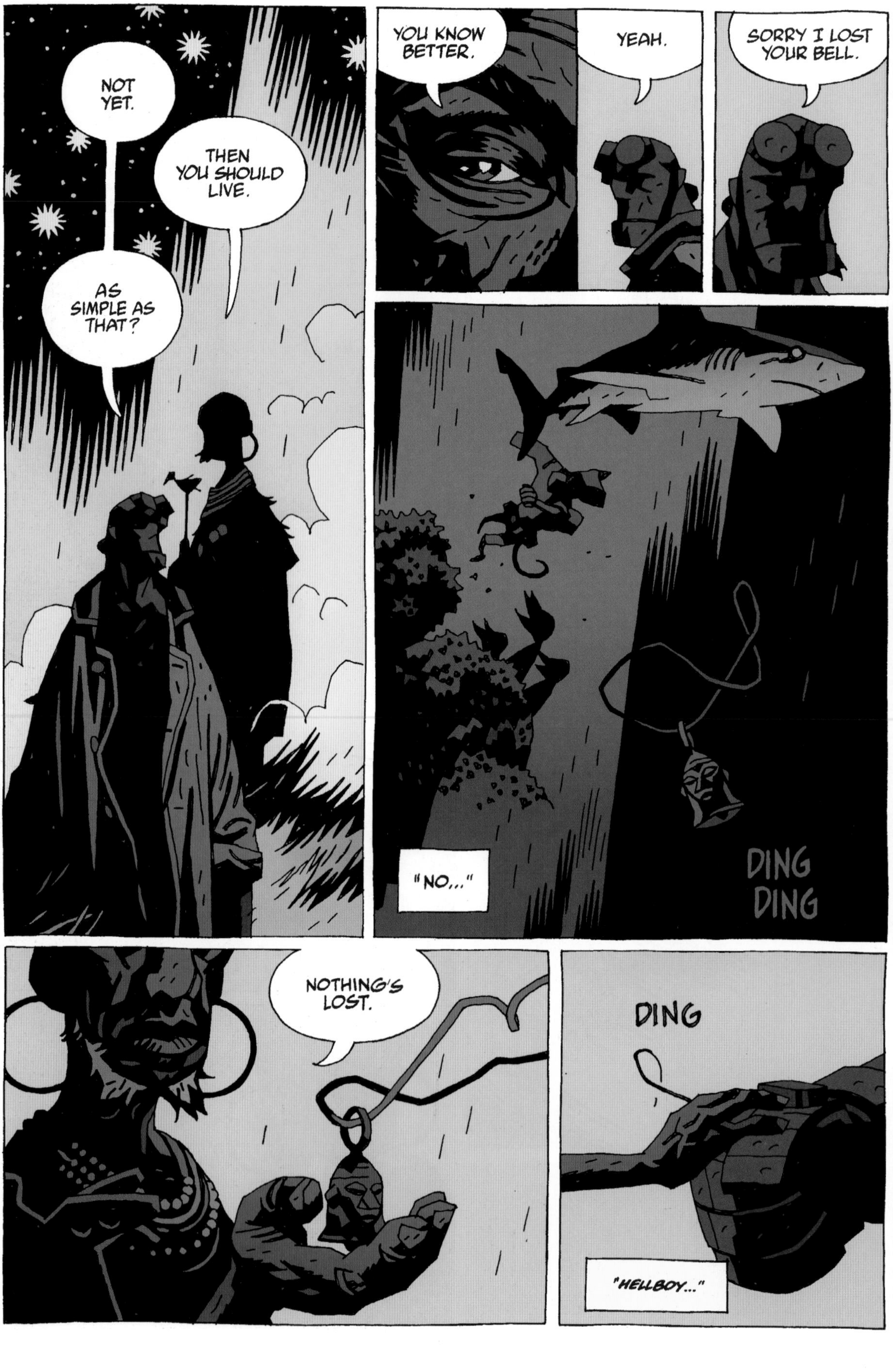
NOT YET.
THEN YOU SHOULD LIVE.
AS SIMPLE AS THAT?
YOU KNOW BETTER.
YEAH.
SORRY I LOST YOUR BELL.
"NO..."
DING DING
NOTHING'S LOST.
DING
"HELLBOY..."

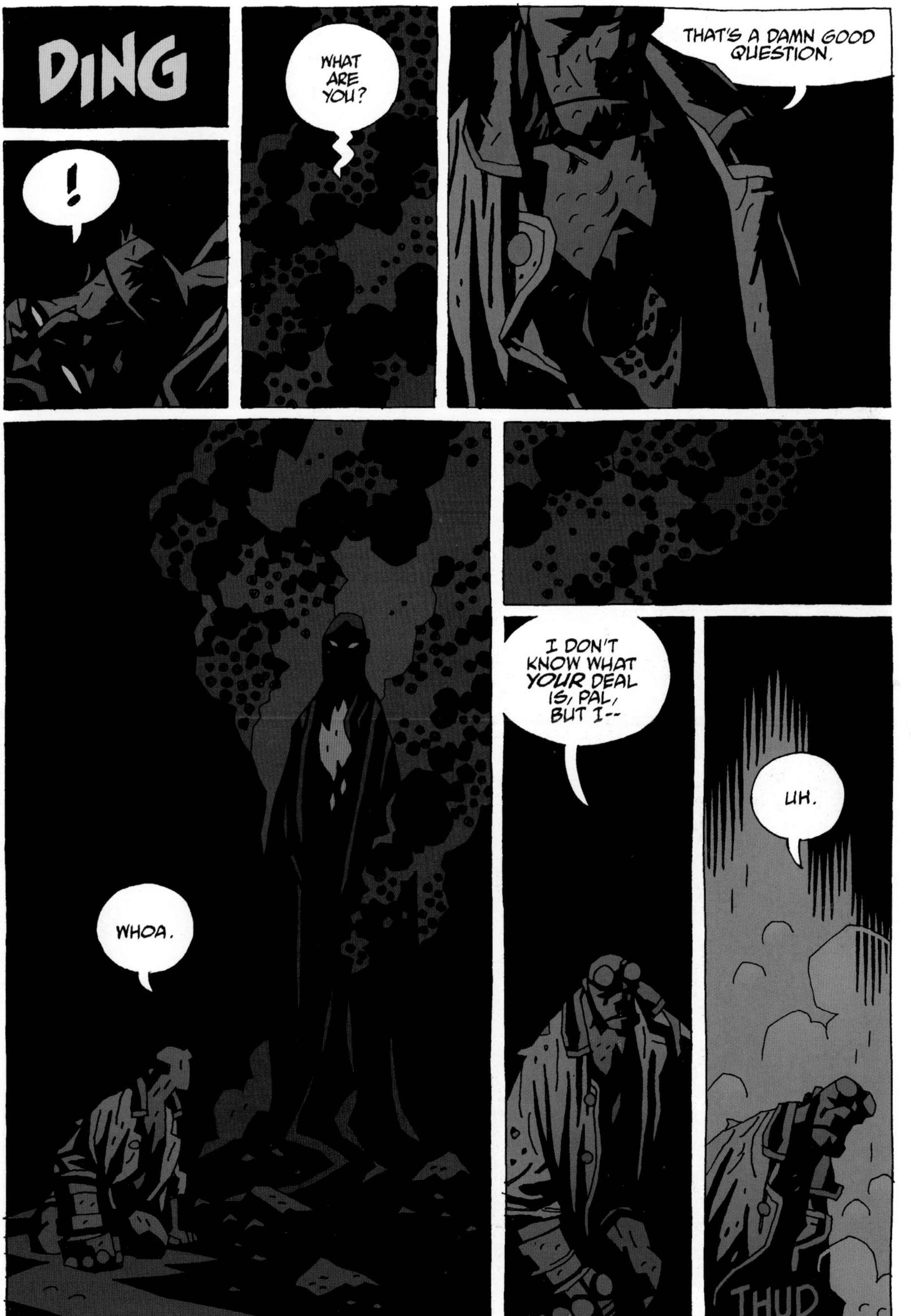
DING
!
WHAT ARE YOU?
THAT'S A DAMN GOOD QUESTION.
WHOA.
I DON'T KNOW WHAT YOUR DEAL IS, PAL, BUT I--
UH.
THUD

DAMN.

WHAT ARE YOU?

WHAT *WERE* YOU?

AND THEREFORE, WHAT AM I?

YOU SEE THIS SKIN, THIS BODY...

"IT IS WOVEN FROM YOUR BLOOD--*ALL* YOUR BLOOD. I AM RECREATED FROM *YOU.* I AM ALL THAT *YOU* WERE..."

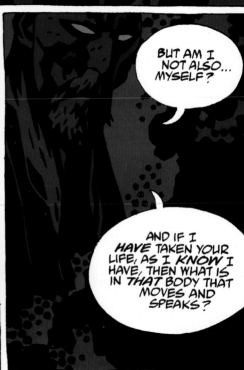

BUT AM I NOT ALSO... MYSELF?

AND IF I *HAVE* TAKEN YOUR LIFE, AS I *KNOW* I HAVE, THEN WHAT IS IN *THAT* BODY THAT MOVES AND SPEAKS?

JESUS, PAL, YOU'RE MAKING ME DIZZY.

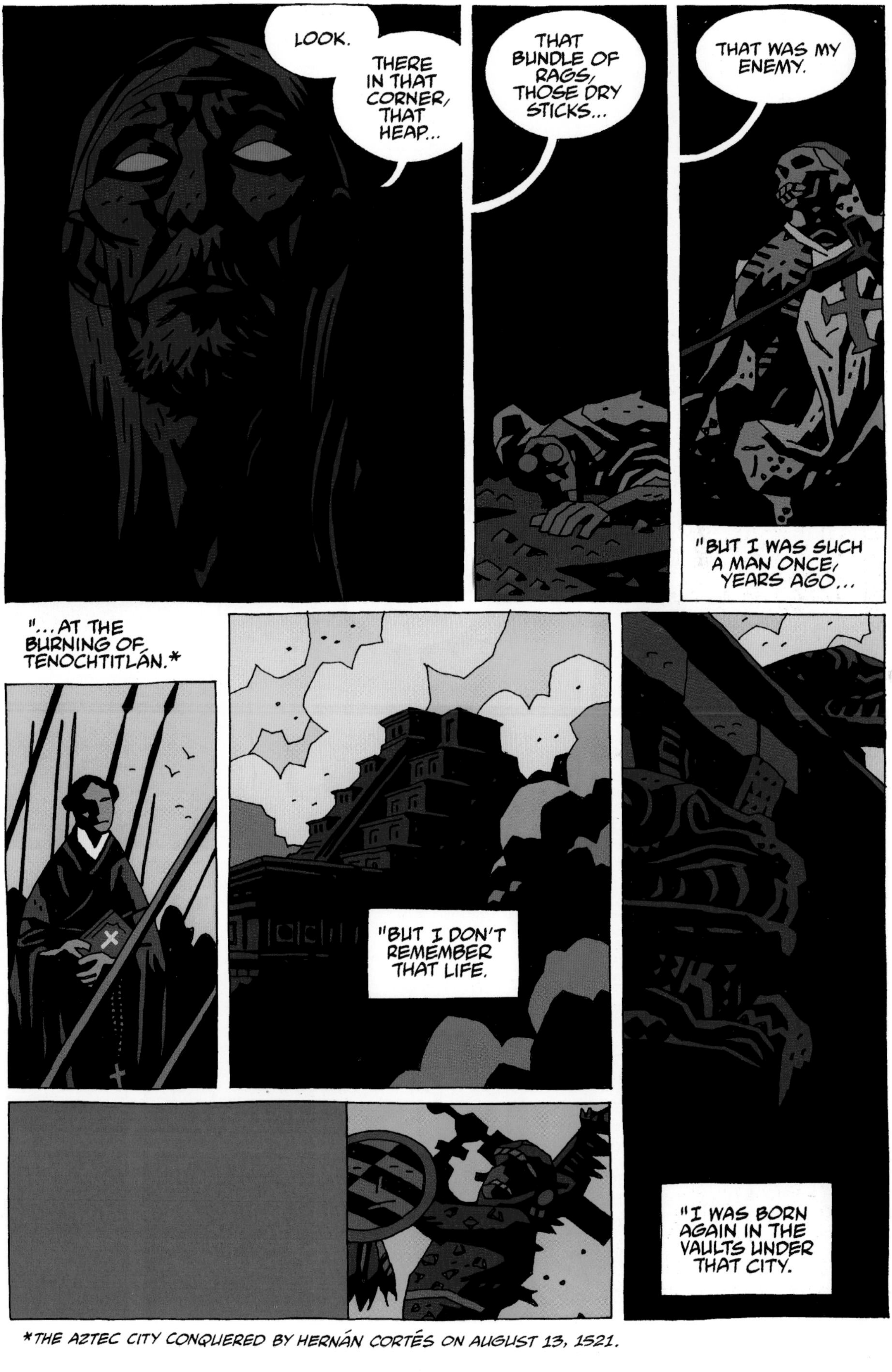
LOOK.
THERE IN THAT CORNER, THAT HEAP...
THAT BUNDLE OF RAGS, THOSE DRY STICKS...
THAT WAS MY ENEMY.
"BUT I WAS SUCH A MAN ONCE, YEARS AGO...
"...AT THE BURNING OF TENOCHTITLÁN.*
"BUT I DON'T REMEMBER THAT LIFE.
"I WAS BORN AGAIN IN THE VAULTS UNDER THAT CITY.

**THE AZTEC CITY CONQUERED BY HERNÁN CORTÉS ON AUGUST 13, 1521.*

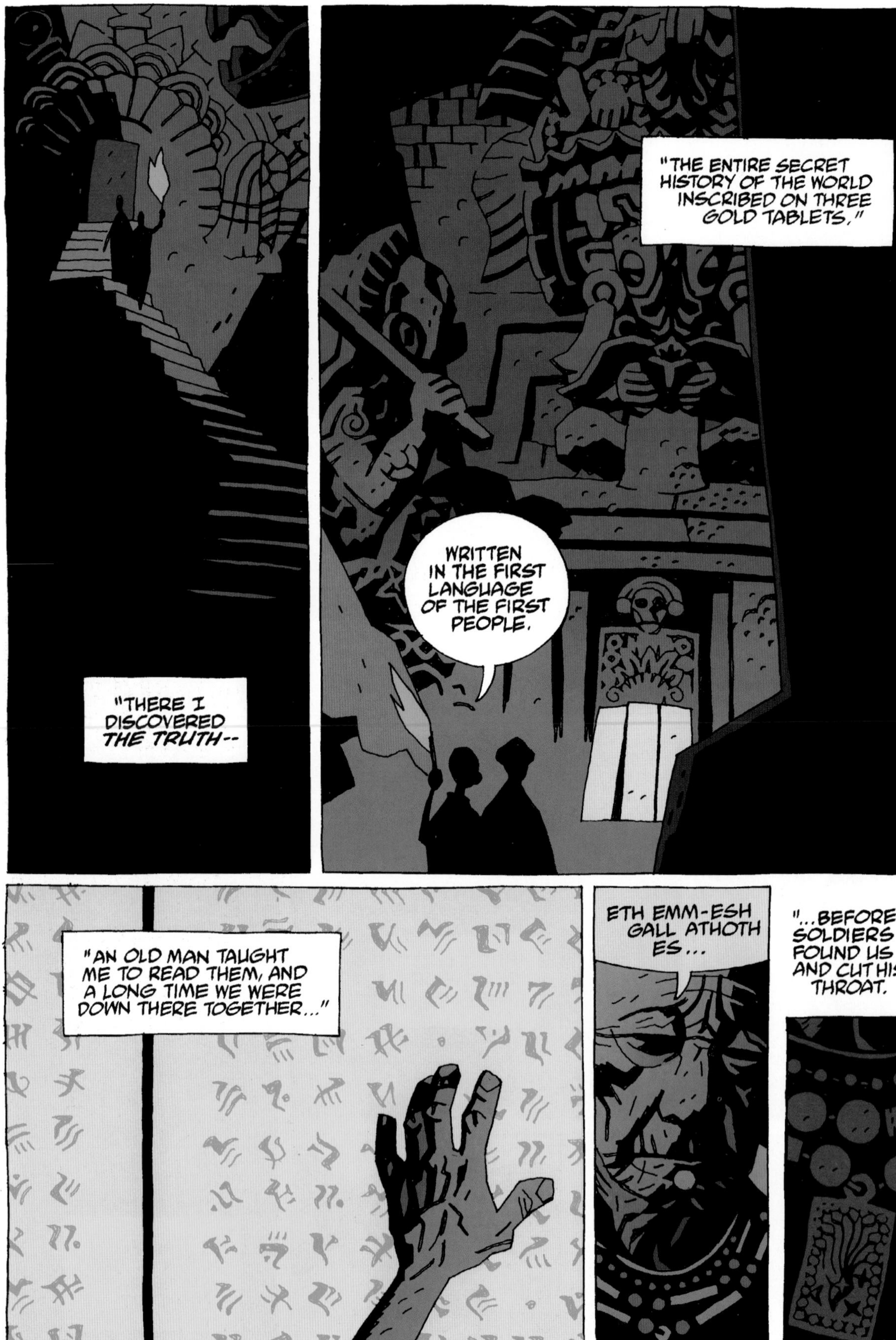
"THE ENTIRE SECRET HISTORY OF THE WORLD INSCRIBED ON THREE GOLD TABLETS."
"THERE I DISCOVERED THE TRUTH--
WRITTEN IN THE FIRST LANGUAGE OF THE FIRST PEOPLE.
"AN OLD MAN TAUGHT ME TO READ THEM, AND A LONG TIME WE WERE DOWN THERE TOGETHER..."
ETH EMM-ESH GALL ATHOTH ES...
"...BEFORE SOLDIERS FOUND US AND CUT HIS THROAT.

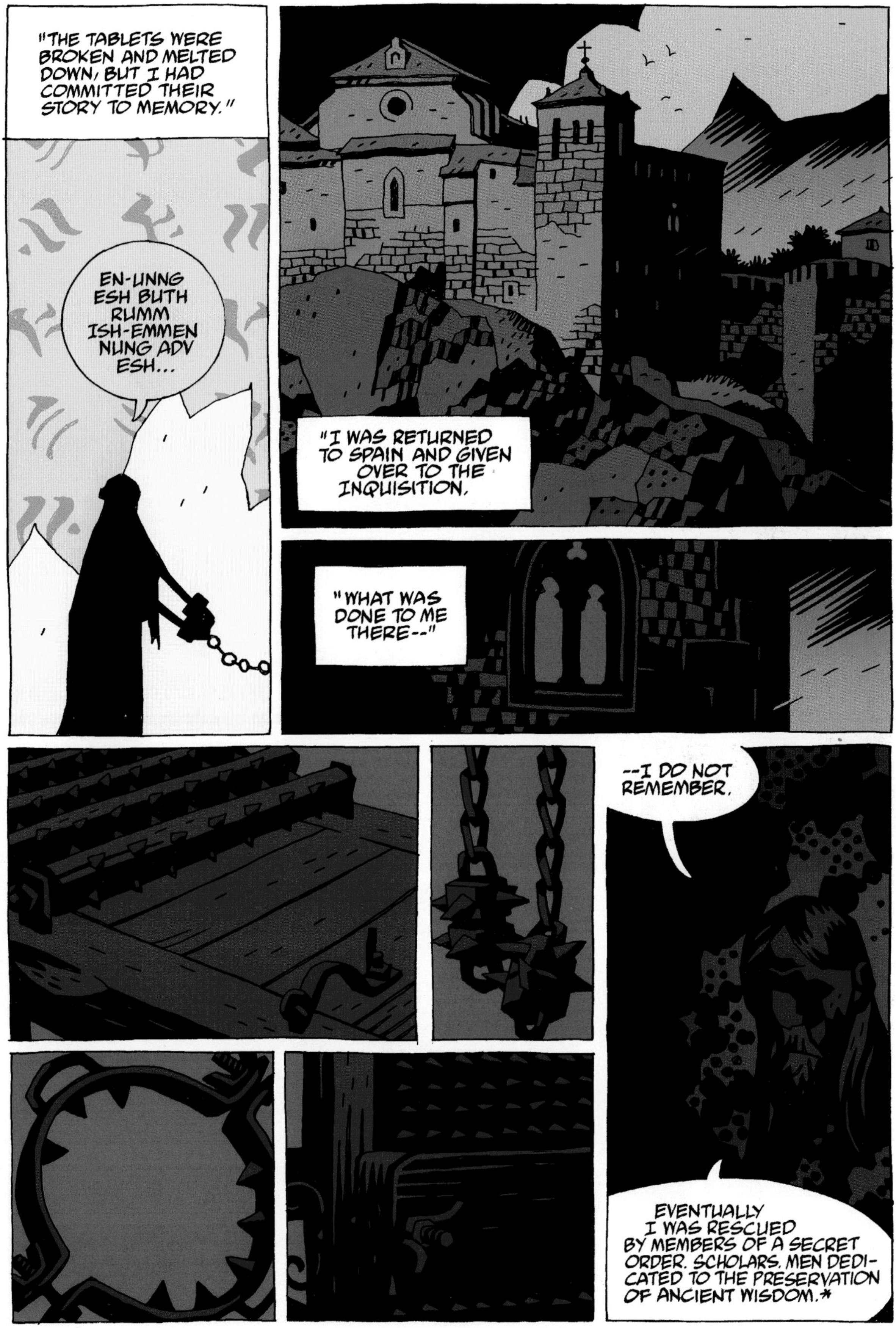
"THE TABLETS WERE BROKEN AND MELTED DOWN, BUT I HAD COMMITTED THEIR STORY TO MEMORY."
EN-UNNG ESH BUTH RUMM ISH-EMMEN NUNG ADV ESH...
"I WAS RETURNED TO SPAIN AND GIVEN OVER TO THE INQUISITION.
"WHAT WAS DONE TO ME THERE--"
--I DO NOT REMEMBER.
EVENTUALLY I WAS RESCUED BY MEMBERS OF A SECRET ORDER. SCHOLARS. MEN DEDICATED TO THE PRESERVATION OF ANCIENT WISDOM.*

*PROBABLY THE ROSICRUCIANS, FOUNDED BY CHRISTIAN ROSENKREUTZ (1378-1484?).

THEY BROUGHT ME TO THIS, THEIR MOST SECRET PLACE.

TO HIDE ME.

"HERE THEY HAD GATHERED ALL THEIR TREASURES FROM THE FOUR CORNERS OF THE GLOBE-- CARVED STONE AND CLAY POTS, BRONZE AND PARCHMENT.

"BITS OF ATLANTIS, LEMURIA, AND URR.

"SCRAPS OF BABYLON.

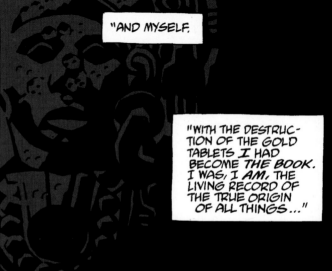

"AND MYSELF.

"WITH THE DESTRUCTION OF THE GOLD TABLETS I HAD BECOME THE BOOK. I WAS, I AM, THE LIVING RECORD OF THE TRUE ORIGIN OF ALL THINGS..."

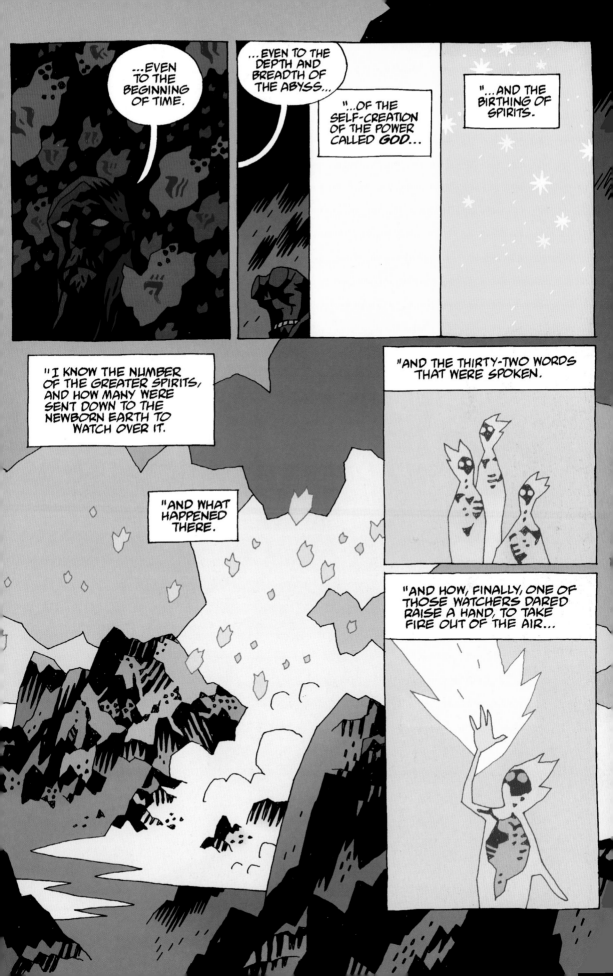

...EVEN TO THE BEGINNING OF TIME.

...EVEN TO THE DEPTH AND BREADTH OF THE ABYSS...

"...OF THE SELF-CREATION OF THE POWER CALLED GOD...

"...AND THE BIRTHING OF SPIRITS.

"I KNOW THE NUMBER OF THE GREATER SPIRITS, AND HOW MANY WERE SENT DOWN TO THE NEWBORN EARTH TO WATCH OVER IT.

"AND THE THIRTY-TWO WORDS THAT WERE SPOKEN.

"AND WHAT HAPPENED THERE.

"AND HOW, FINALLY, ONE OF THOSE WATCHERS DARED RAISE A HAND, TO TAKE FIRE OUT OF THE AIR...

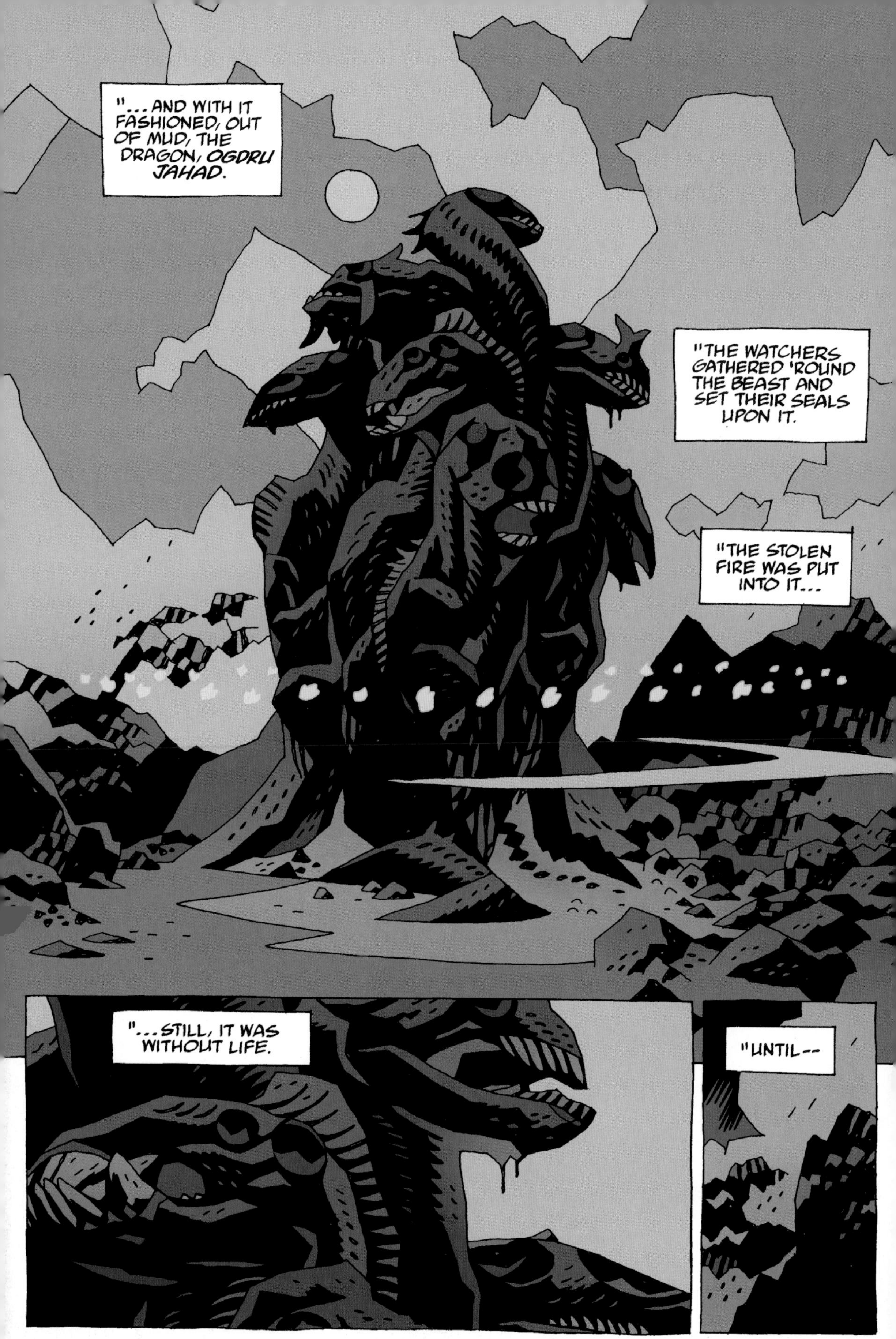
"...AND WITH IT FASHIONED, OUT OF MUD, THE DRAGON, OGDRU JAHAD.
"THE WATCHERS GATHERED 'ROUND THE BEAST AND SET THEIR SEALS UPON IT.
"THE STOLEN FIRE WAS PUT INTO IT...
"...STILL, IT WAS WITHOUT LIFE.
"UNTIL--

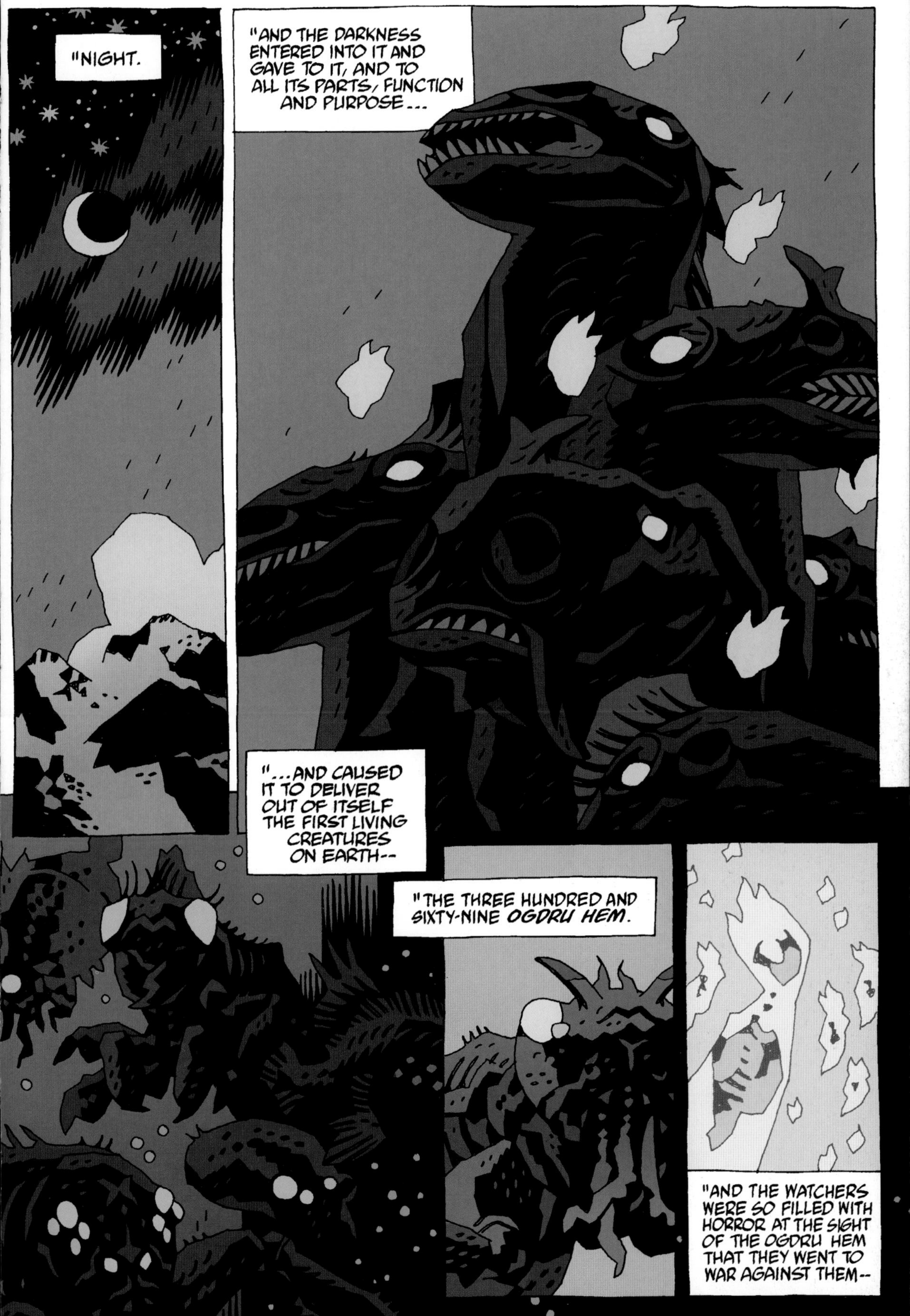
"NIGHT.
"AND THE DARKNESS ENTERED INTO IT AND GAVE TO IT, AND TO ALL ITS PARTS, FUNCTION AND PURPOSE...
"...AND CAUSED IT TO DELIVER OUT OF ITSELF THE FIRST LIVING CREATURES ON EARTH--
"THE THREE HUNDRED AND SIXTY-NINE *OGDRU HEM*.
"AND THE WATCHERS WERE SO FILLED WITH HORROR AT THE SIGHT OF THE OGDRU HEM THAT THEY WENT TO WAR AGAINST THEM--

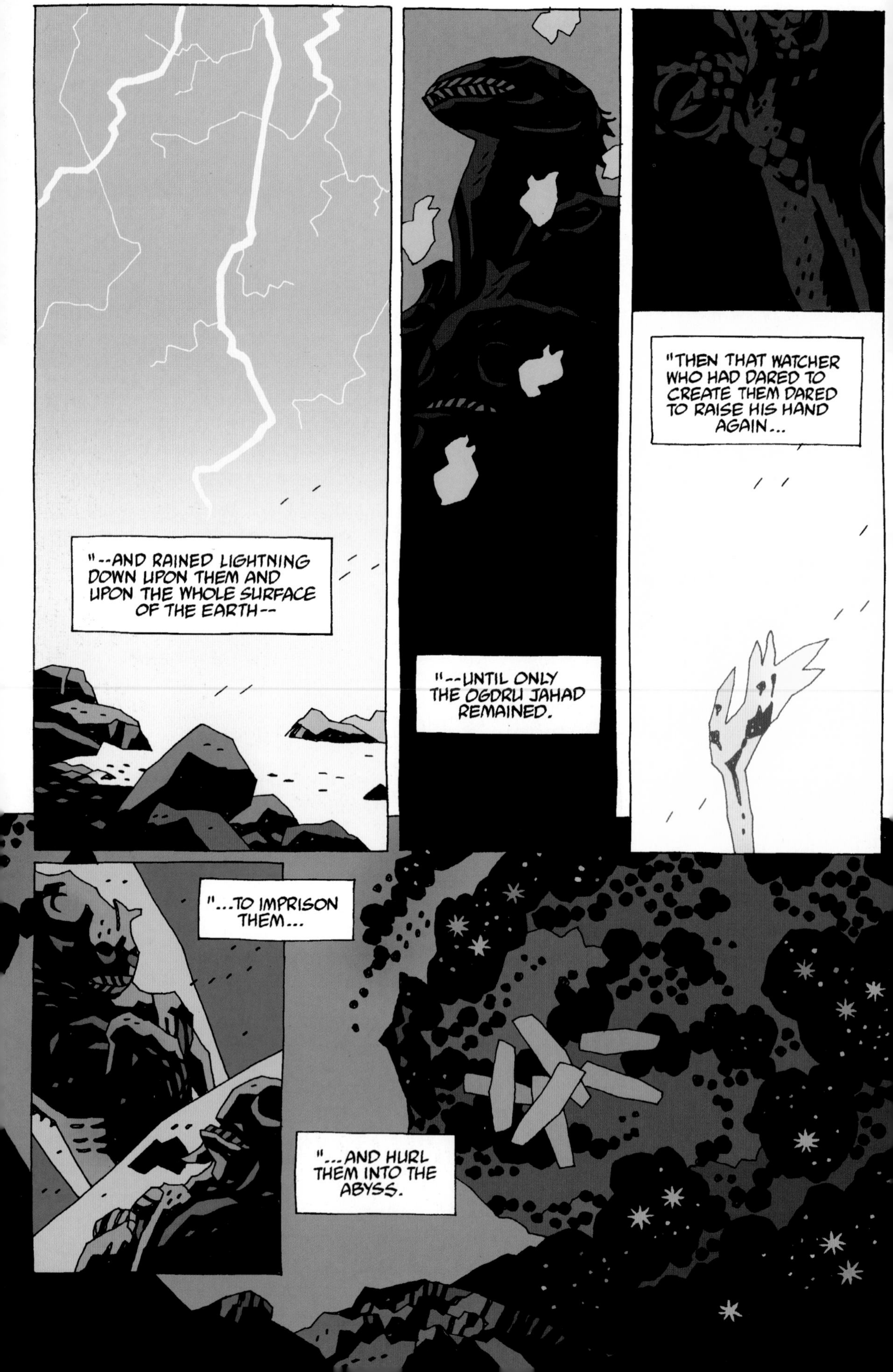
"--AND RAINED LIGHTNING DOWN UPON THEM AND UPON THE WHOLE SURFACE OF THE EARTH--
"--UNTIL ONLY THE OGDRU JAHAD REMAINED.
"THEN THAT WATCHER WHO HAD DARED TO CREATE THEM DARED TO RAISE HIS HAND AGAIN...
"...TO IMPRISON THEM...
"...AND HURL THEM INTO THE ABYSS.

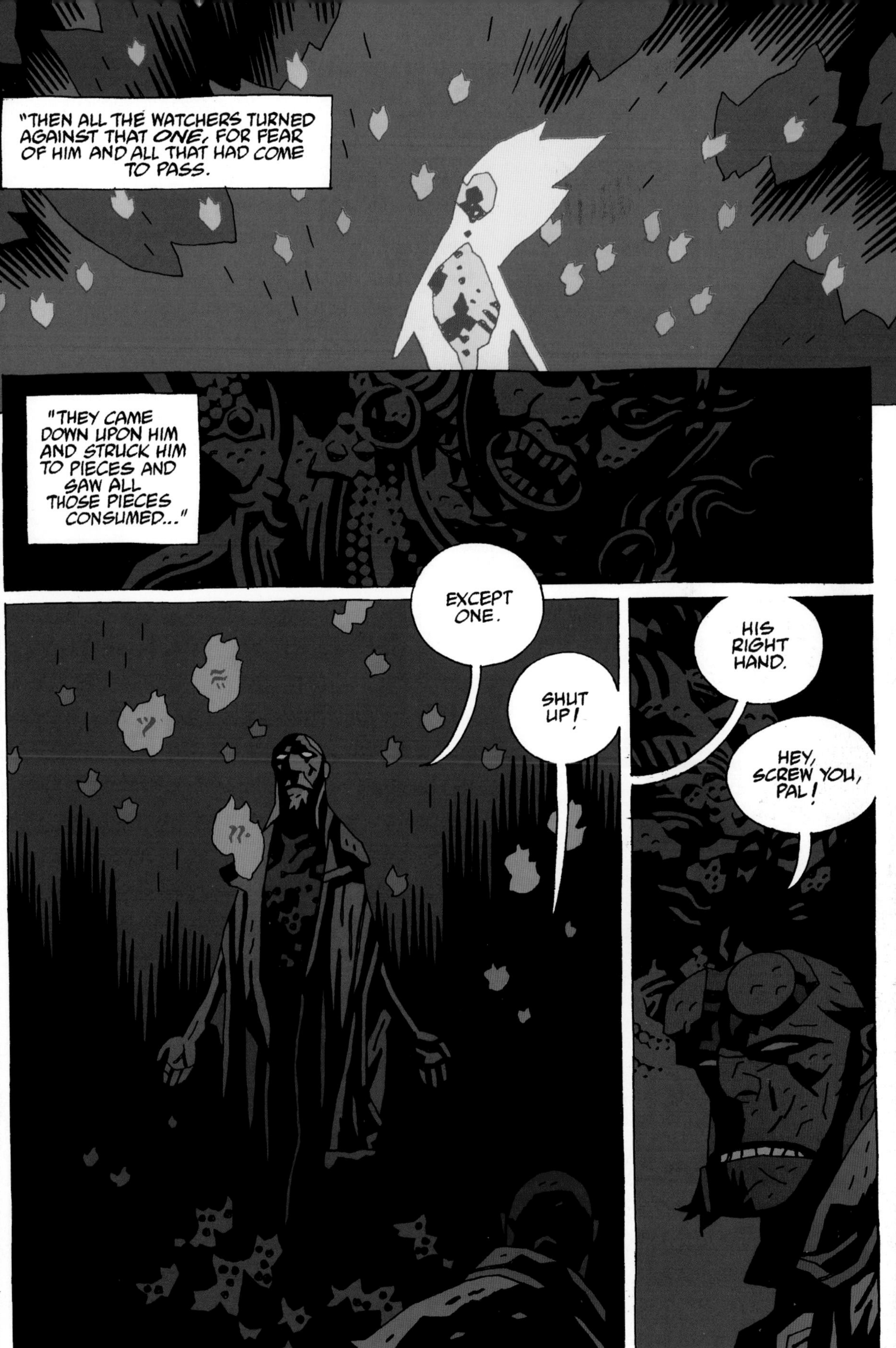
"THEN ALL THE WATCHERS TURNED AGAINST THAT ONE, FOR FEAR OF HIM AND ALL THAT HAD COME TO PASS.
"THEY CAME DOWN UPON HIM AND STRUCK HIM TO PIECES AND SAW ALL THOSE PIECES CONSUMED..."
EXCEPT ONE.
SHUT UP!
HIS RIGHT HAND.
HEY, SCREW YOU, PAL!

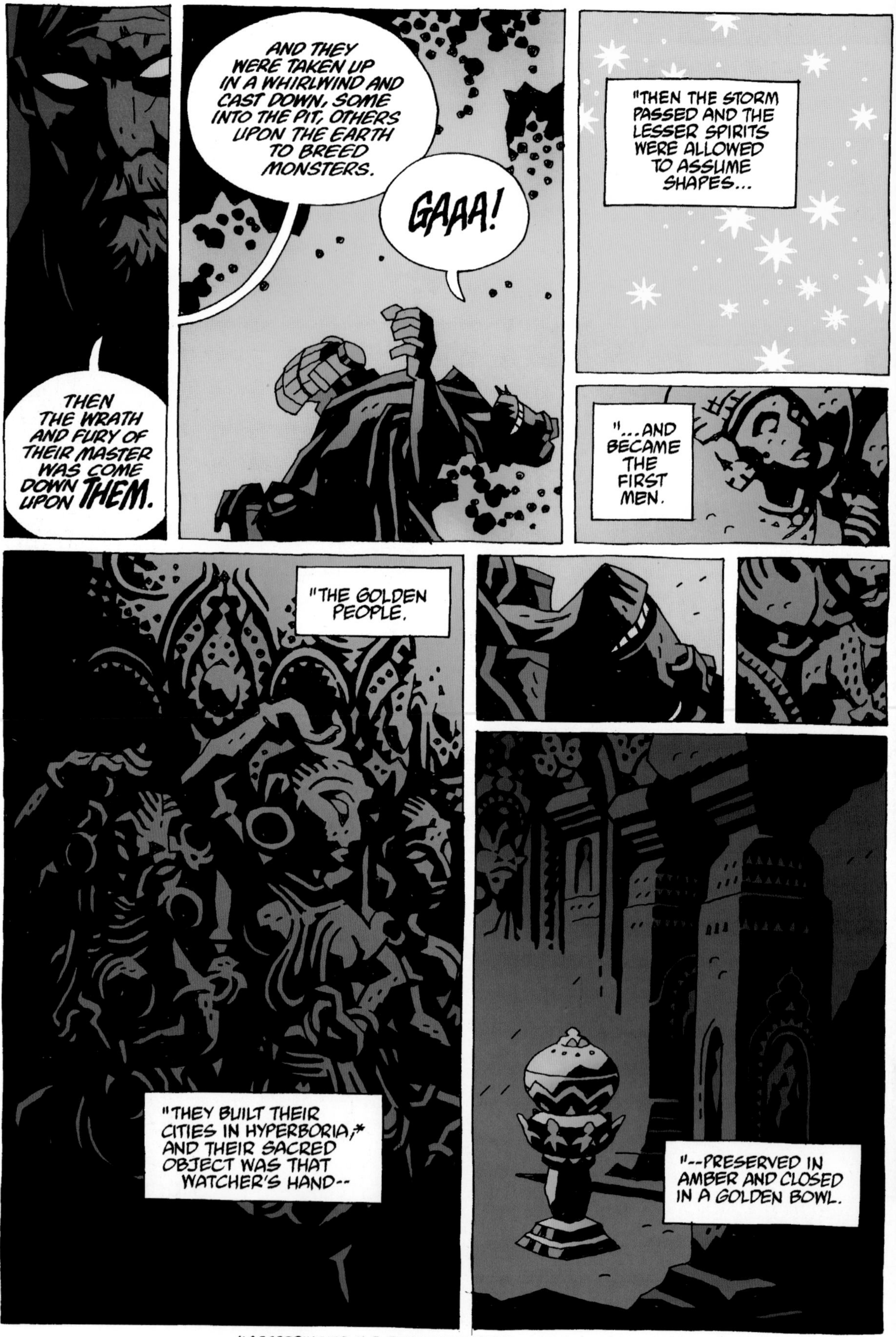
THEN THE WRATH AND FURY OF THEIR MASTER WAS COME DOWN UPON THEM.
AND THEY WERE TAKEN UP IN A WHIRLWIND AND CAST DOWN, SOME INTO THE PIT, OTHERS UPON THE EARTH TO BREED MONSTERS.
GAAA!
"THEN THE STORM PASSED AND THE LESSER SPIRITS WERE ALLOWED TO ASSUME SHAPES...
"...AND BECAME THE FIRST MEN.
"THE GOLDEN PEOPLE.
"THEY BUILT THEIR CITIES IN HYPERBORIA,* AND THEIR SACRED OBJECT WAS THAT WATCHER'S HAND--
"--PRESERVED IN AMBER AND CLOSED IN A GOLDEN BOWL.

*ACCORDING TO H.P. BLAVATSKY (1831-1891), THE "IMPERISHABLE SACRED LAND," WHICH COVERED THE ENTIRE NORTH POLE AND IS NOW BURIED UNDER "POLARIAN" ICE.

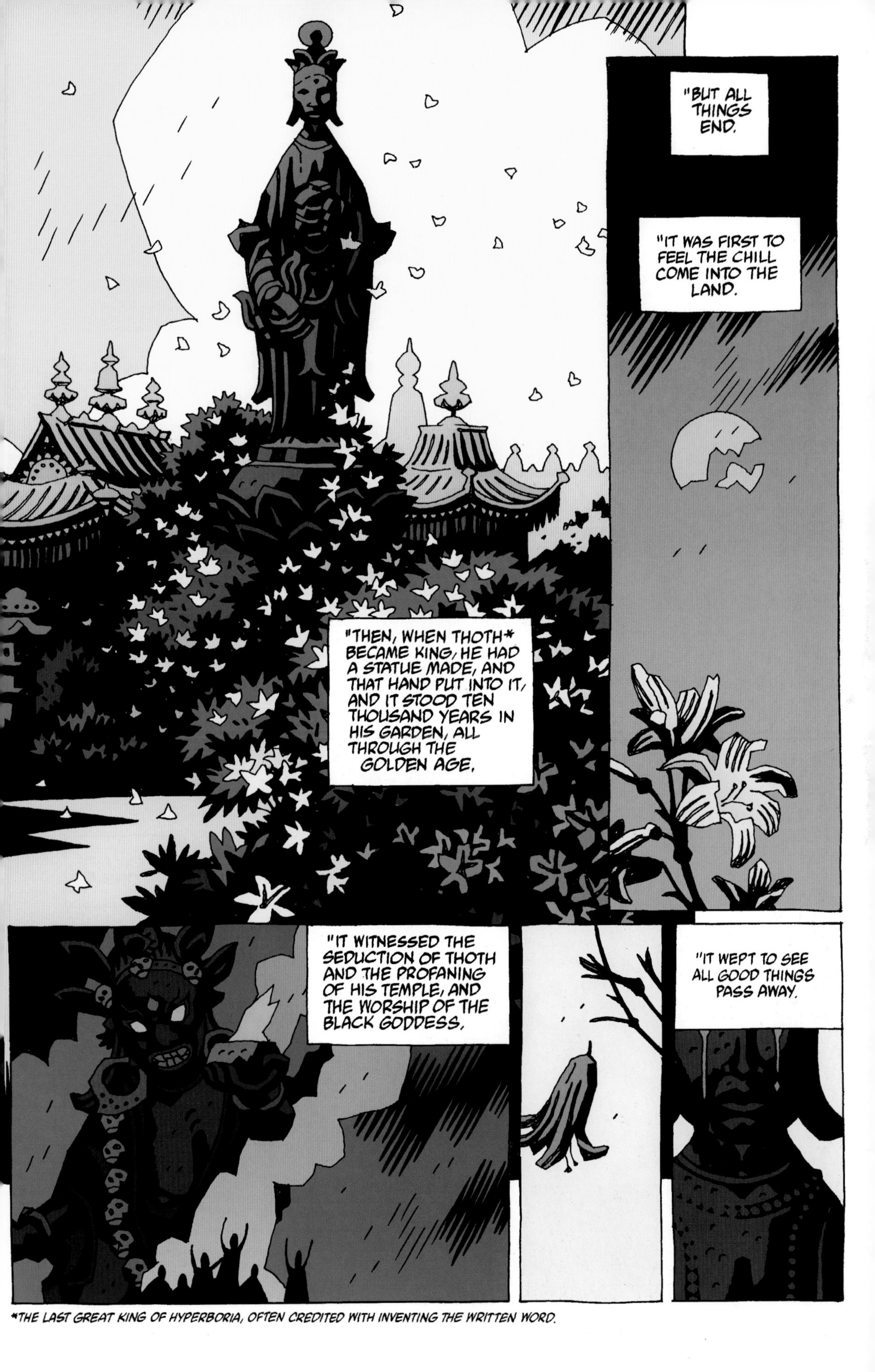
"BUT ALL THINGS END.
"IT WAS FIRST TO FEEL THE CHILL COME INTO THE LAND.
"THEN, WHEN THOTH* BECAME KING, HE HAD A STATUE MADE, AND THAT HAND PUT INTO IT, AND IT STOOD TEN THOUSAND YEARS IN HIS GARDEN, ALL THROUGH THE GOLDEN AGE.
"IT WITNESSED THE SEDUCTION OF THOTH AND THE PROFANING OF HIS TEMPLE, AND THE WORSHIP OF THE BLACK GODDESS.
"IT WEPT TO SEE ALL GOOD THINGS PASS AWAY.

*THE LAST GREAT KING OF HYPERBORIA, OFTEN CREDITED WITH INVENTING THE WRITTEN WORD.

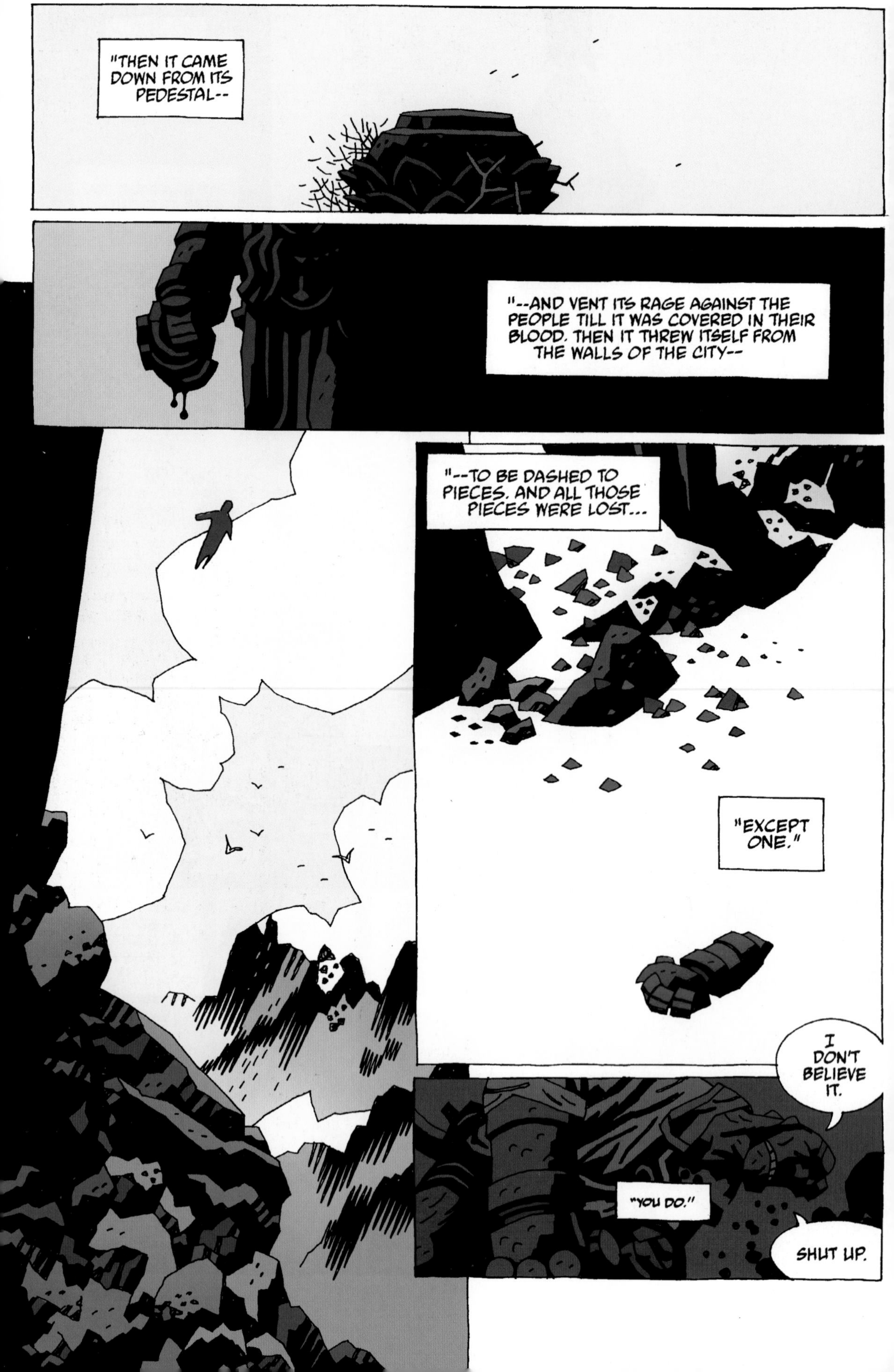
"THEN IT CAME DOWN FROM ITS PEDESTAL--
"--AND VENT ITS RAGE AGAINST THE PEOPLE TILL IT WAS COVERED IN THEIR BLOOD. THEN IT THREW ITSELF FROM THE WALLS OF THE CITY--
"--TO BE DASHED TO PIECES. AND ALL THOSE PIECES WERE LOST...
"EXCEPT ONE."
I DON'T BELIEVE IT.
"YOU DO."
SHUT UP.

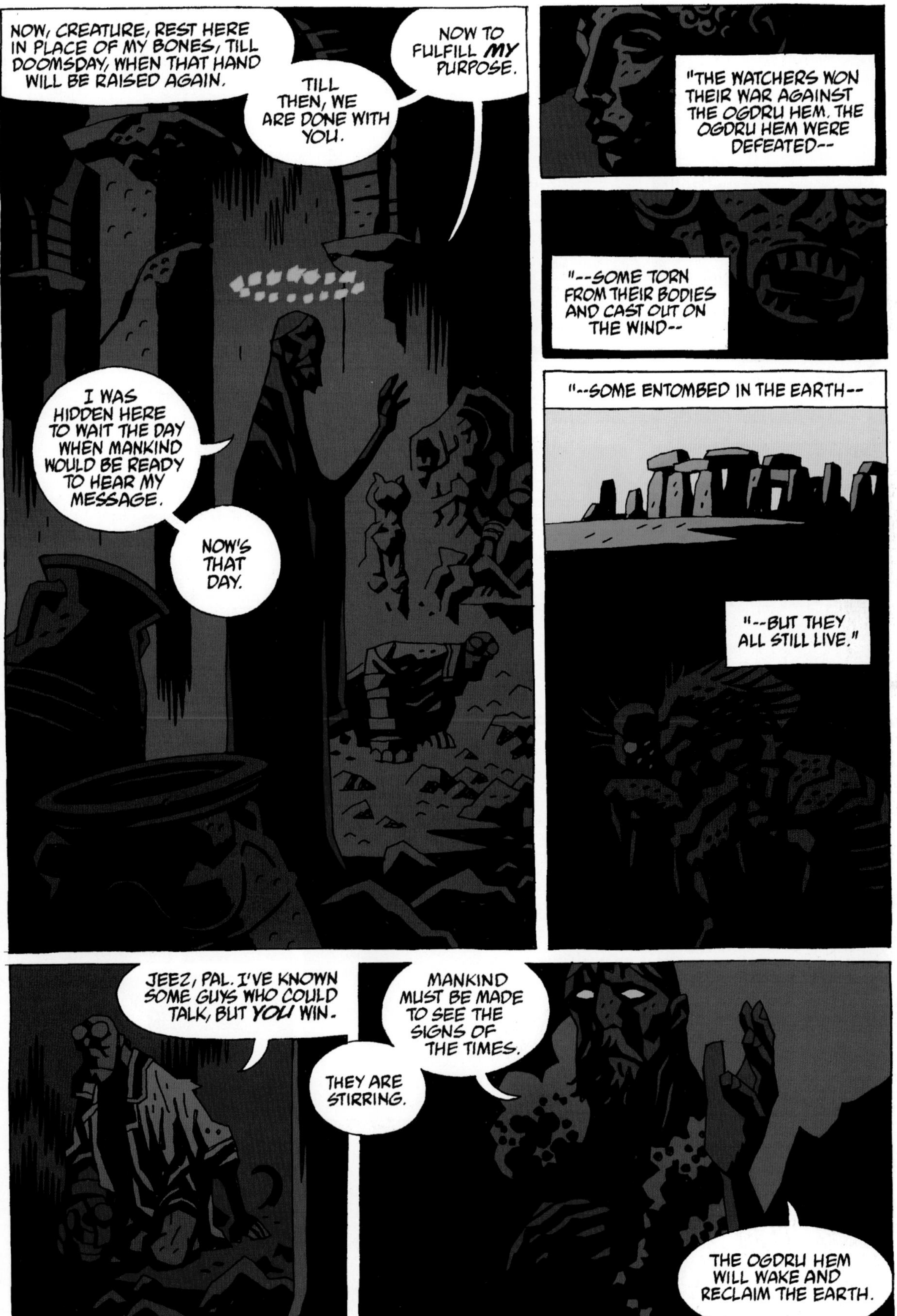
NOW, CREATURE, REST HERE IN PLACE OF MY BONES, TILL DOOMSDAY, WHEN THAT HAND WILL BE RAISED AGAIN.
TILL THEN, WE ARE DONE WITH YOU.
NOW TO FULFILL MY PURPOSE.
I WAS HIDDEN HERE TO WAIT THE DAY WHEN MANKIND WOULD BE READY TO HEAR MY MESSAGE.
NOW'S THAT DAY.
"THE WATCHERS WON THEIR WAR AGAINST THE OGDRU HEM. THE OGDRU HEM WERE DEFEATED--
"--SOME TORN FROM THEIR BODIES AND CAST OUT ON THE WIND--
"--SOME ENTOMBED IN THE EARTH--
"--BUT THEY ALL STILL LIVE."
JEEZ, PAL. I'VE KNOWN SOME GUYS WHO COULD TALK, BUT YOU WIN.
MANKIND MUST BE MADE TO SEE THE SIGNS OF THE TIMES.
THEY ARE STIRRING.
THE OGDRU HEM WILL WAKE AND RECLAIM THE EARTH.

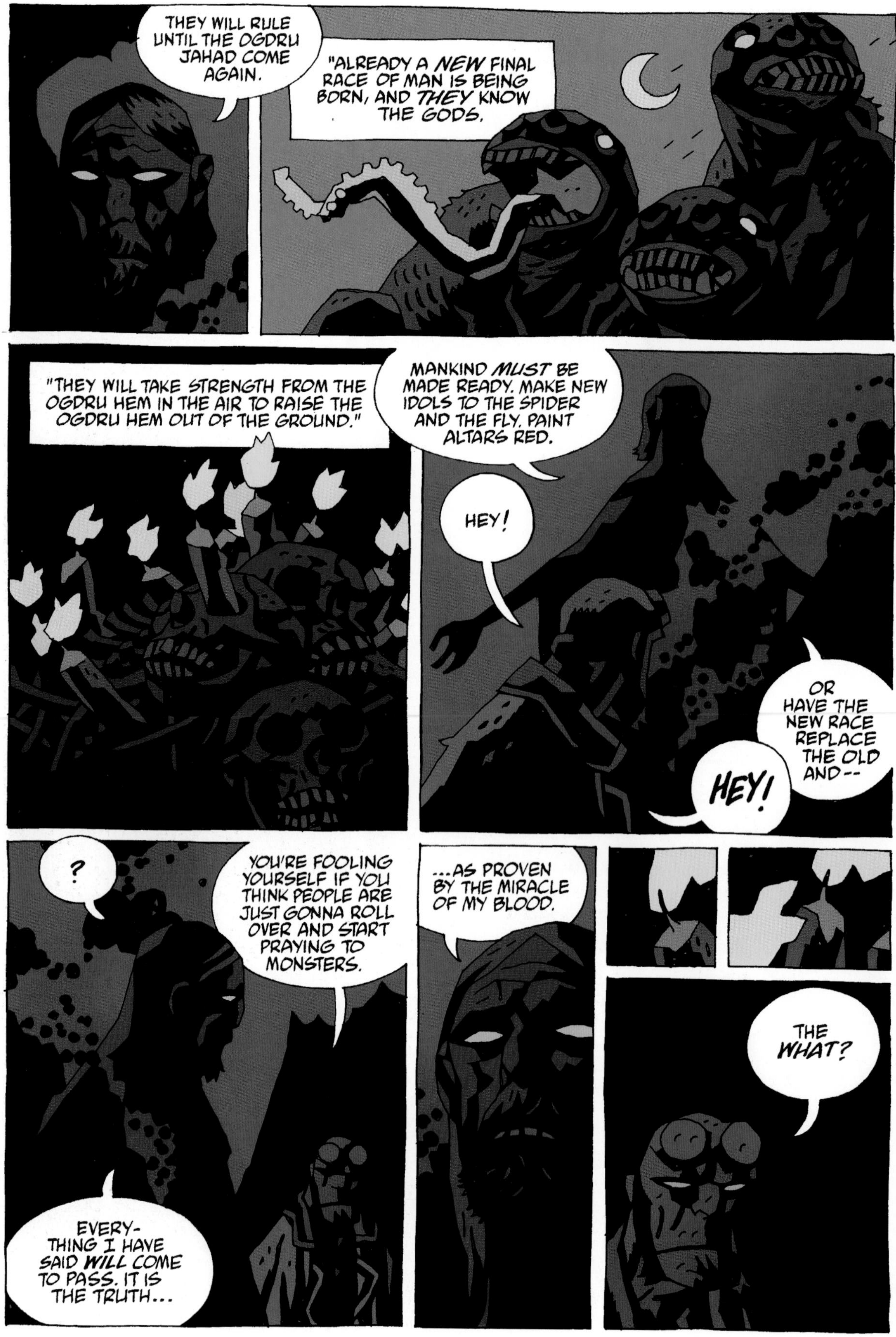
THEY WILL RULE UNTIL THE OGDRU JAHAD COME AGAIN.
"ALREADY A NEW FINAL RACE OF MAN IS BEING BORN, AND THEY KNOW THE GODS.
"THEY WILL TAKE STRENGTH FROM THE OGDRU HEM IN THE AIR TO RAISE THE OGDRU HEM OUT OF THE GROUND."
MANKIND MUST BE MADE READY. MAKE NEW IDOLS TO THE SPIDER AND THE FLY. PAINT ALTARS RED.
HEY!
OR HAVE THE NEW RACE REPLACE THE OLD AND--
HEY!
?
YOU'RE FOOLING YOURSELF IF YOU THINK PEOPLE ARE JUST GONNA ROLL OVER AND START PRAYING TO MONSTERS.
EVERY-THING I HAVE SAID WILL COME TO PASS. IT IS THE TRUTH...
...AS PROVEN BY THE MIRACLE OF MY BLOOD.
THE WHAT?

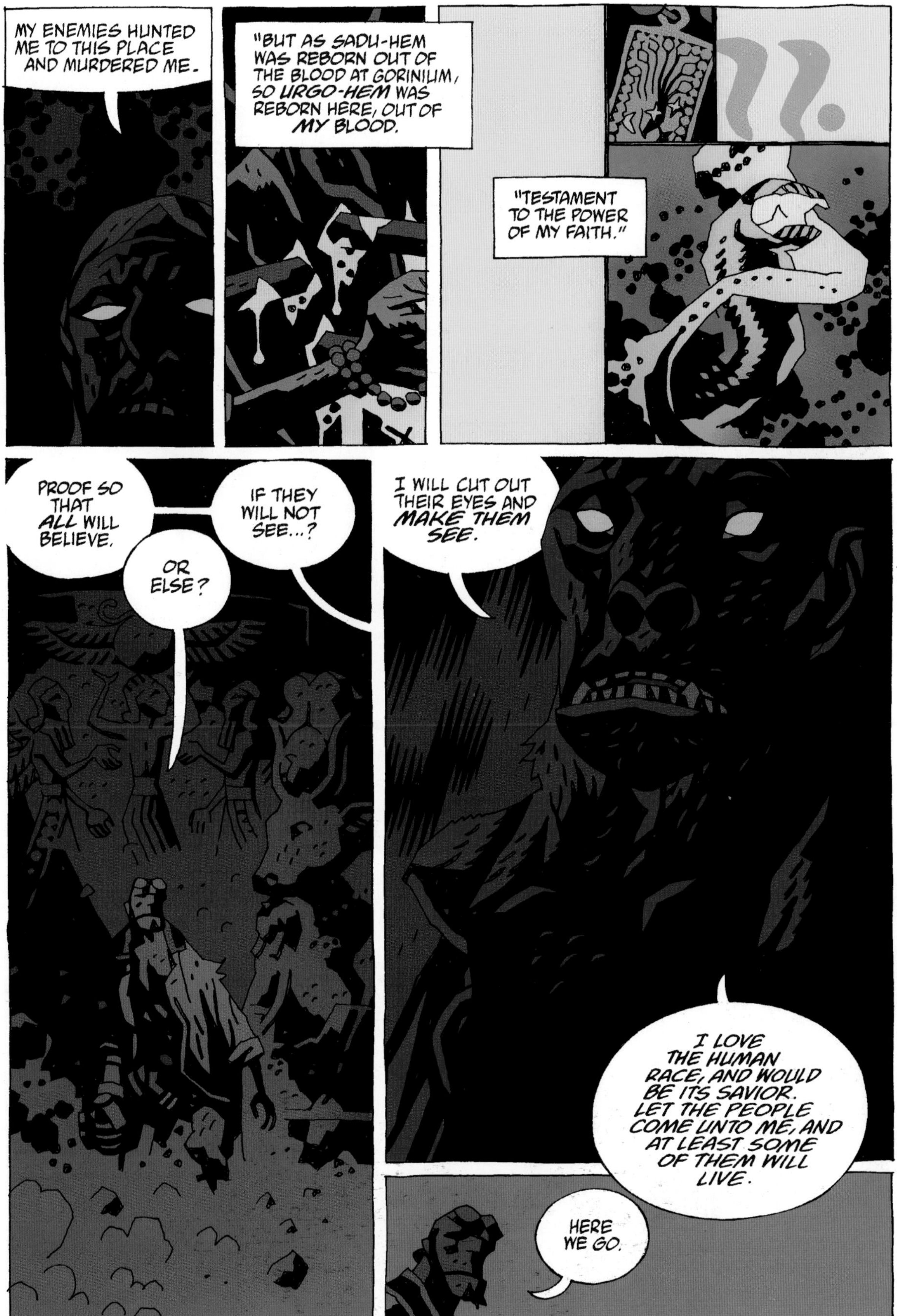
MY ENEMIES HUNTED ME TO THIS PLACE AND MURDERED ME.
"BUT AS SADU-HEM WAS REBORN OUT OF THE BLOOD AT GORINIUM, SO URGO-HEM WAS REBORN HERE, OUT OF MY BLOOD.
"TESTAMENT TO THE POWER OF MY FAITH."
PROOF SO THAT ALL WILL BELIEVE.
IF THEY WILL NOT SEE...?
OR ELSE?
I WILL CUT OUT THEIR EYES AND MAKE THEM SEE.
I LOVE THE HUMAN RACE, AND WOULD BE ITS SAVIOR. LET THE PEOPLE COME UNTO ME, AND AT LEAST SOME OF THEM WILL LIVE.
HERE WE GO.

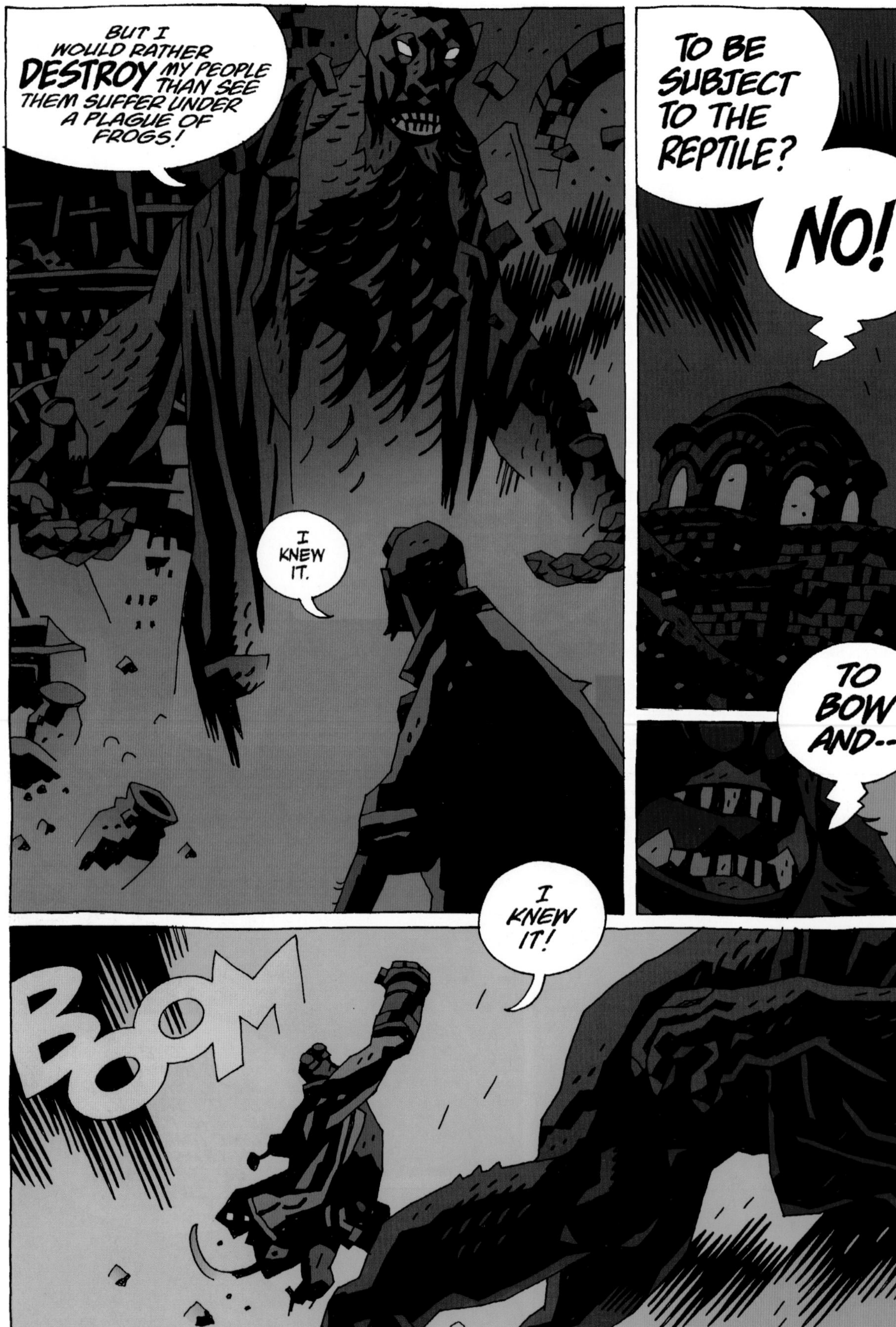
BUT I WOULD RATHER DESTROY MY PEOPLE THAN SEE THEM SUFFER UNDER A PLAGUE OF FROGS!
I KNEW IT.
TO BE SUBJECT TO THE REPTILE?
NO!
TO BOW AND--
I KNEW IT!
BOOM

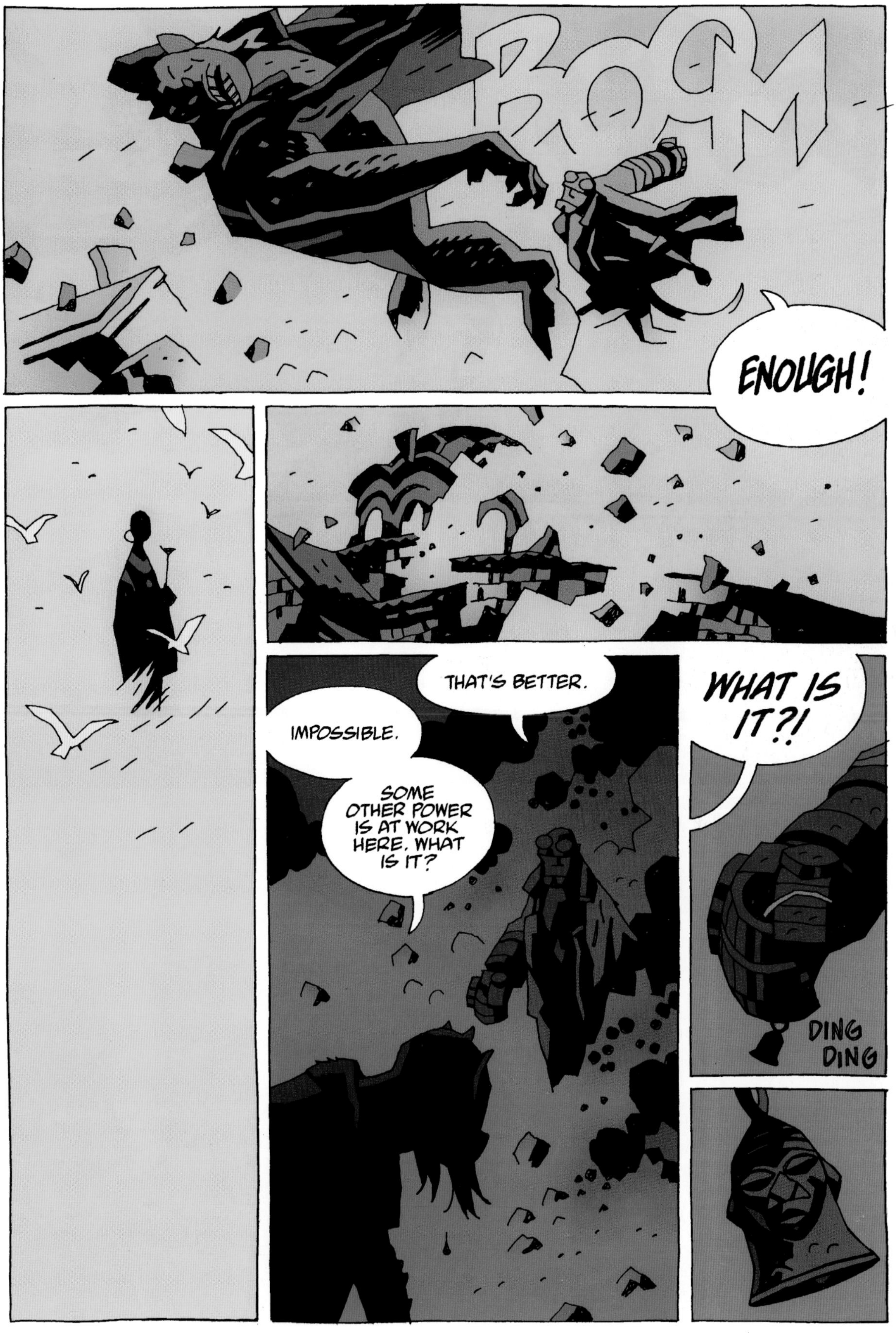
BOOM
ENOUGH!
THAT'S BETTER.
IMPOSSIBLE.
SOME OTHER POWER IS AT WORK HERE. WHAT IS IT?
WHAT IS IT?!
DING DING

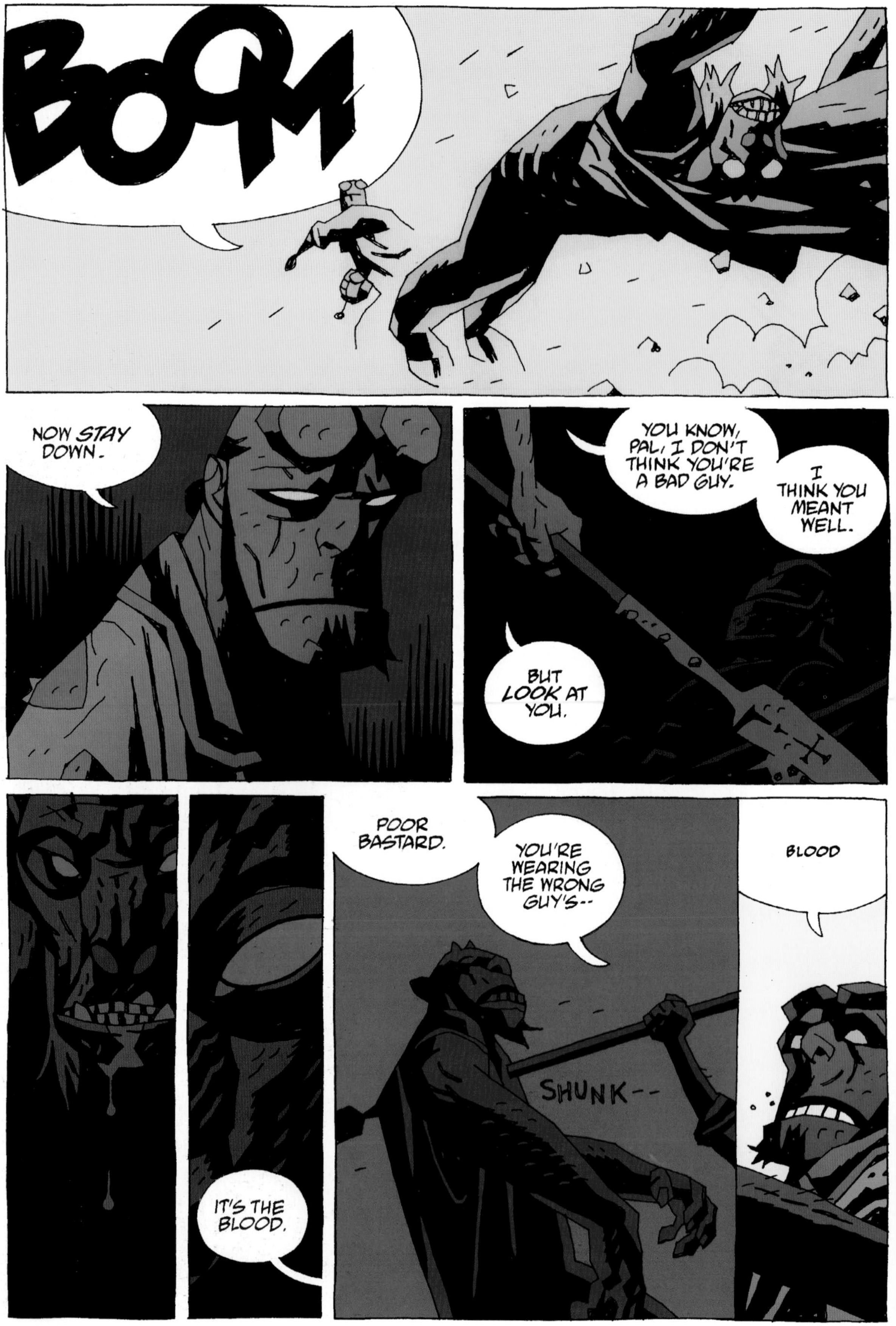
BOOM
NOW STAY DOWN.
YOU KNOW, PAL, I DON'T THINK YOU'RE A BAD GUY.
I THINK YOU MEANT WELL.
BUT LOOK AT YOU.
IT'S THE BLOOD.
POOR BASTARD.
YOU'RE WEARING THE WRONG GUY'S--
SHUNK--
BLOOD

FOOL.

YOU SAID IT YOURSELF. IT'S *YOUR* BLOOD. CUT ME AND WHO BLEEDS FOR IT?

AND WHAT IS THIS?

OH.

A WOODEN SPEAR BECOMES AN IRON STAFF.

WITH A BIRD.

CRAP.

CRAP.

PATHETIC.

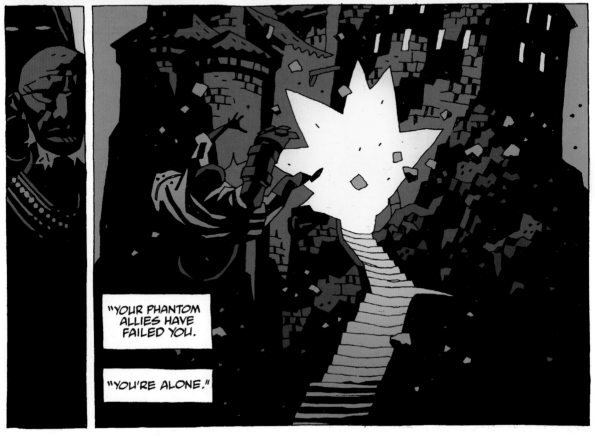

"YOUR PHANTOM ALLIES HAVE FAILED YOU.

"YOU'RE ALONE."

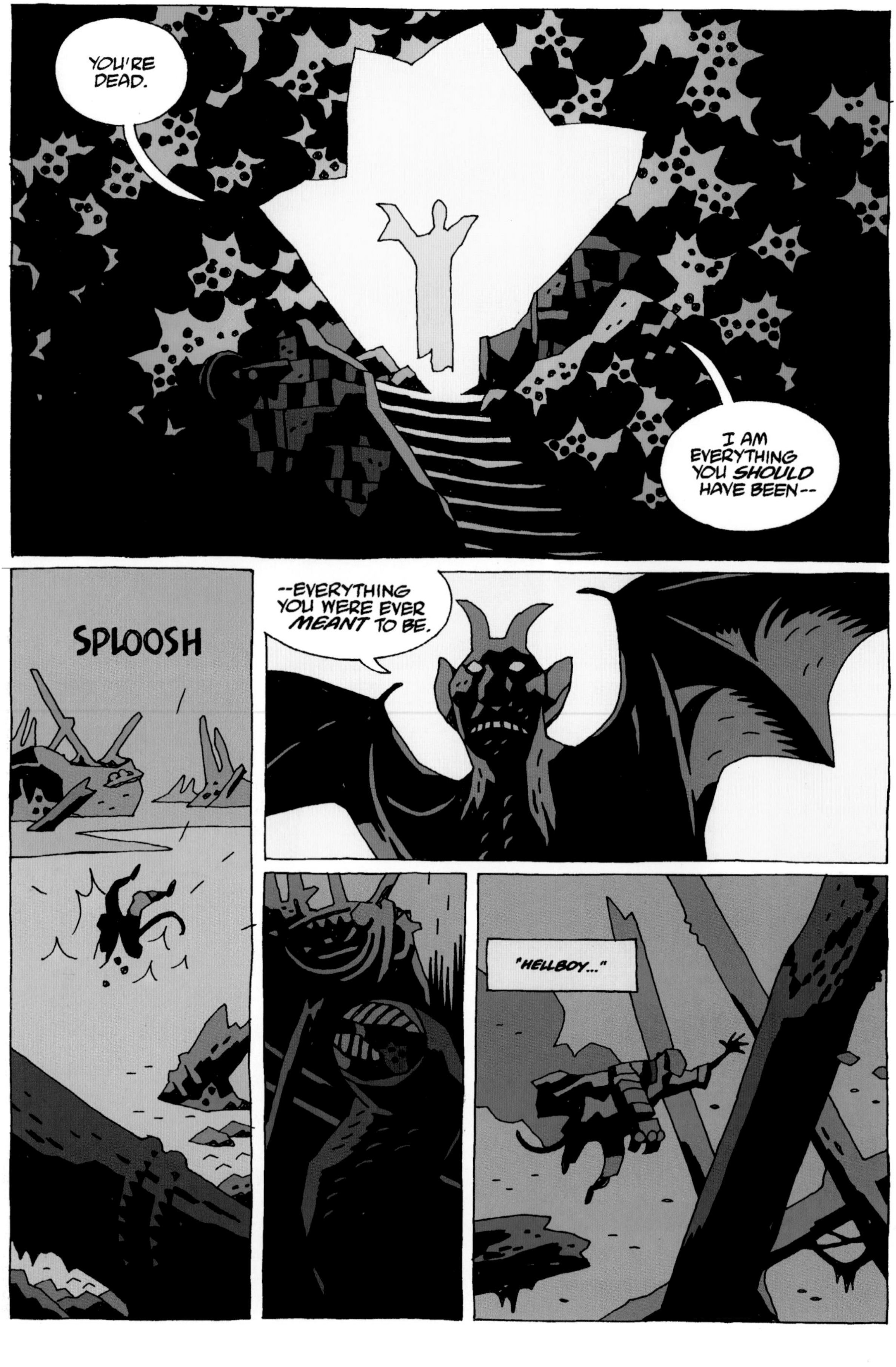
YOU'RE DEAD.
I AM EVERYTHING YOU SHOULD HAVE BEEN--
SPLOOSH
--EVERYTHING YOU WERE EVER MEANT TO BE.
"HELLBOY..."

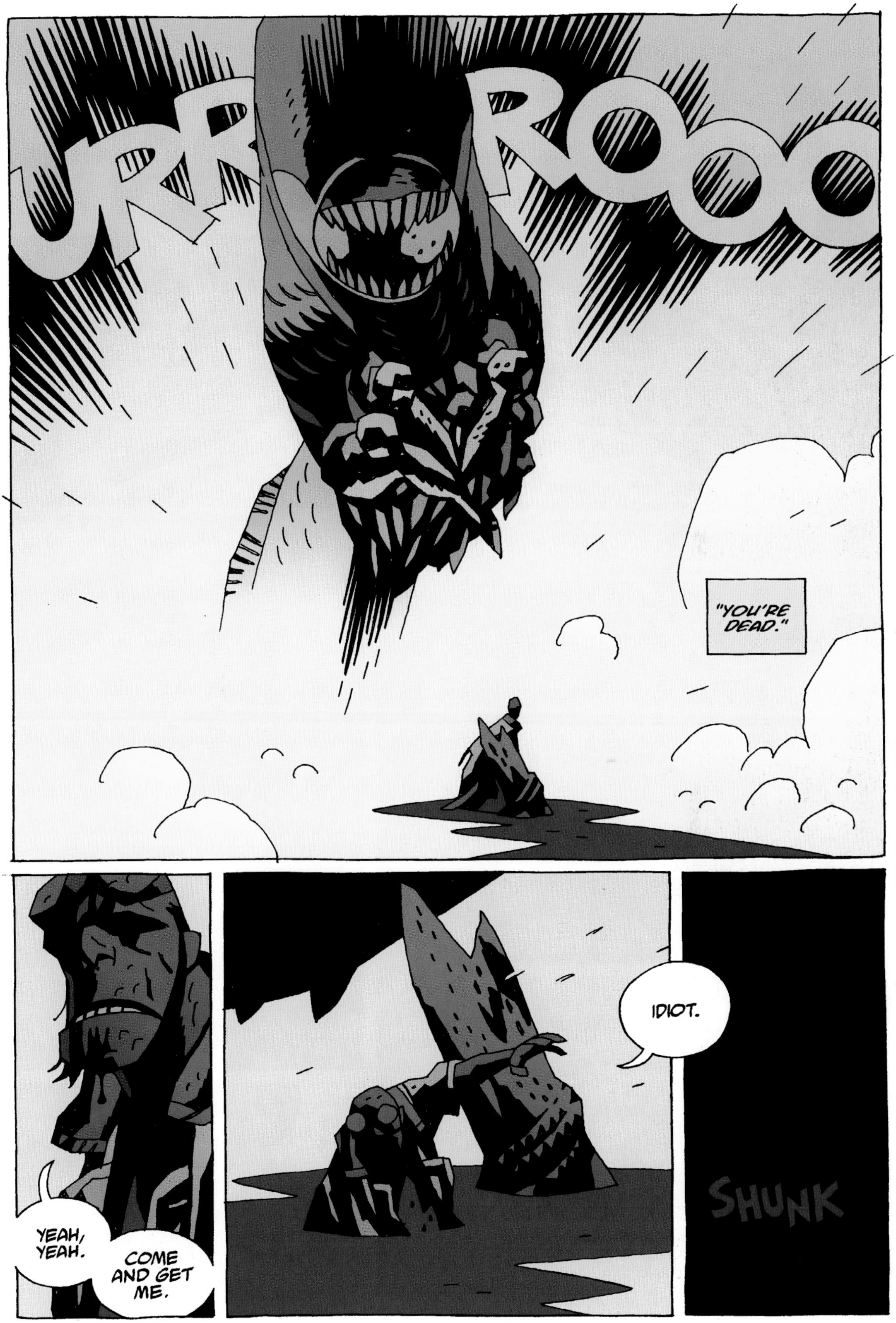

URRROOOO
"YOU'RE DEAD."
YEAH, YEAH.
COME AND GET ME.
IDIOT.
SHUNK

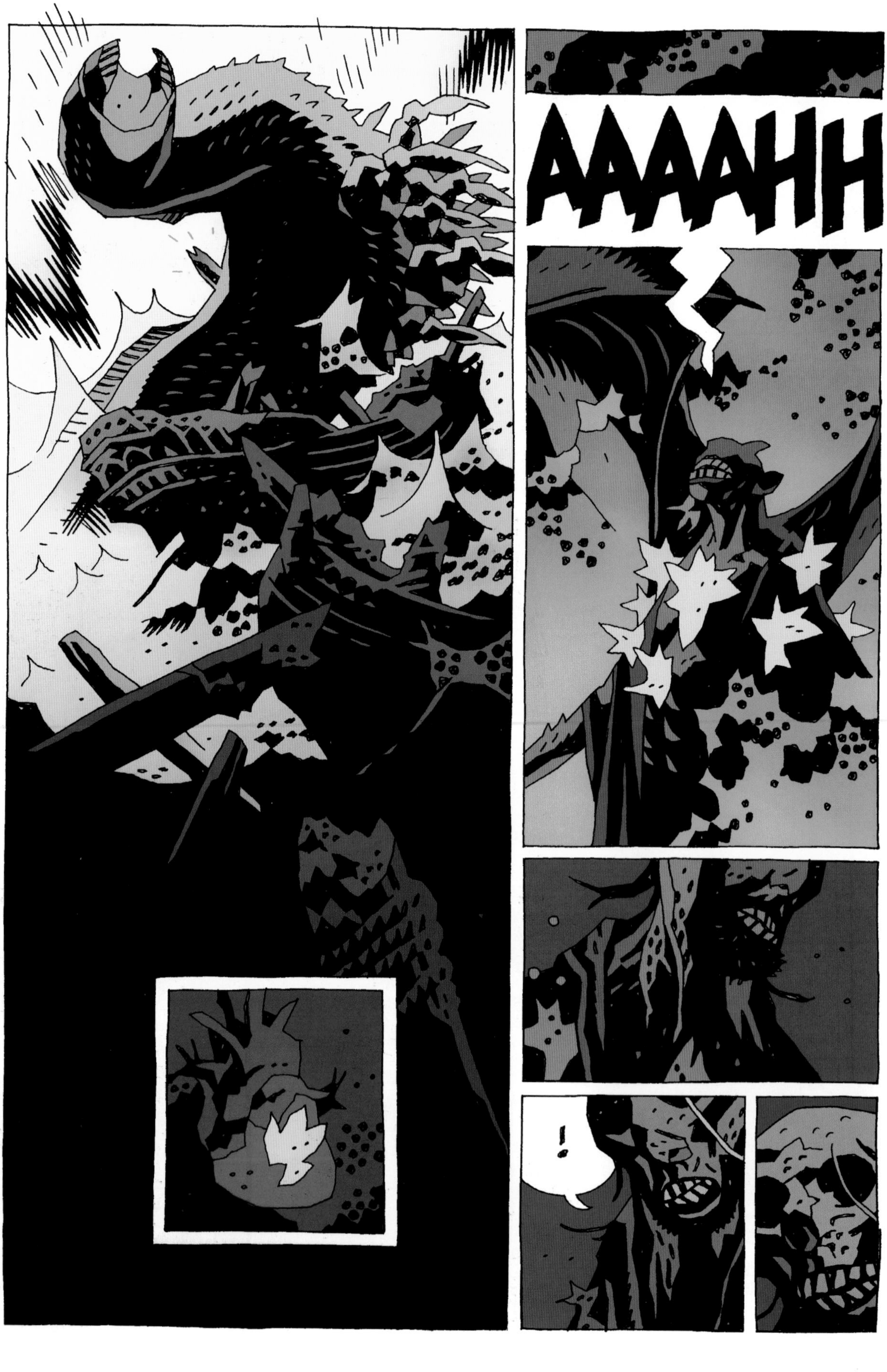
AAAAHH
!

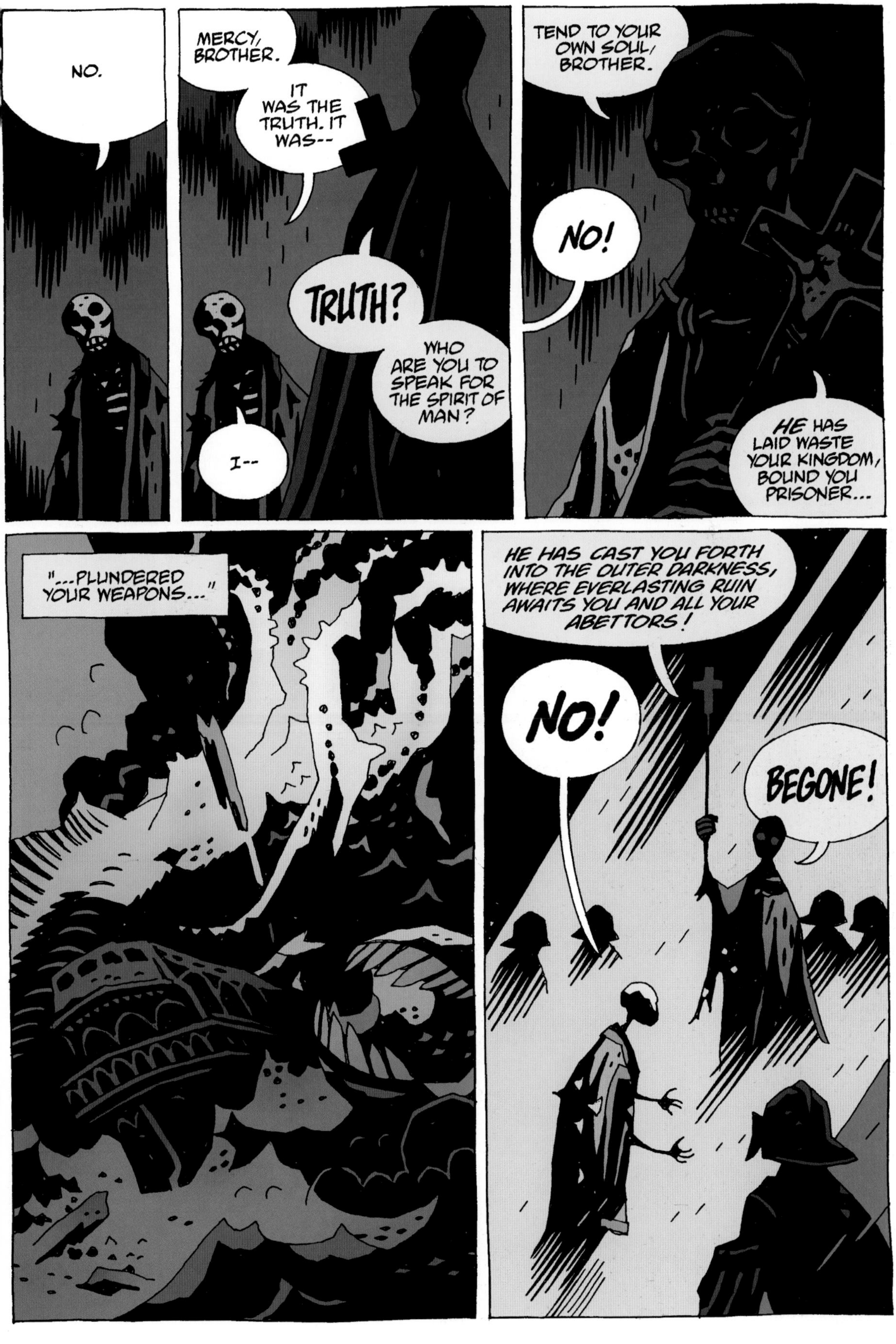
NO.
MERCY, BROTHER.
IT WAS THE TRUTH. IT WAS--
TRUTH?
WHO ARE YOU TO SPEAK FOR THE SPIRIT OF MAN?
I--
TEND TO YOUR OWN SOUL, BROTHER.
NO!
HE HAS LAID WASTE YOUR KINGDOM, BOUND YOU PRISONER...
"...PLUNDERED YOUR WEAPONS..."
HE HAS CAST YOU FORTH INTO THE OUTER DARKNESS, WHERE EVERLASTING RUIN AWAITS YOU AND ALL YOUR ABETTORS!
NO!
BEGONE!

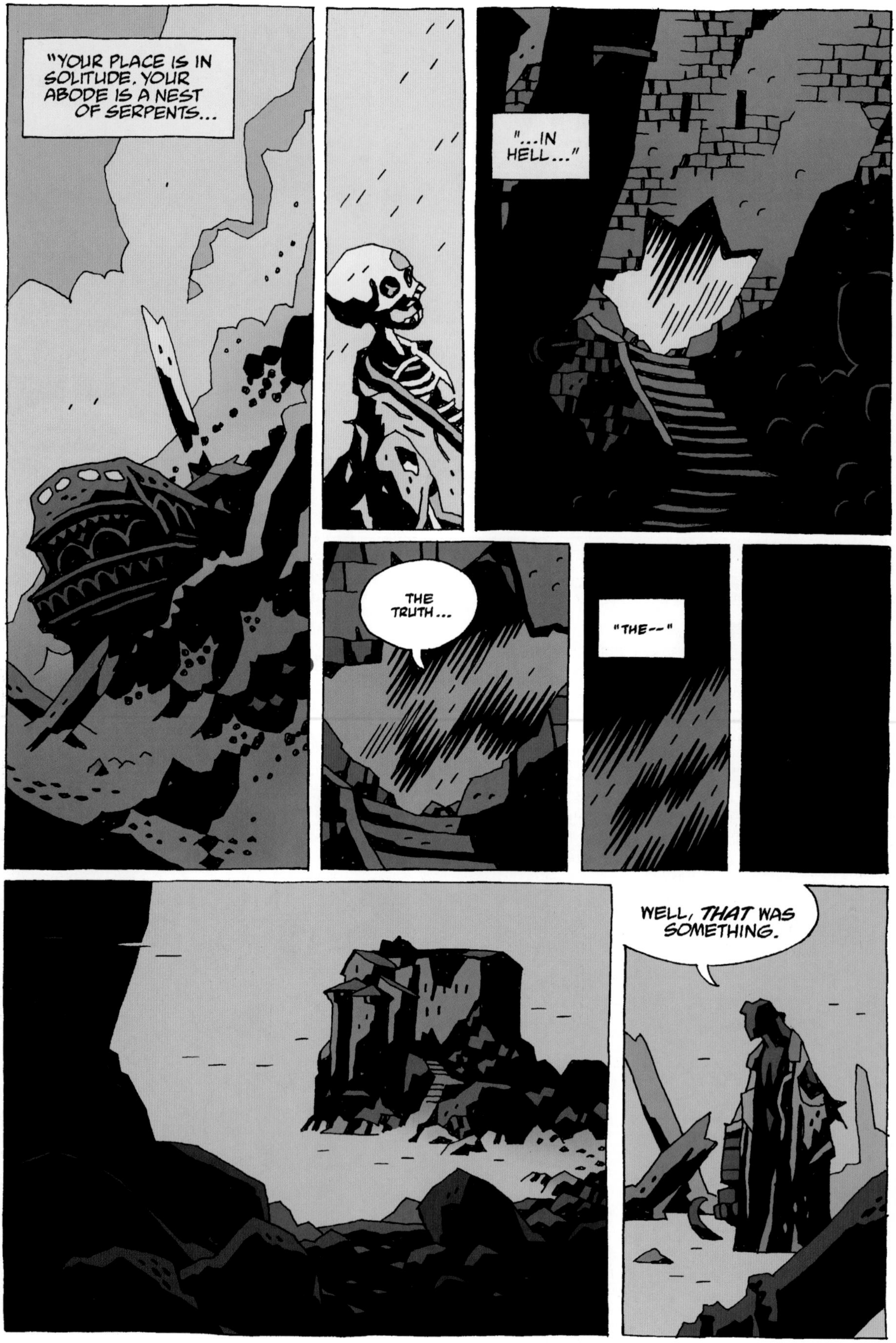
"YOUR PLACE IS IN SOLITUDE. YOUR ABODE IS A NEST OF SERPENTS...
"...IN HELL..."
THE TRUTH...
"THE--"
WELL, *THAT* WAS SOMETHING.

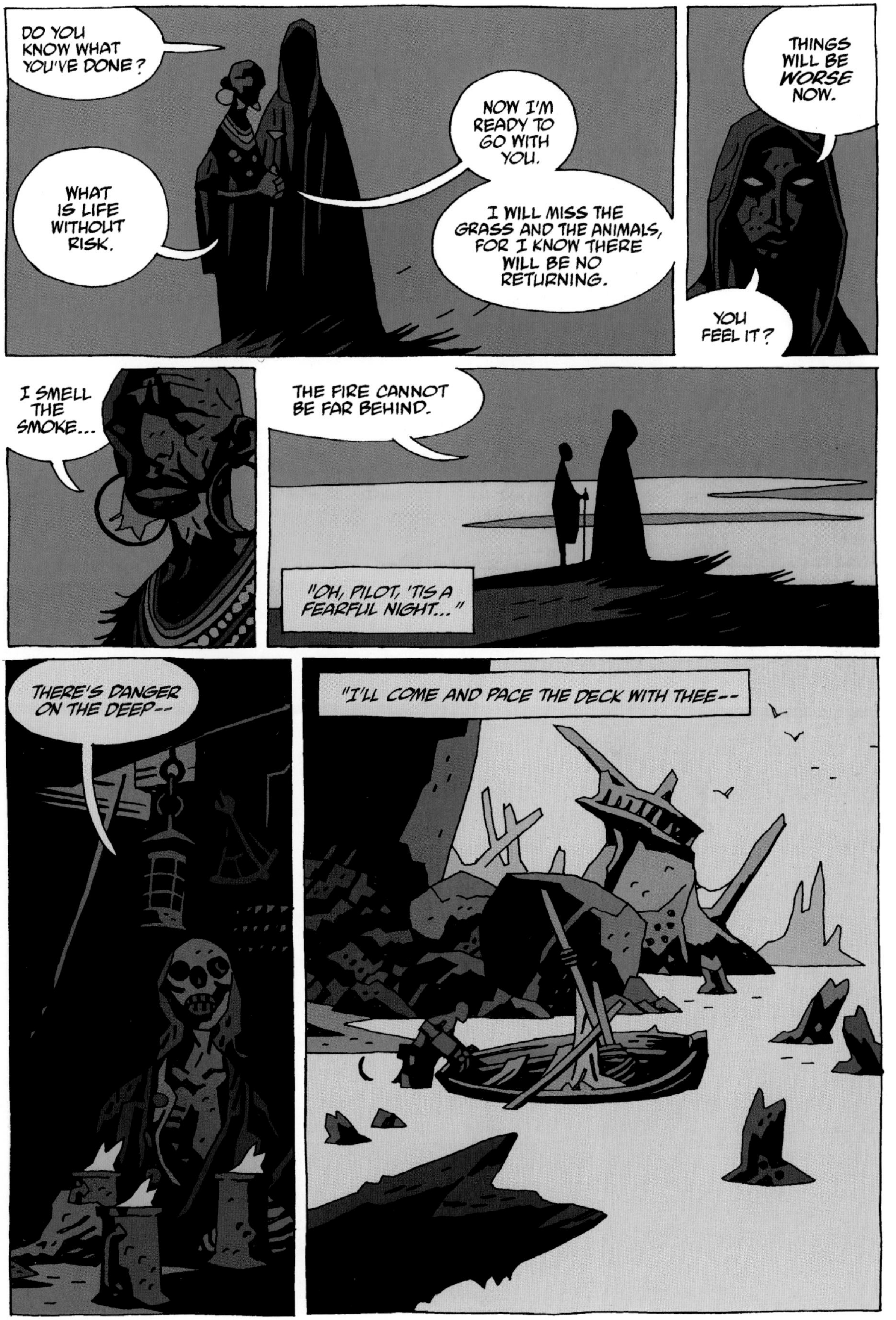
DO YOU KNOW WHAT YOU'VE DONE?
WHAT IS LIFE WITHOUT RISK.
NOW I'M READY TO GO WITH YOU.
I WILL MISS THE GRASS AND THE ANIMALS, FOR I KNOW THERE WILL BE NO RETURNING.
THINGS WILL BE WORSE NOW.
YOU FEEL IT?
I SMELL THE SMOKE...
THE FIRE CANNOT BE FAR BEHIND.
"OH, PILOT, 'TIS A FEARFUL NIGHT..."
THERE'S DANGER ON THE DEEP--
"I'LL COME AND PACE THE DECK WITH THEE--

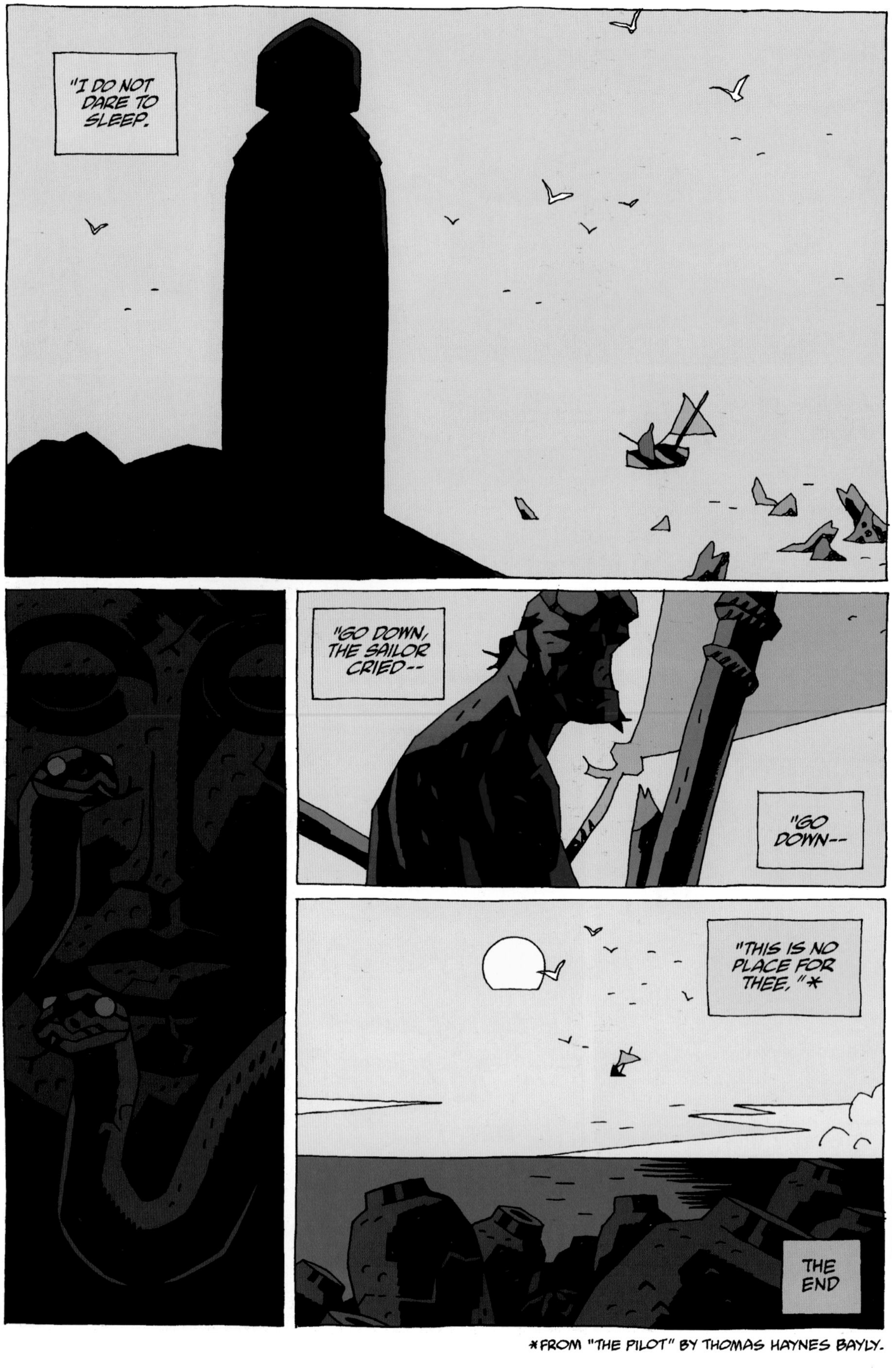
"I DO NOT DARE TO SLEEP.
"GO DOWN, THE SAILOR CRIED--
"GO DOWN--
"THIS IS NO PLACE FOR THEE."*
THE END

*FROM "THE PILOT" BY THOMAS HAYNES BAYLY.

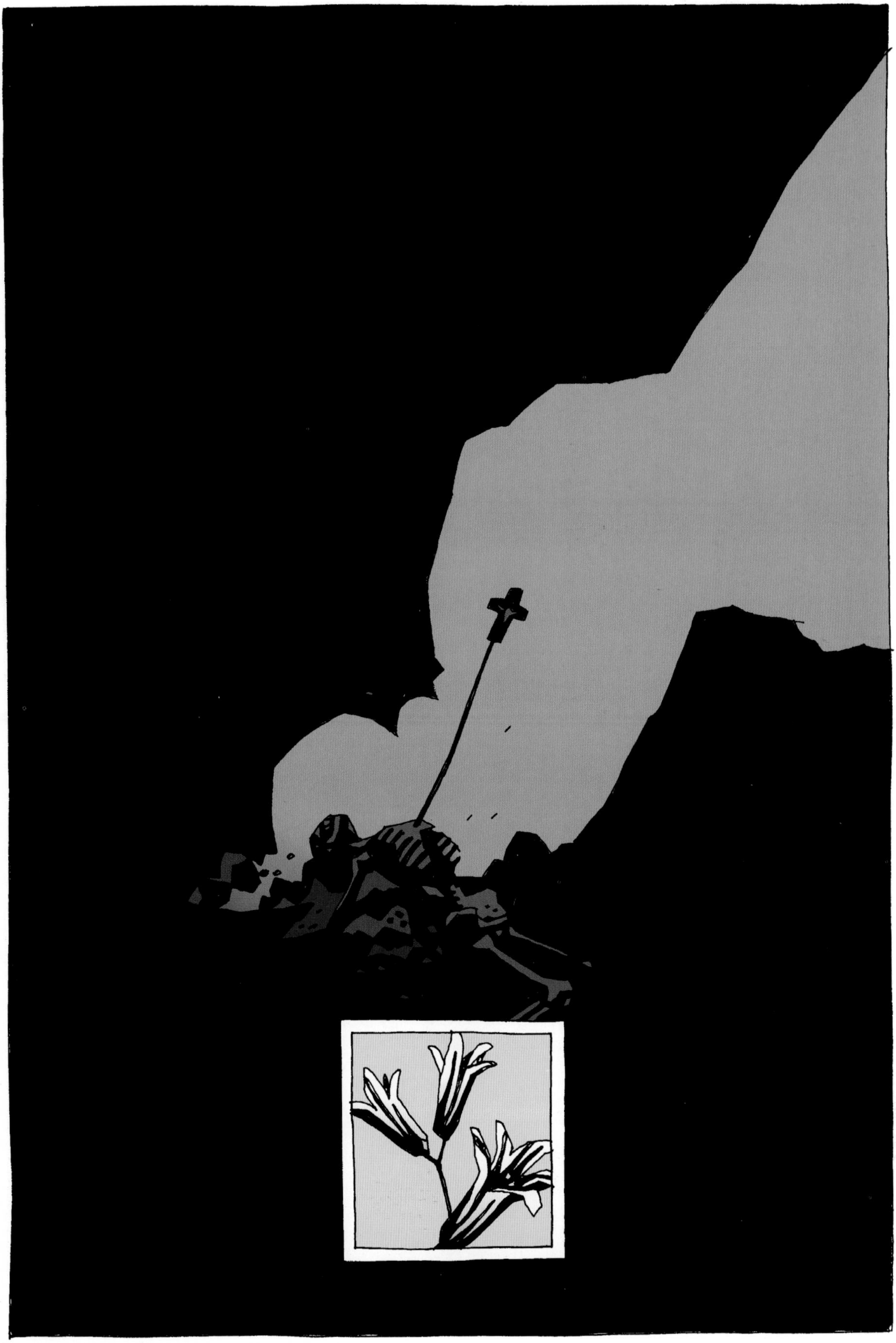

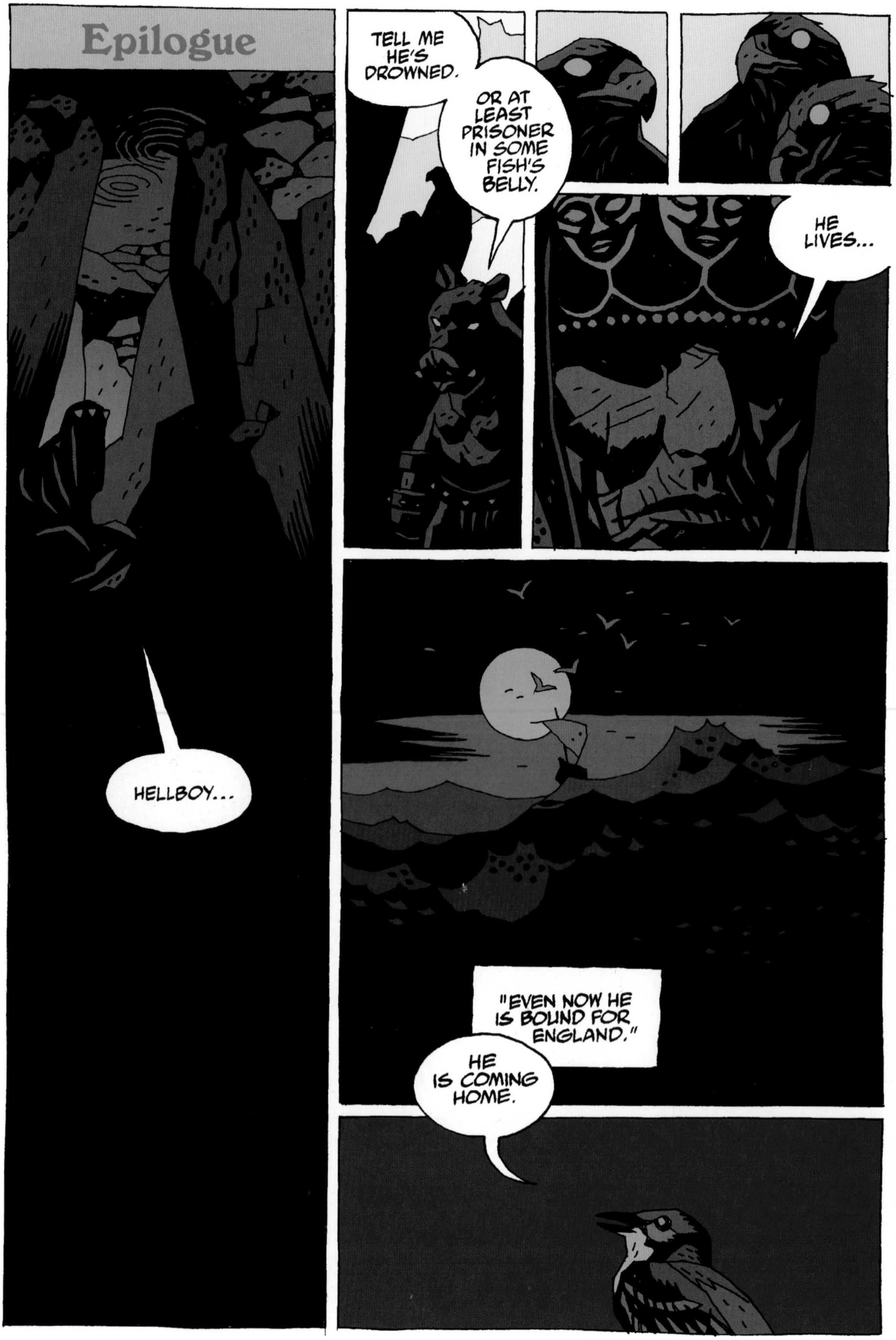
Epilogue
HELLBOY...
TELL ME HE'S DROWNED.
OR AT LEAST PRISONER IN SOME FISH'S BELLY.
HE LIVES...
"EVEN NOW HE IS BOUND FOR ENGLAND."
HE IS COMING HOME.

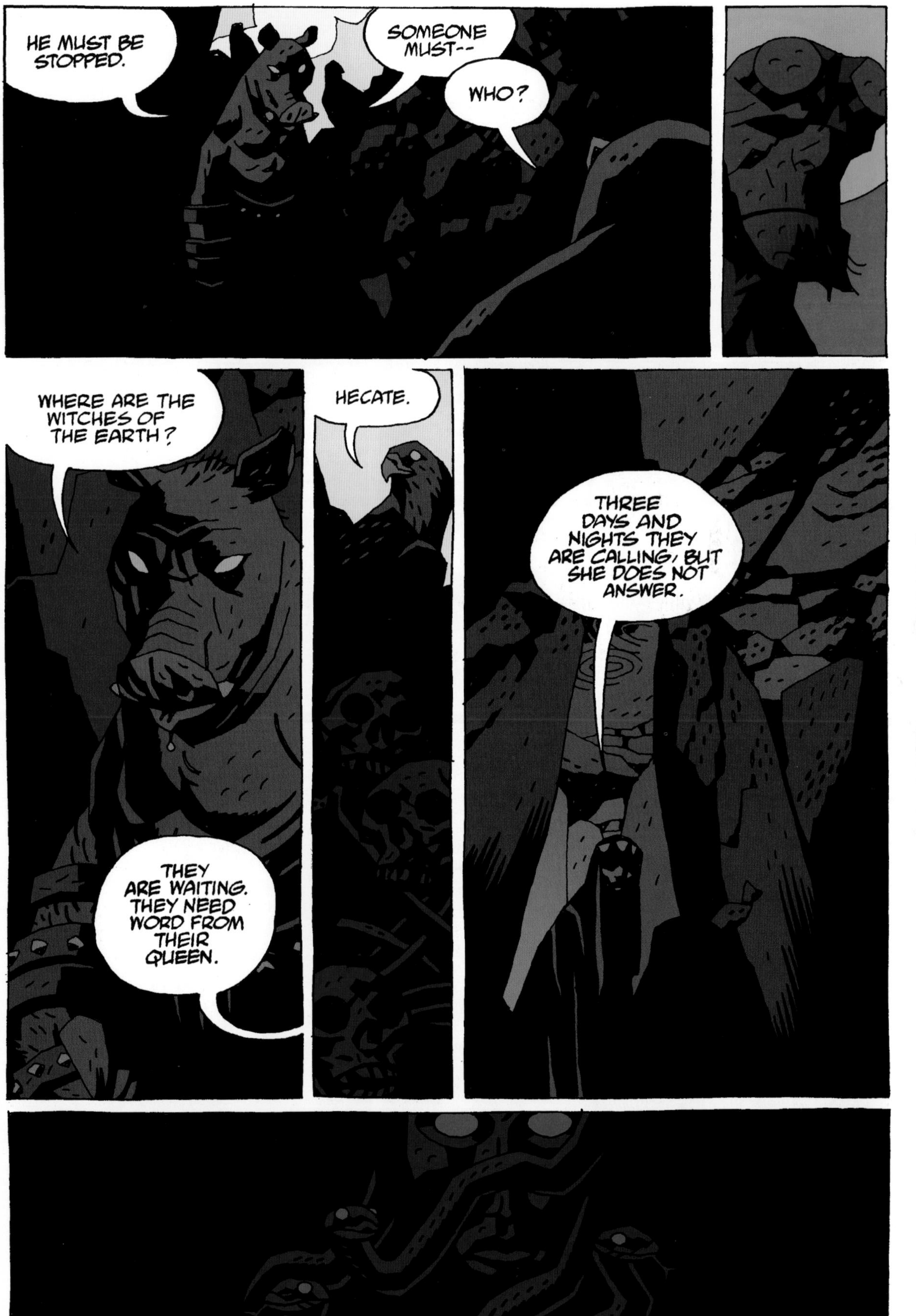
HE MUST BE STOPPED.
SOMEONE MUST--
WHO?
WHERE ARE THE WITCHES OF THE EARTH?
THEY ARE WAITING. THEY NEED WORD FROM THEIR QUEEN.
HECATE.
THREE DAYS AND NIGHTS THEY ARE CALLING, BUT SHE DOES NOT ANSWER.

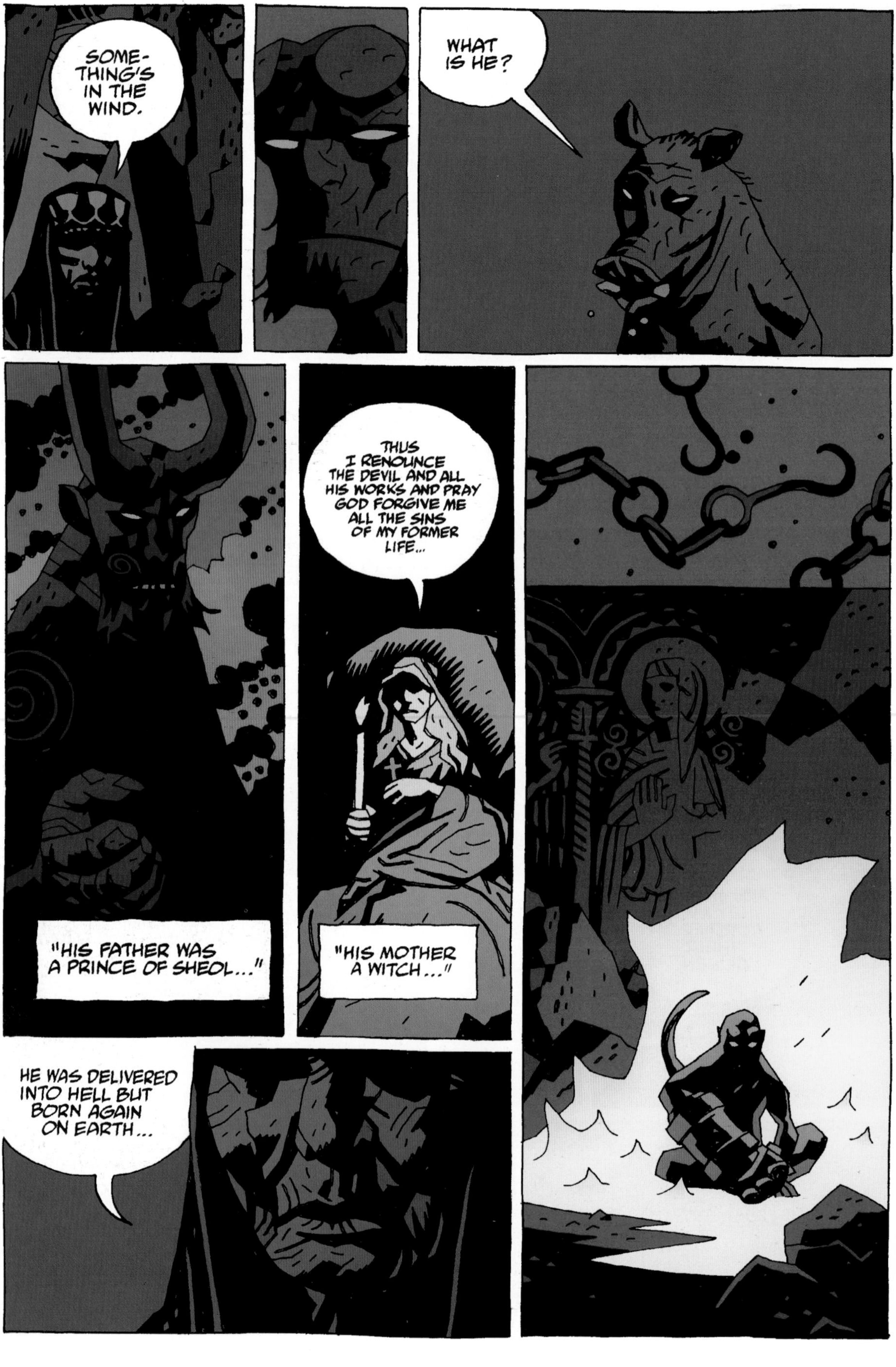
SOME-THING'S IN THE WIND.
WHAT IS HE?
"HIS FATHER WAS A PRINCE OF SHEOL..."
THUS I RENOUNCE THE DEVIL AND ALL HIS WORKS AND PRAY GOD FORGIVE ME ALL THE SINS OF MY FORMER LIFE...
"HIS MOTHER A WITCH..."
HE WAS DELIVERED INTO HELL BUT BORN AGAIN ON EARTH...

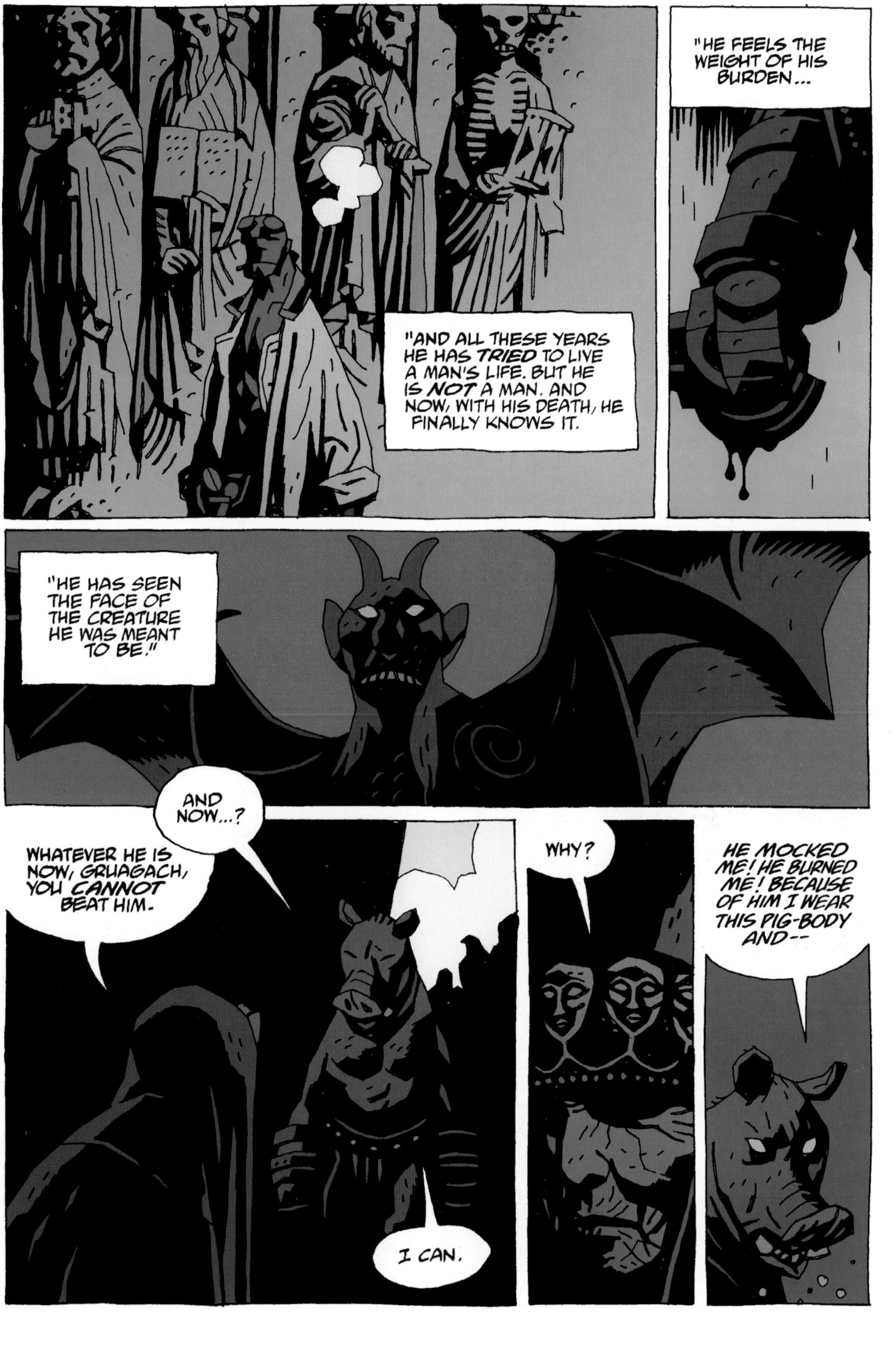
"AND ALL THESE YEARS HE HAS TRIED TO LIVE A MAN'S LIFE. BUT HE IS NOT A MAN. AND NOW, WITH HIS DEATH, HE FINALLY KNOWS IT.
"HE FEELS THE WEIGHT OF HIS BURDEN...
"HE HAS SEEN THE FACE OF THE CREATURE HE WAS MEANT TO BE."
WHATEVER HE IS NOW, GRUAGACH, YOU CANNOT BEAT HIM.
AND NOW...?
I CAN.
WHY?
HE MOCKED ME! HE BURNED ME! BECAUSE OF HIM I WEAR THIS PIG-BODY AND--

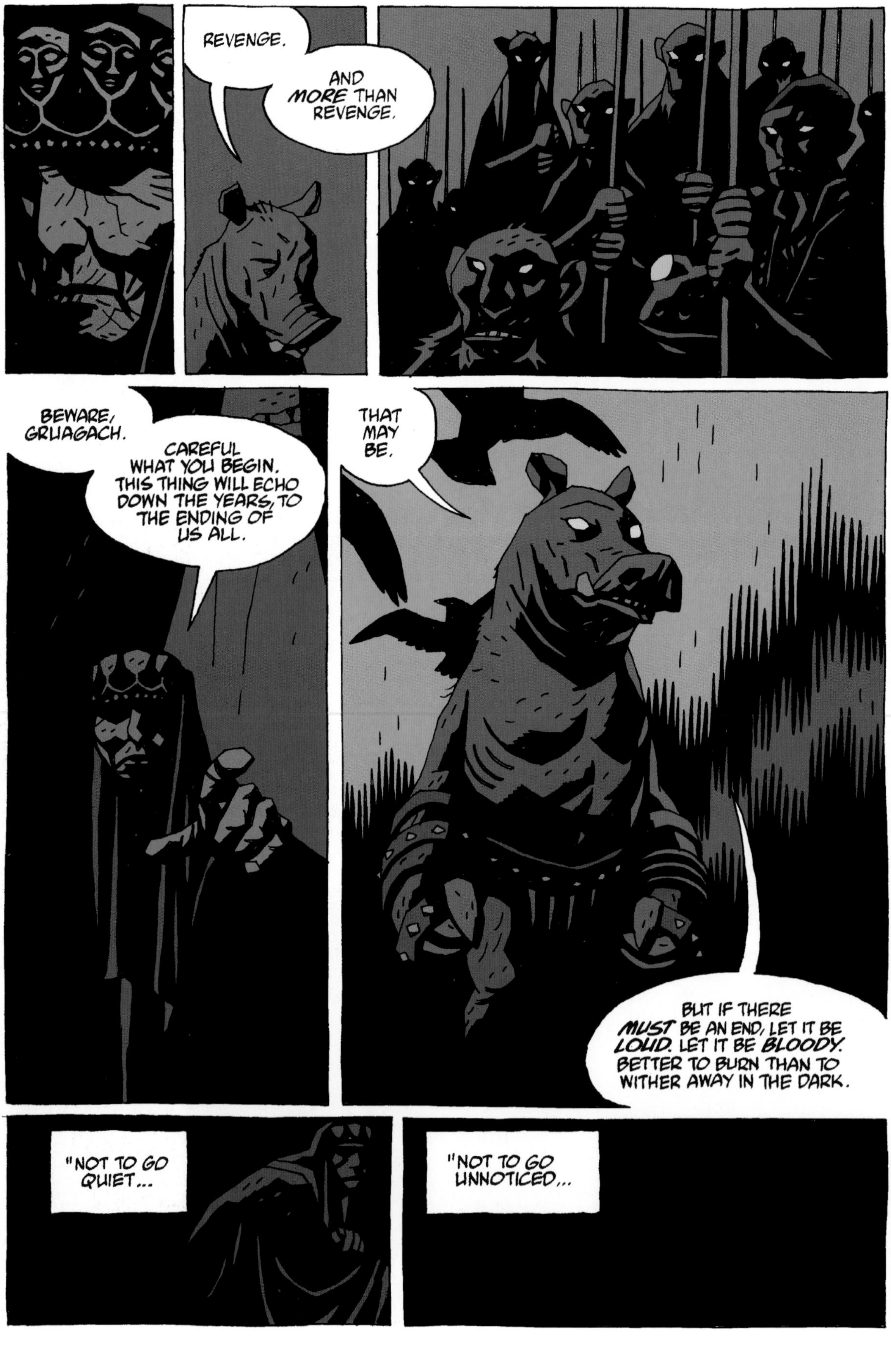
REVENGE.
AND MORE THAN REVENGE.
BEWARE, GRUAGACH.
CAREFUL WHAT YOU BEGIN. THIS THING WILL ECHO DOWN THE YEARS, TO THE ENDING OF US ALL.
THAT MAY BE.
BUT IF THERE MUST BE AN END, LET IT BE LOUD. LET IT BE BLOODY. BETTER TO BURN THAN TO WITHER AWAY IN THE DARK.
"NOT TO GO QUIET...
"NOT TO GO UNNOTICED...

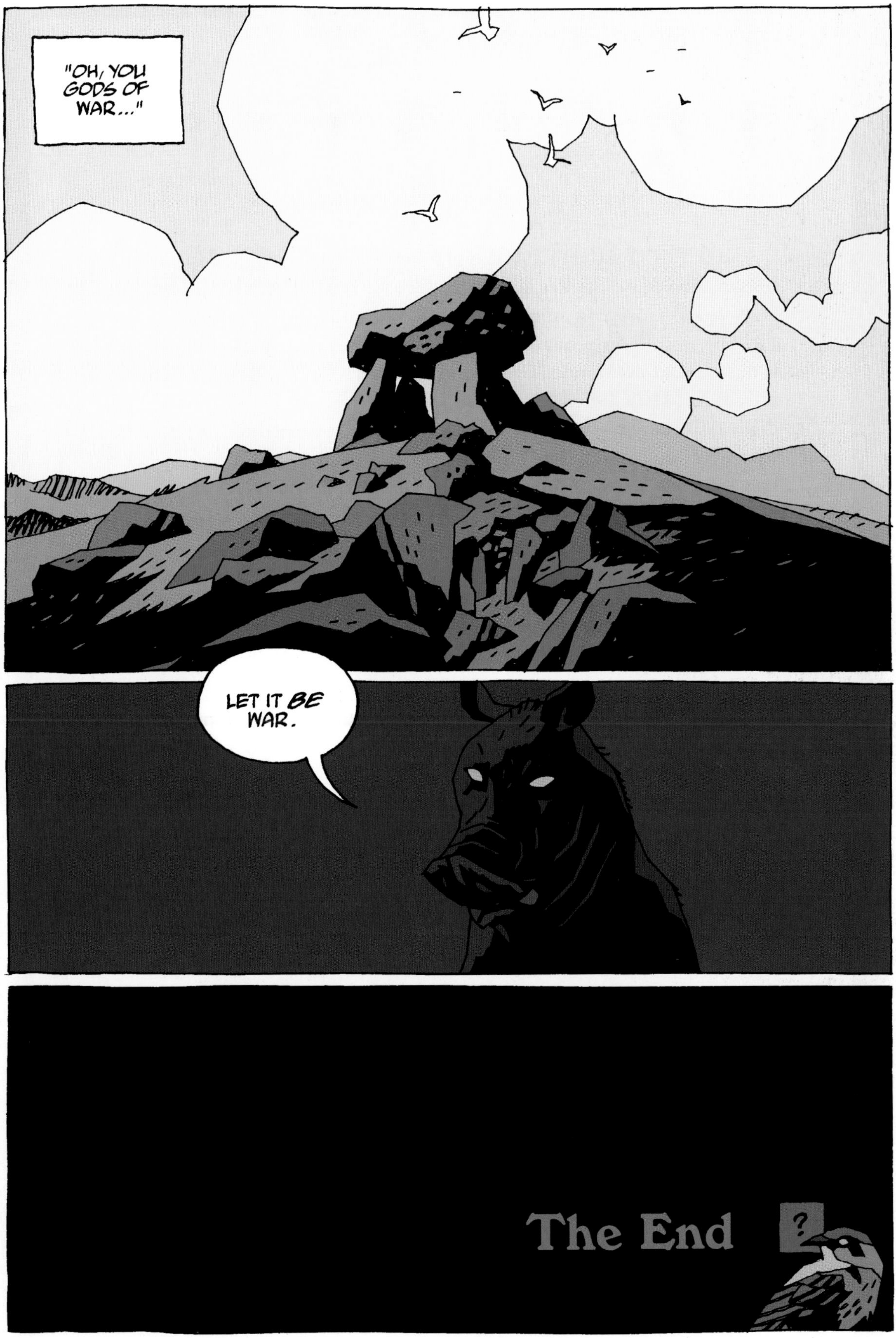
"OH, YOU GODS OF WAR..."
LET IT *BE* WAR.
The End ?

THE FIRST EIGHT PAGES to follow (inked and colored specifically for this book) are the beginning of the first version of *The Island*. This version was closest in spirit to the old William Hope Hodgson stories. Hellboy is called up out of the sea by witches and finds himself on a spooky island surrounded by fog and wrecked ships. He finds the remains of a sailor who's killed himself to avoid the fate of his shipmates. His diary tells the tale—despair, madness, and men turned to fungus. And, of course, that night the fungus men attack. The bit with the witches and the little carved Hellboy is being used to better effect in the next Hellboy miniseries, *Darkness Calls*. Strangely enough, Hellboy's last line on page eight was going to be, "This isn't going to work." As is so often the case, he was right.

The next pages (in pencil) are part of my second attempt. With a little redrawing, I was able to use the first twelve pages of this version as the beginning of the published story. These pages (which would have been thirteen through nineteen) show the original design of the big weird house, the old man and his servant, and a longer sequence with the fungus men. You can also clearly see the panel where I ran out of gas. I don't want to say too much about what was going to happen in this version of the story. It's a good one, and I do plan to do it right one of these days.

Following the unused pages are a few pages from my sketchbook, and there you go.

That's it.

MIKE MYGNOLA

Somewhere in Southern California

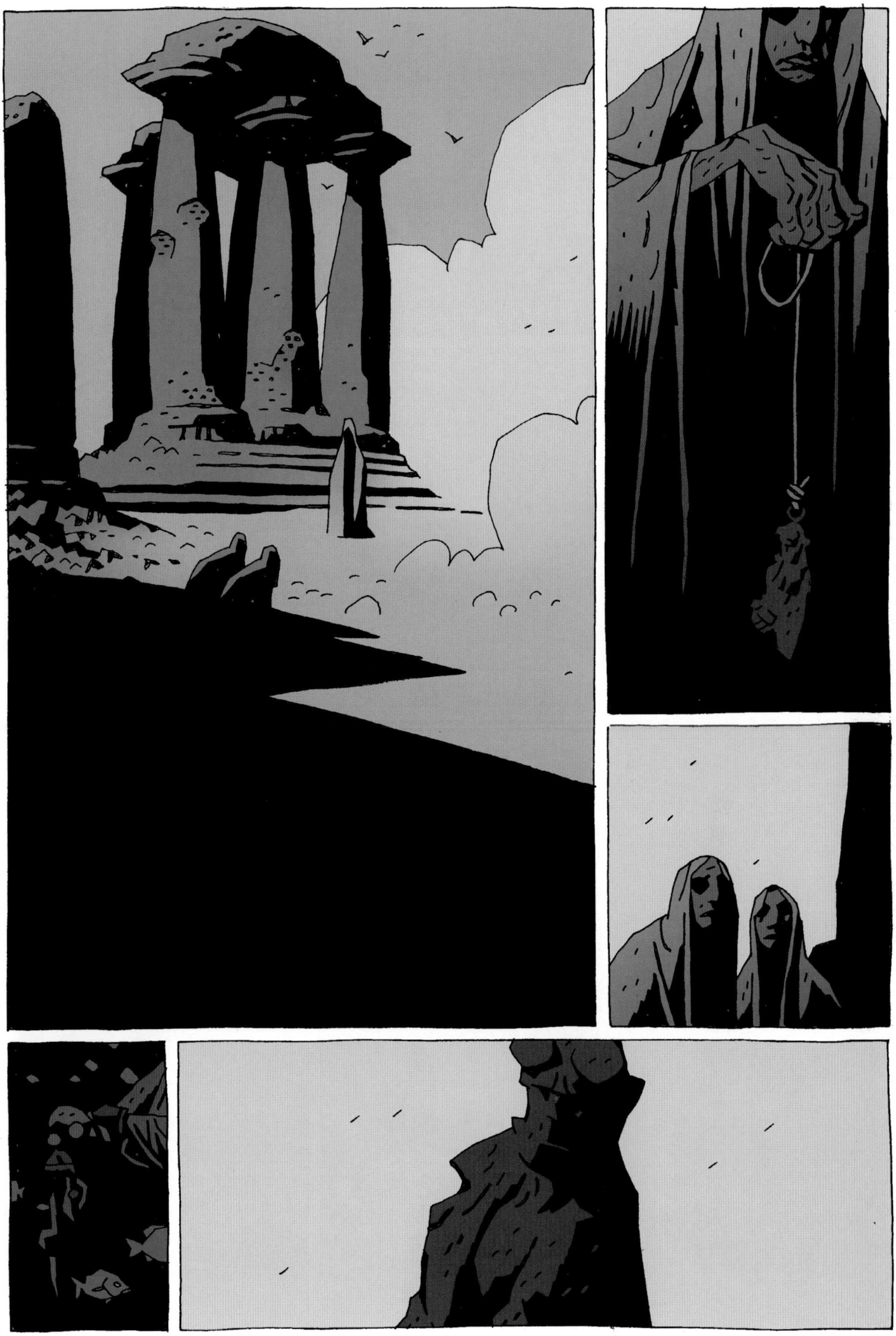

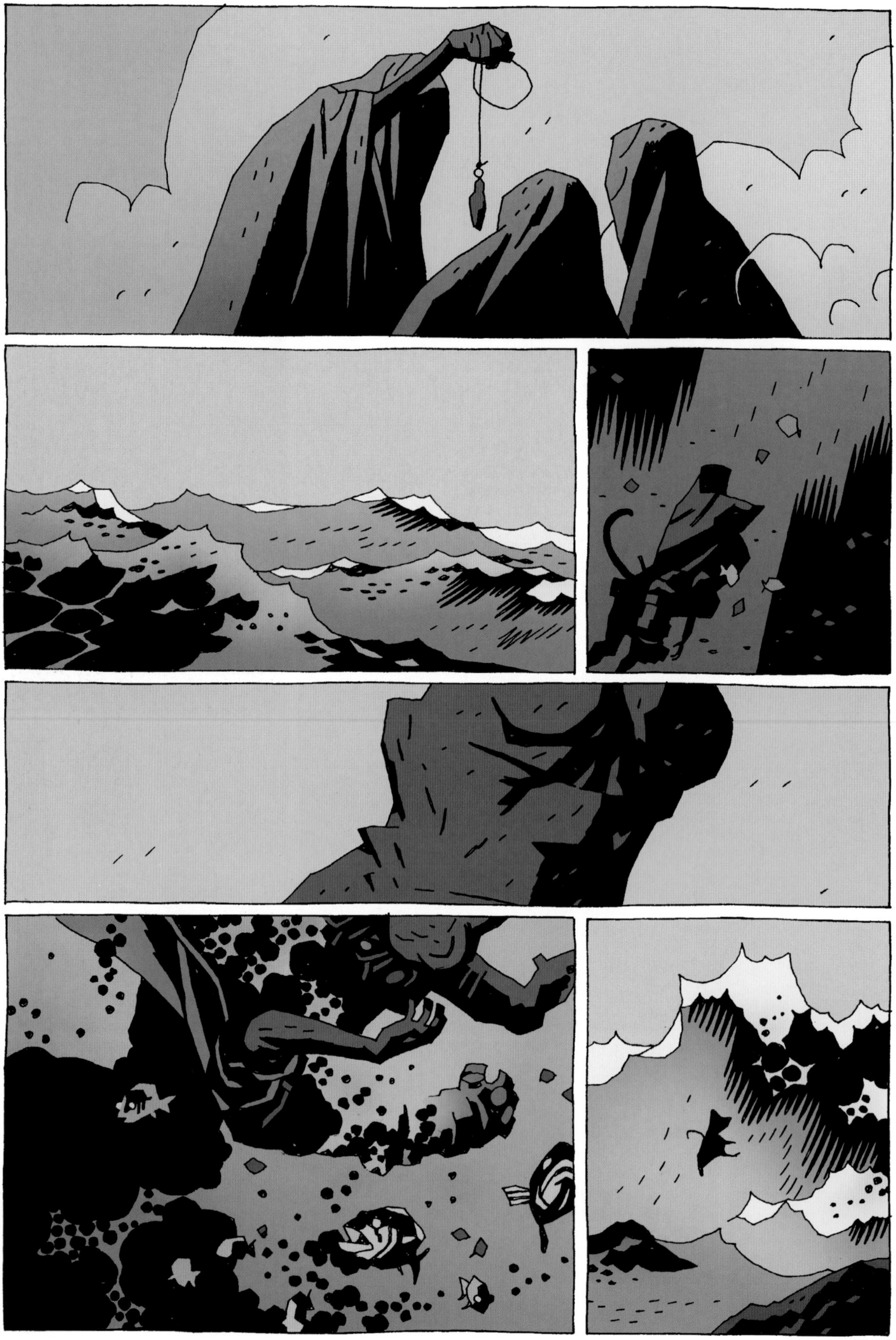

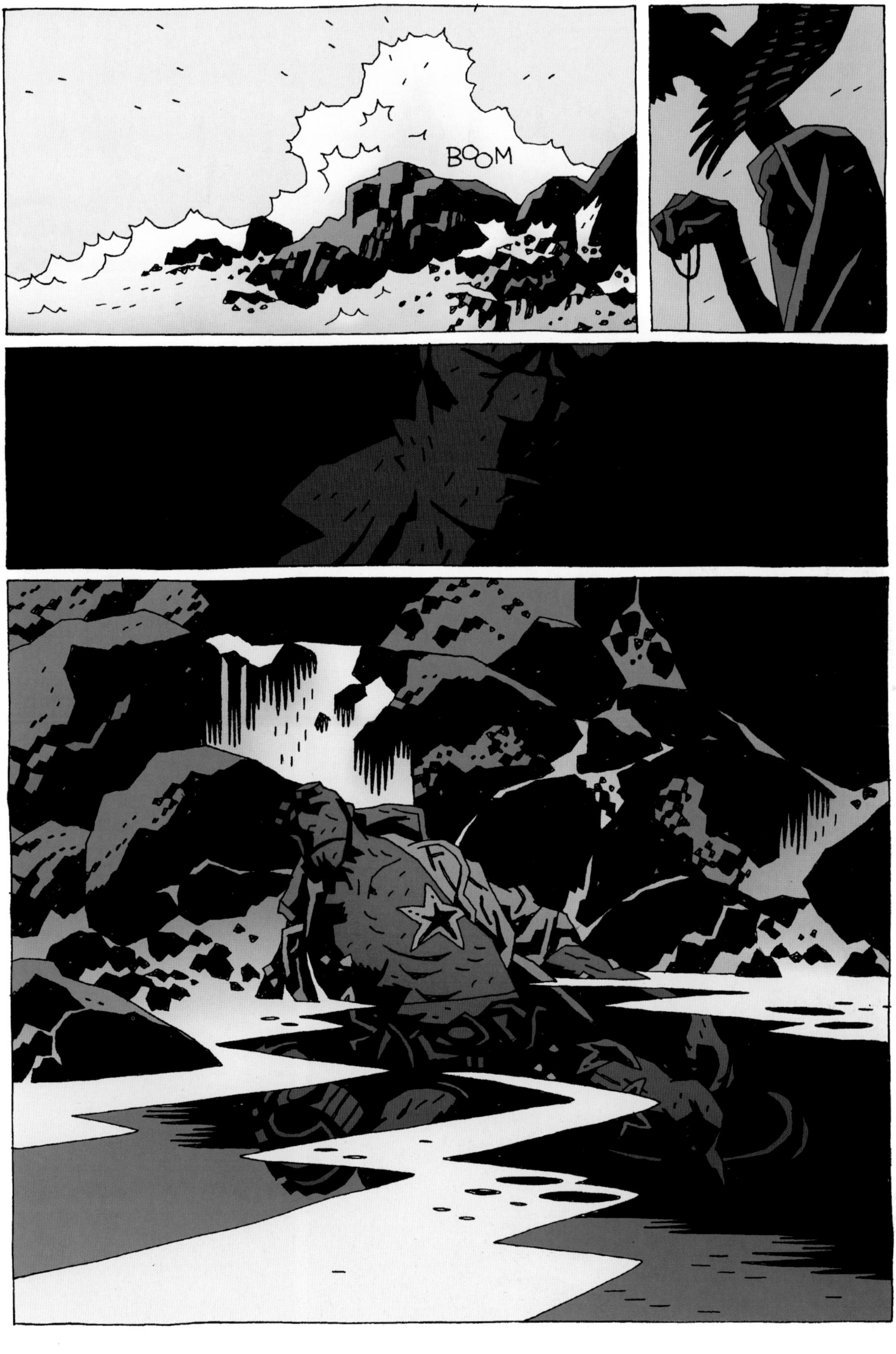
BOOM

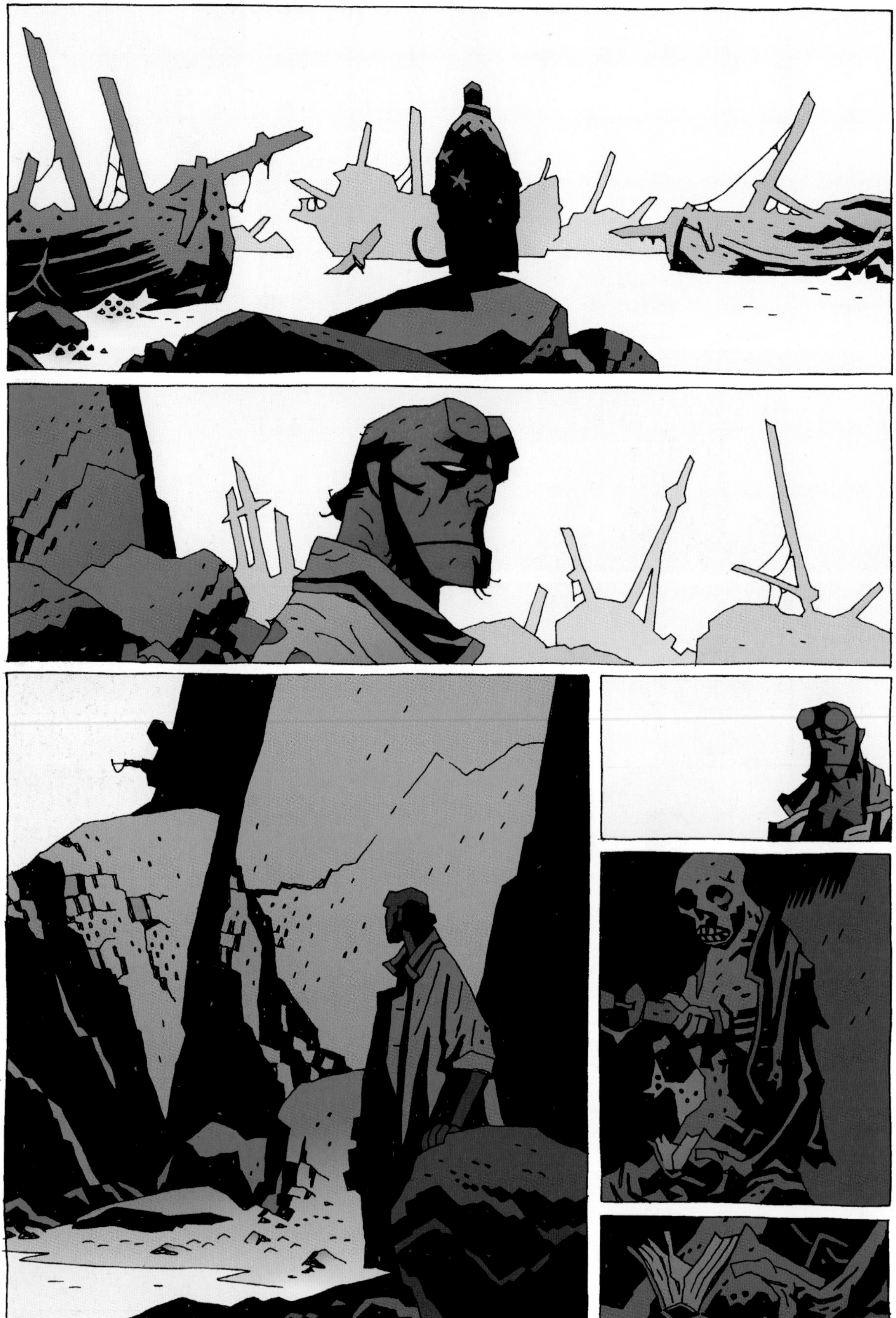

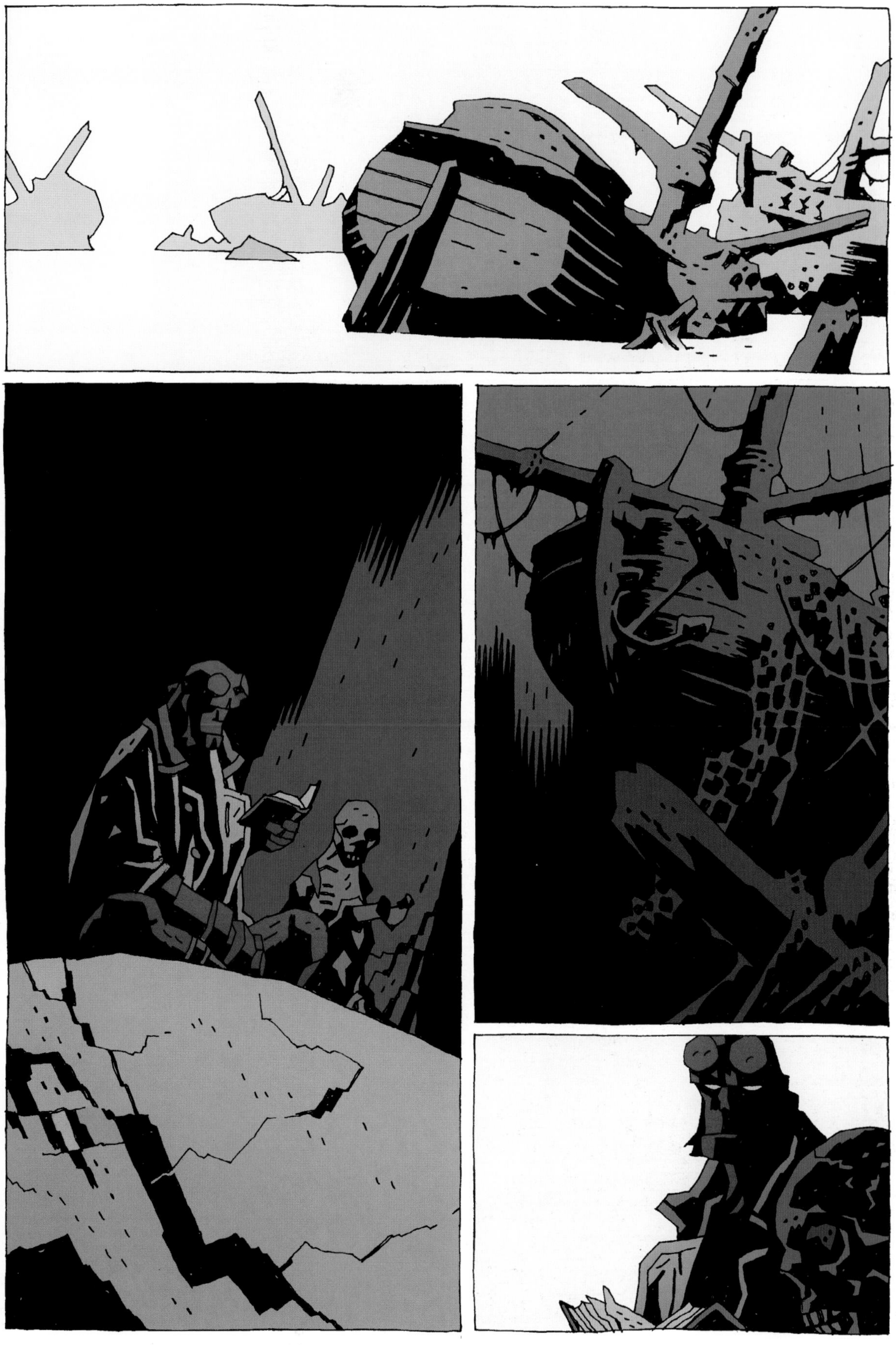

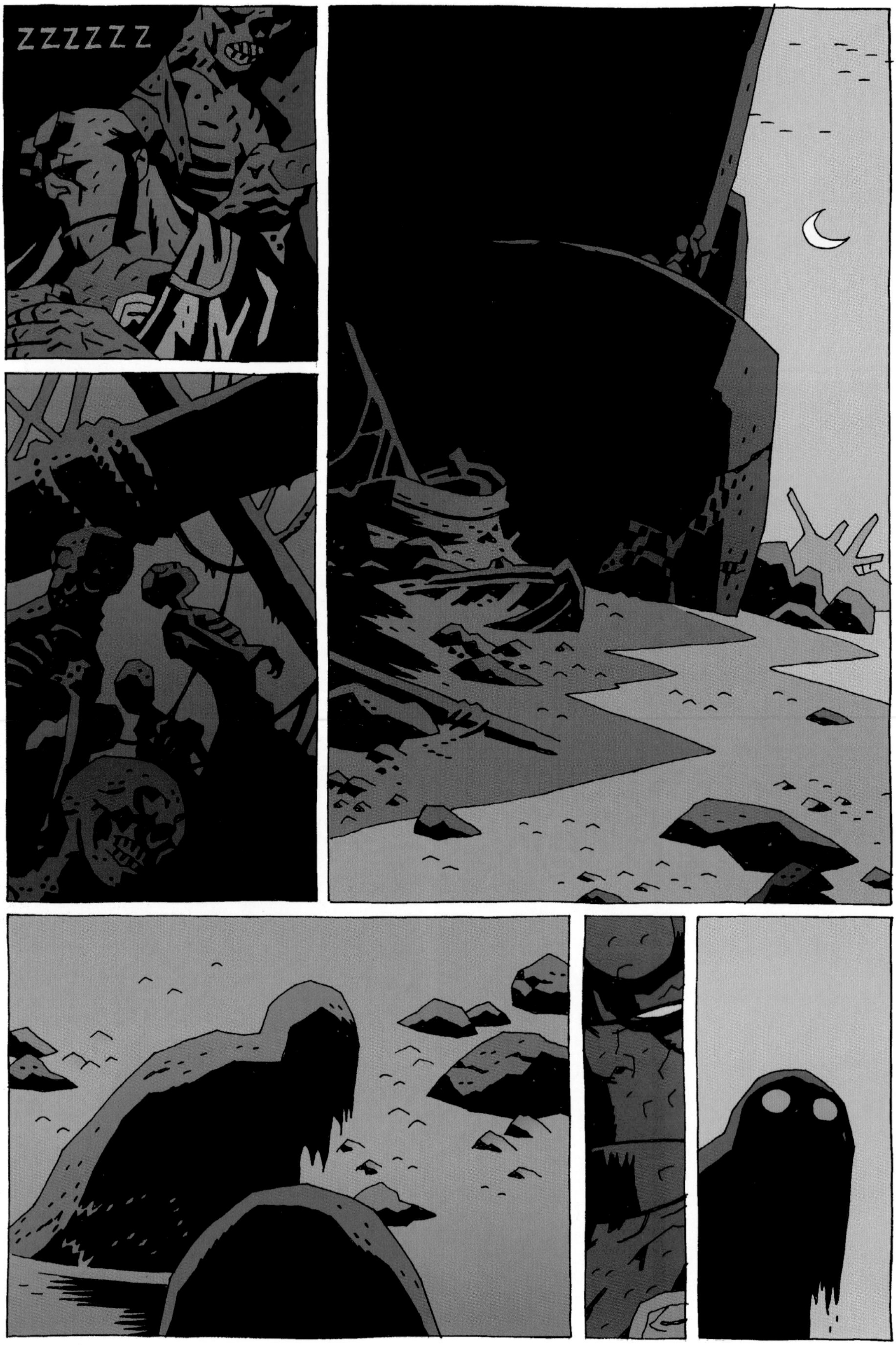
ZZZZZZ

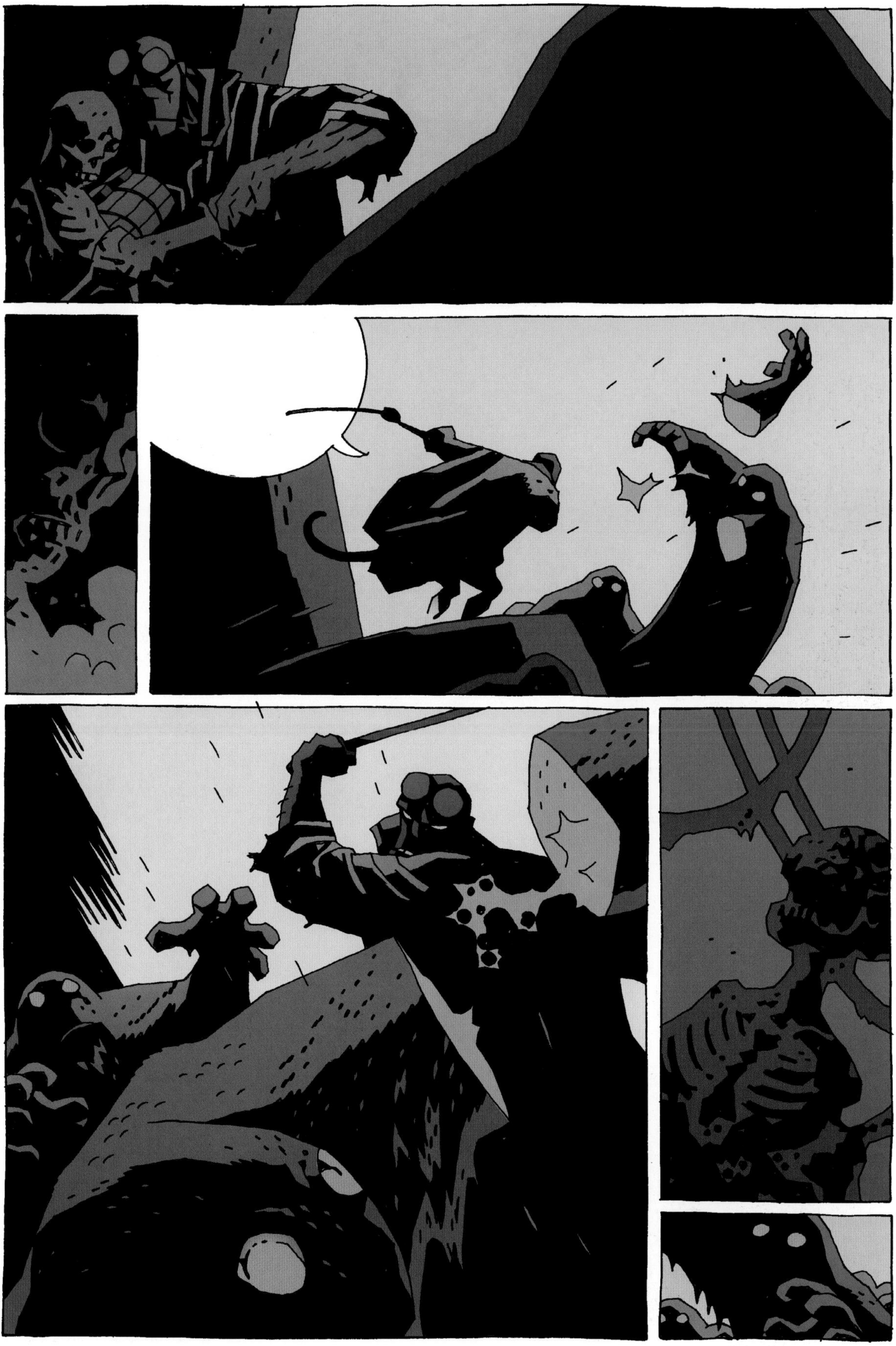

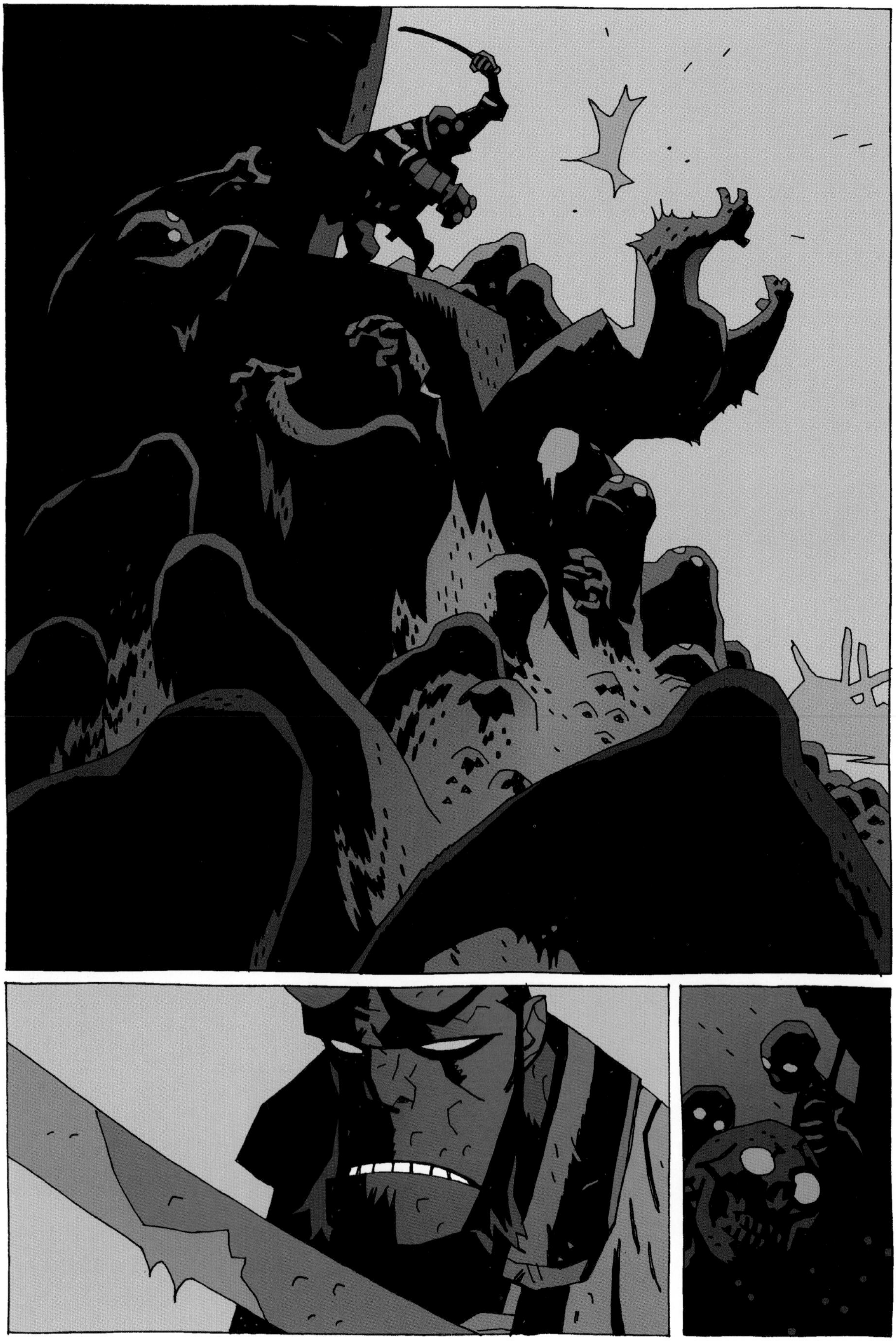

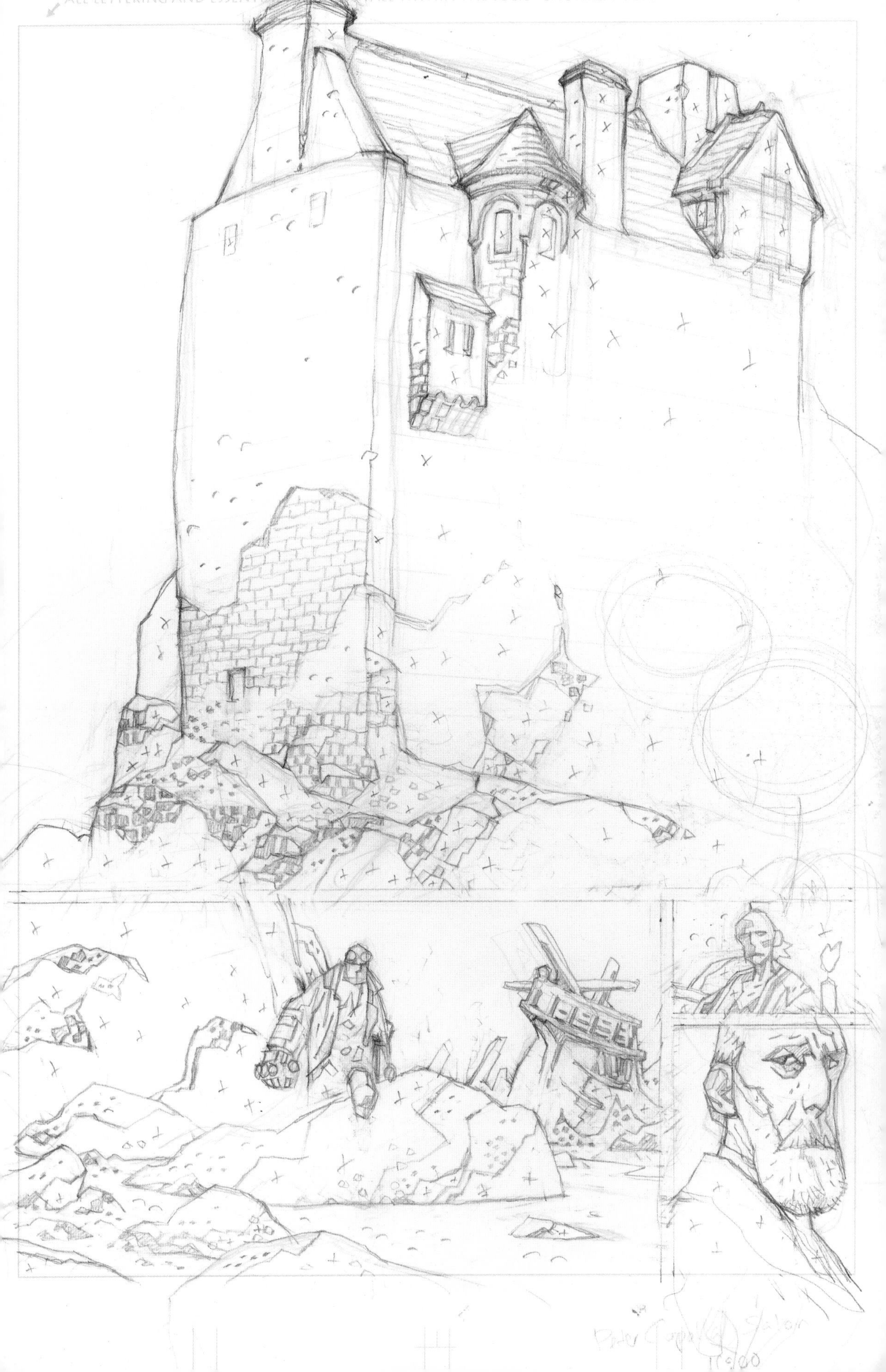

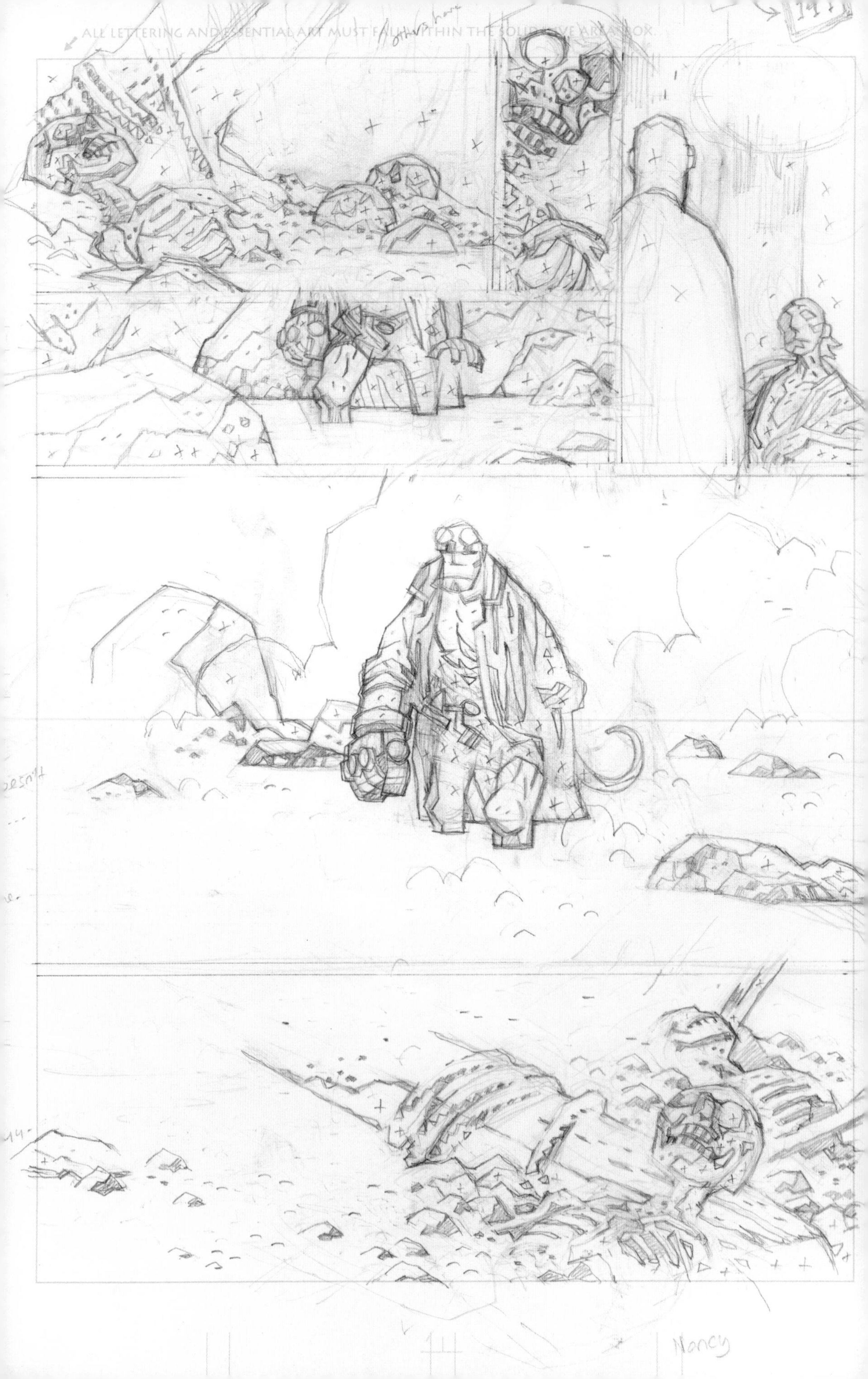
14
Nancy

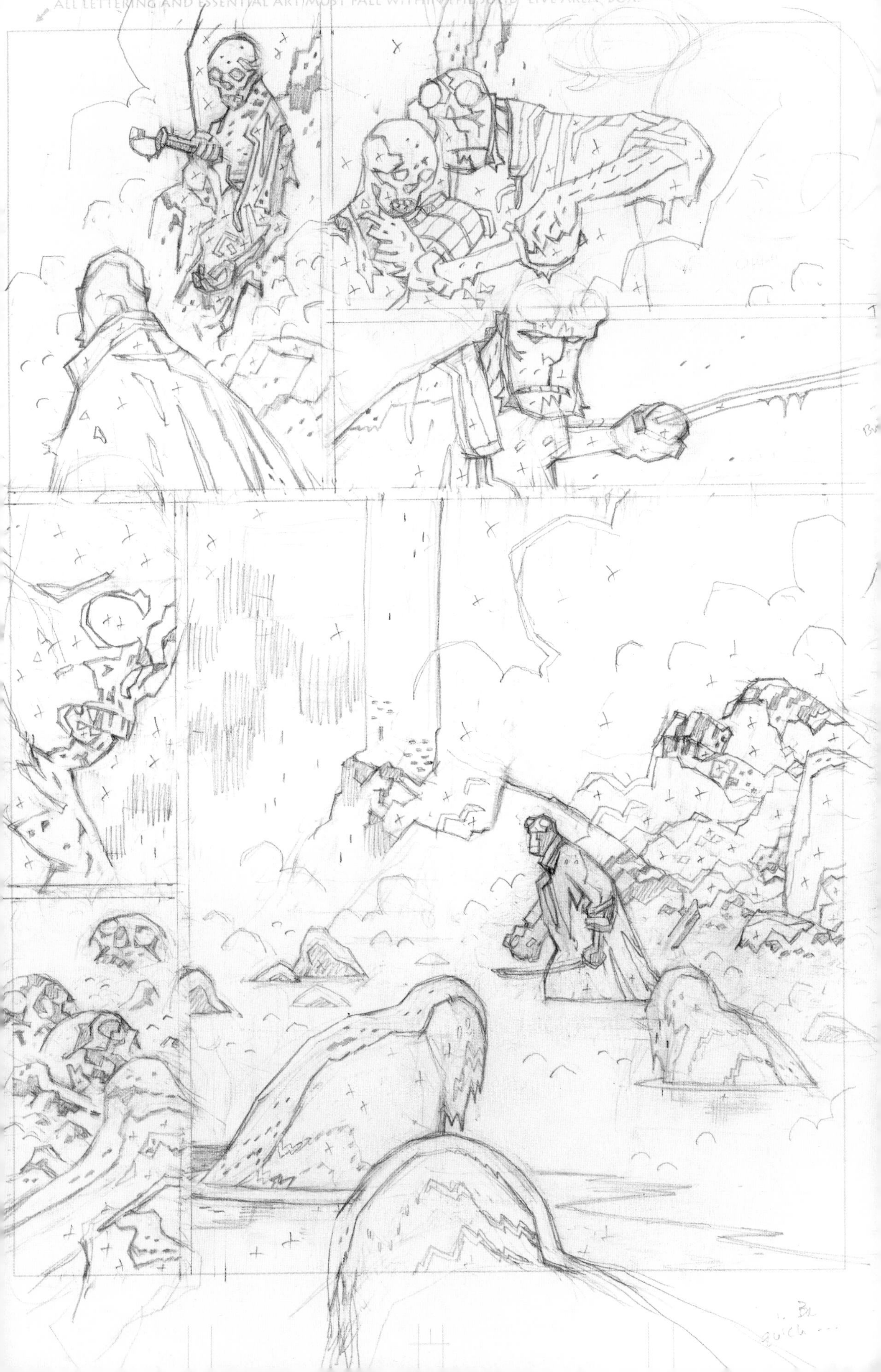

ALL LETTERING AND ESSENTIAL ART MUST FALL WITHIN THE SOLID "LIVE AREA" BOX.

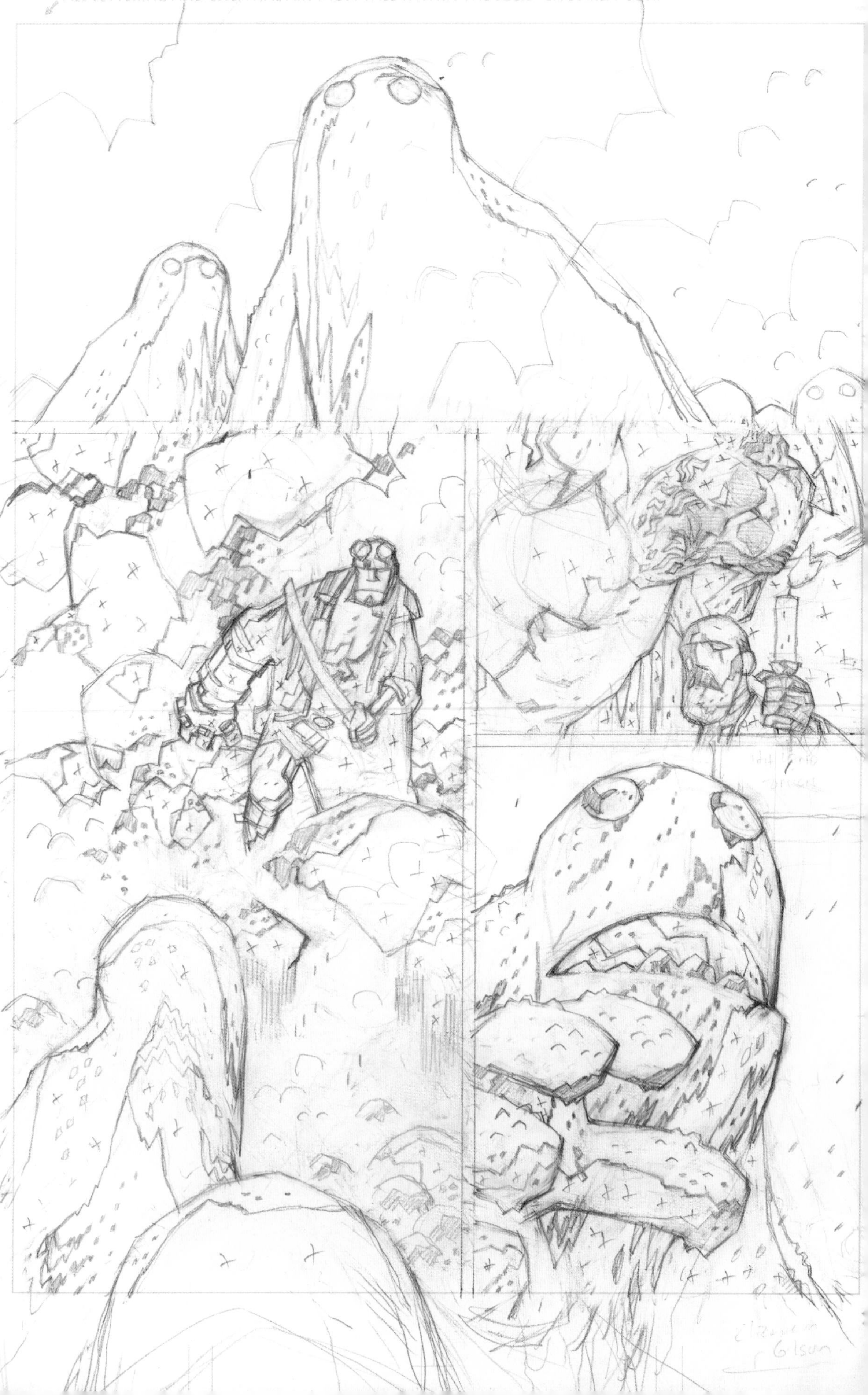

ALL LETTERING AND ESSENTIAL ART MUST FALL WITHIN THE SOLID "LIVE AREA" BOX.

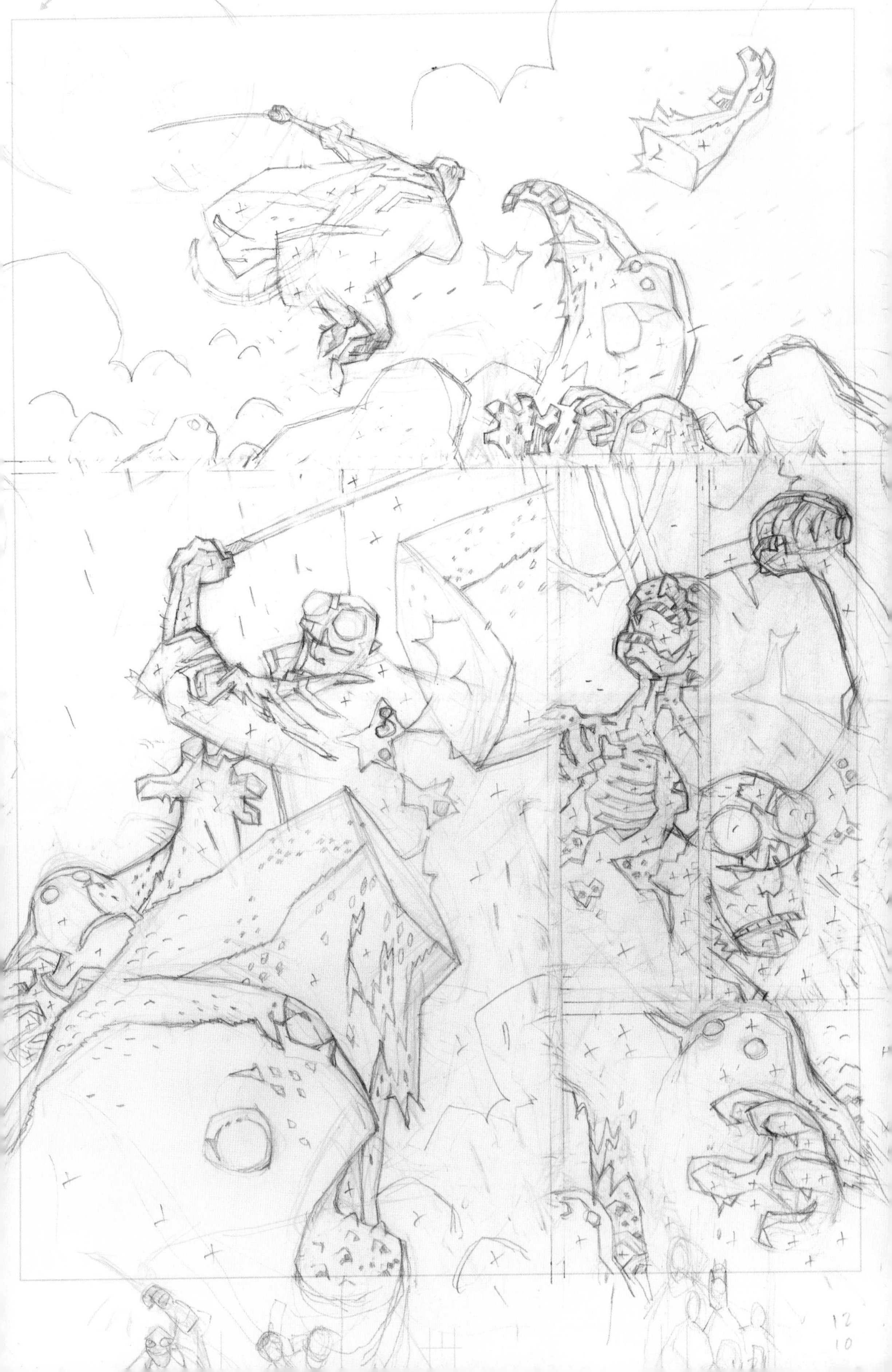

12
10

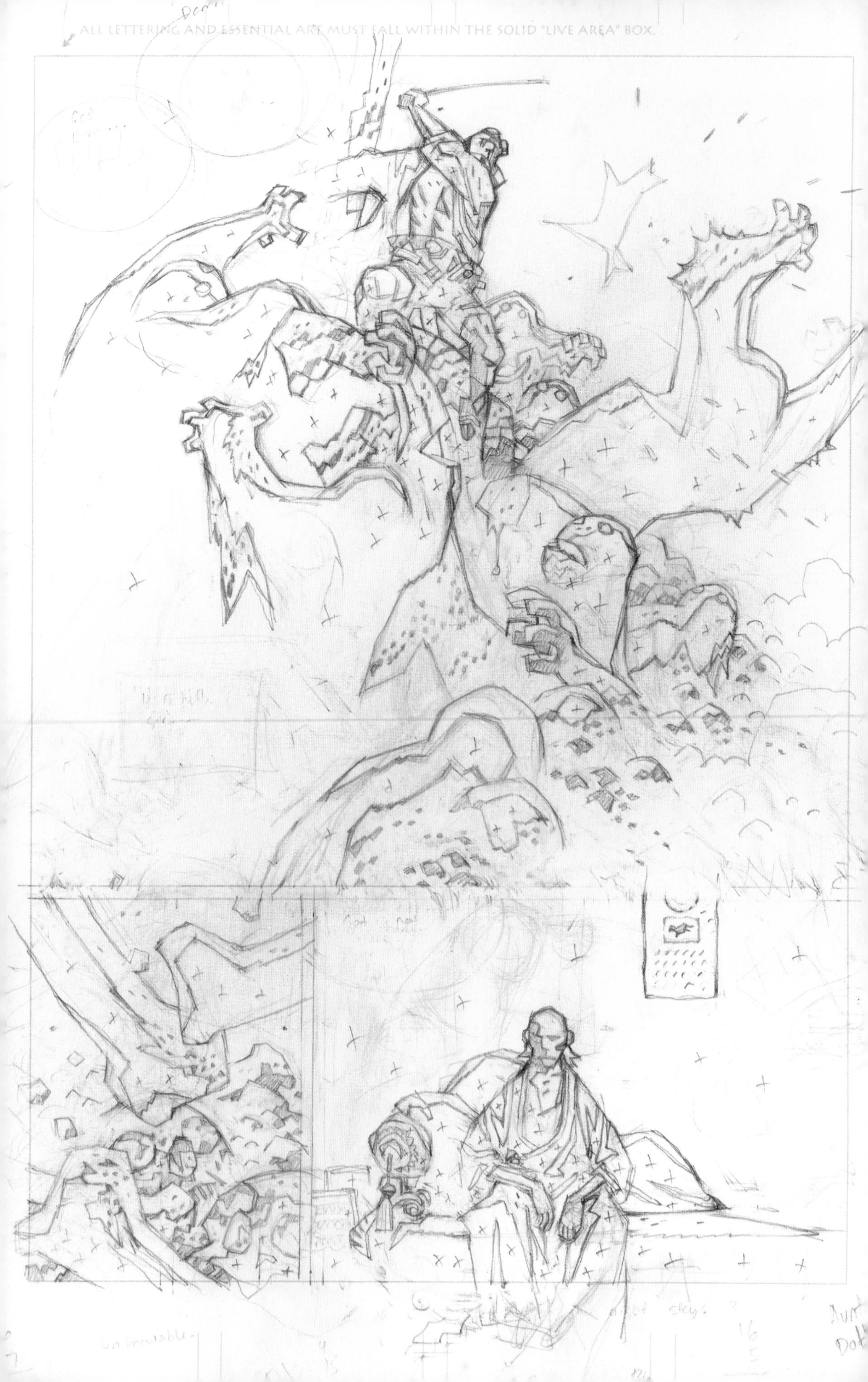
ALL LETTERING AND ESSENTIAL ART MUST FALL WITHIN THE SOLID "LIVE AREA" BOX.

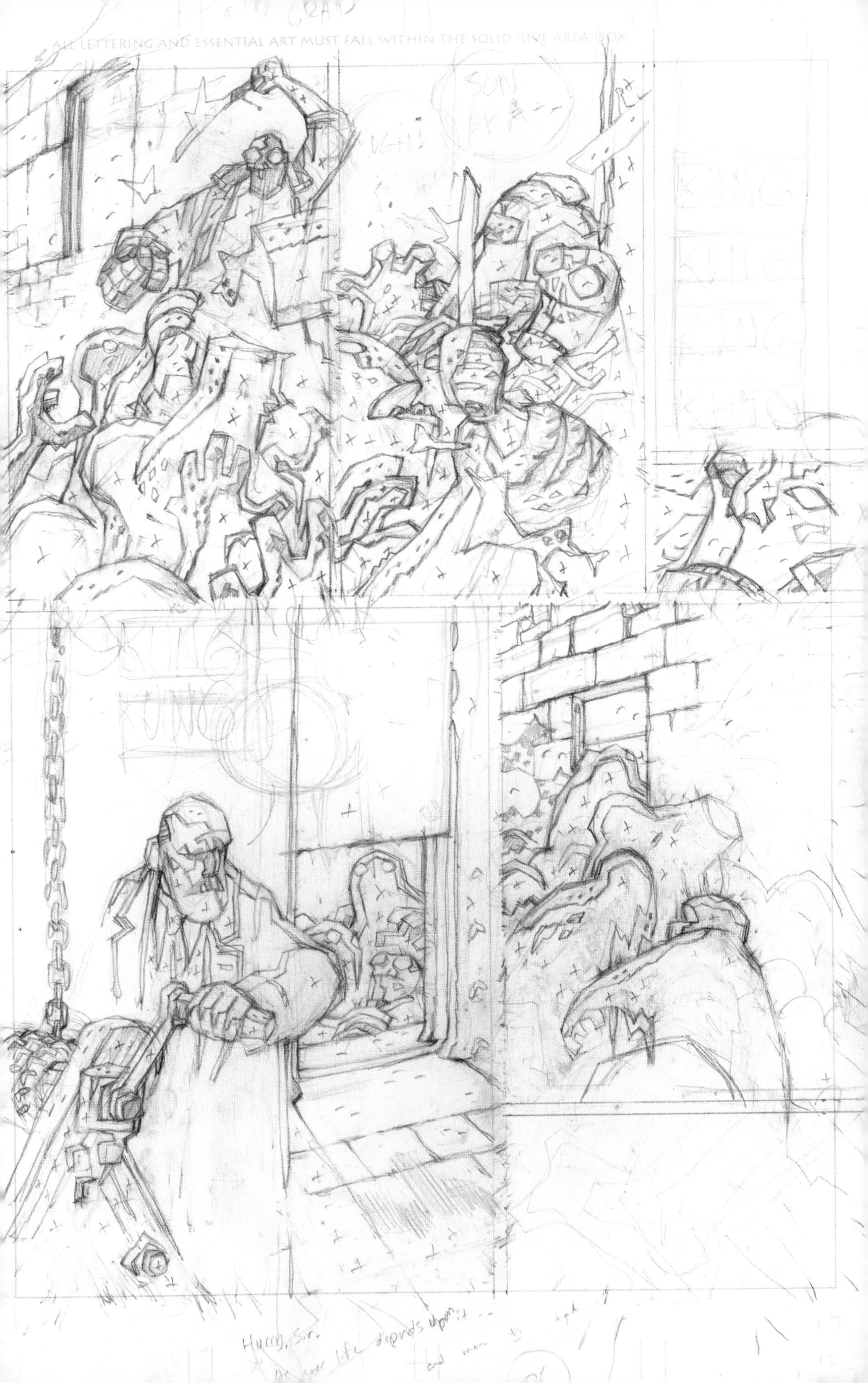
ALL LETTERING AND ESSENTIAL ART MUST FALL WITHIN THE SOLID "LIVE AREA" BOX.
UGH!
SON OF A--
KUNG
your life depends upon it...

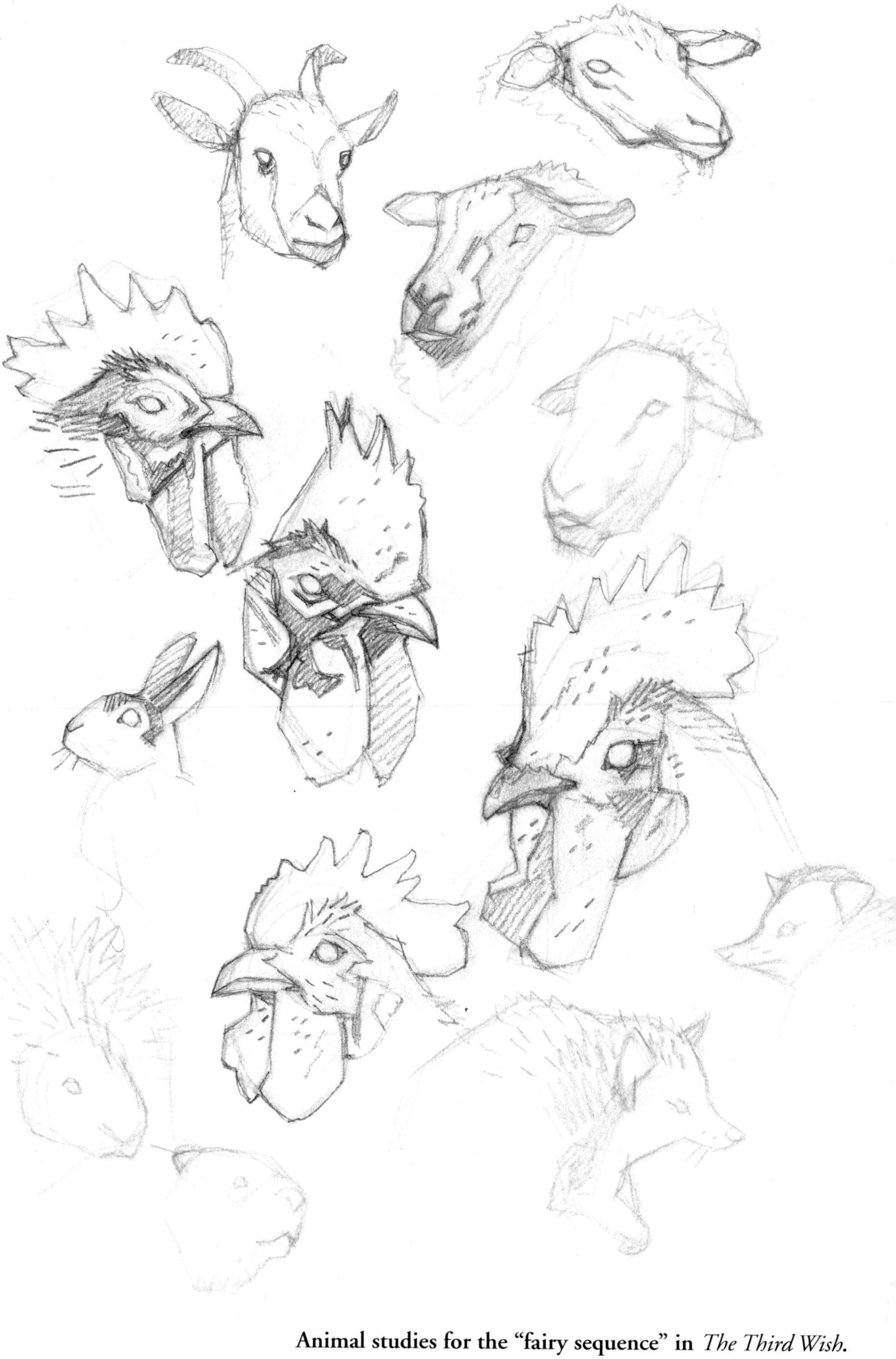

Animal studies for the "fairy sequence" in *The Third Wish*.

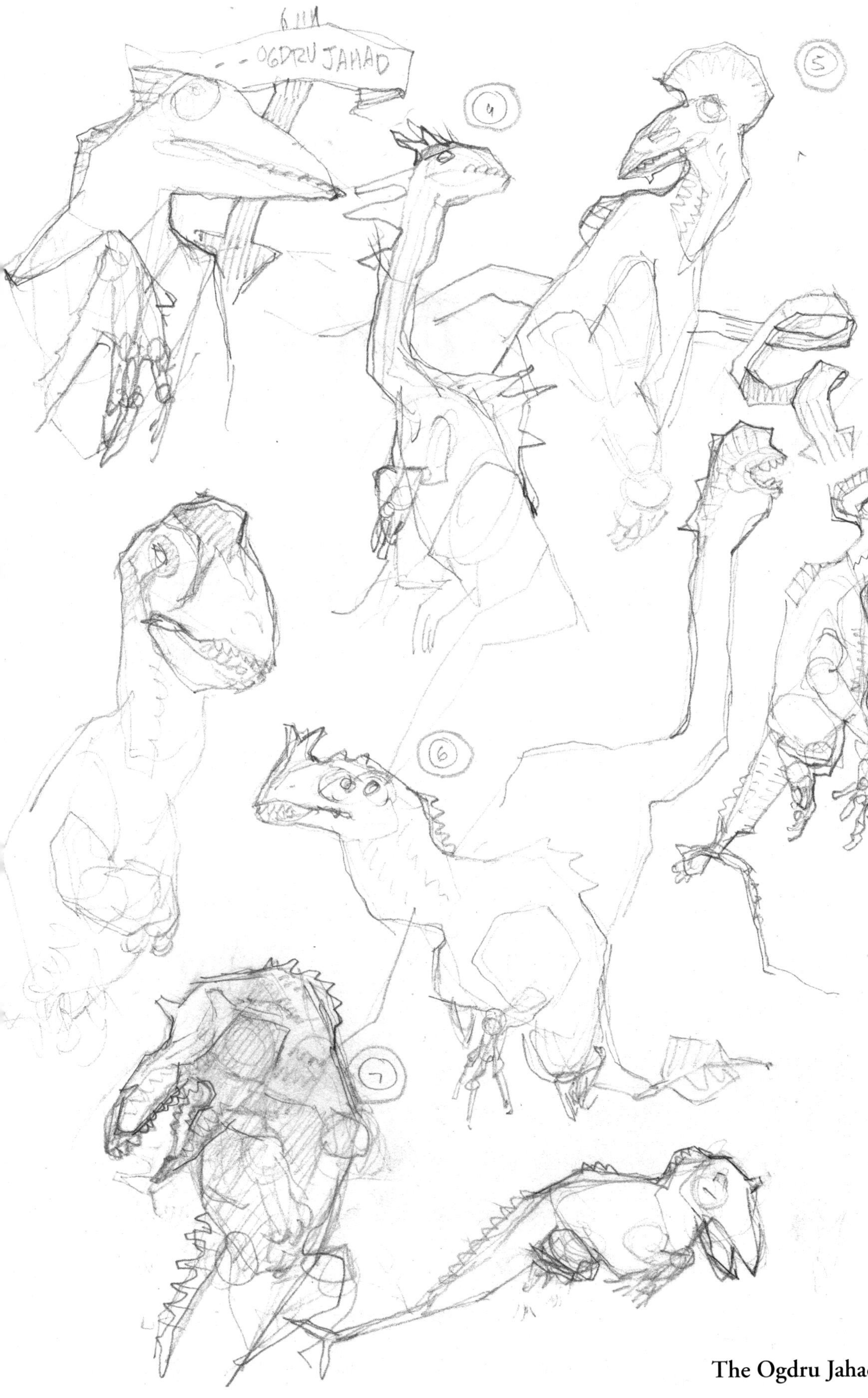
OGDRU JAHAD
4
5
6
7

The Ogdru Jahad.

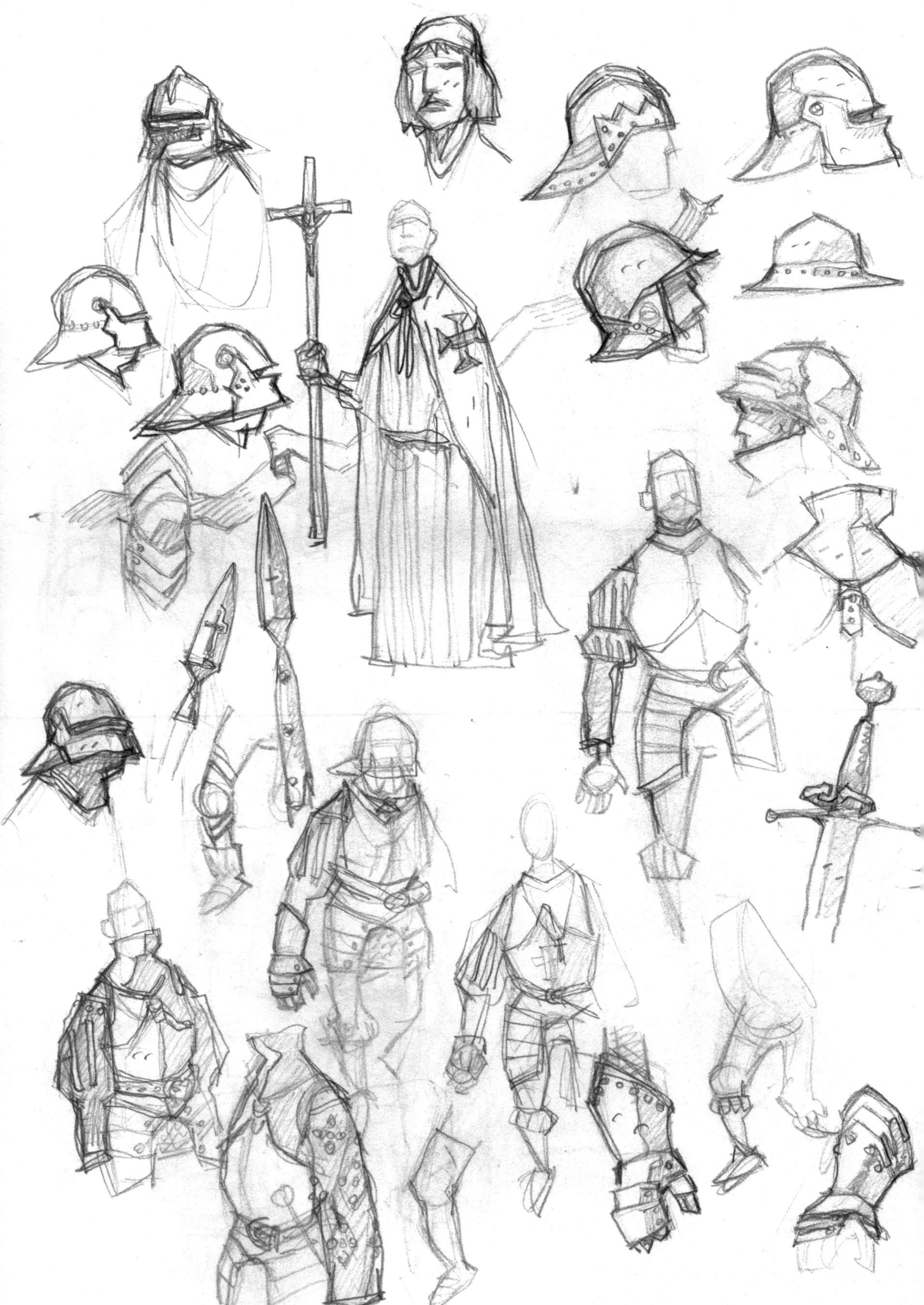

The priest and the Inquisition soldiers.

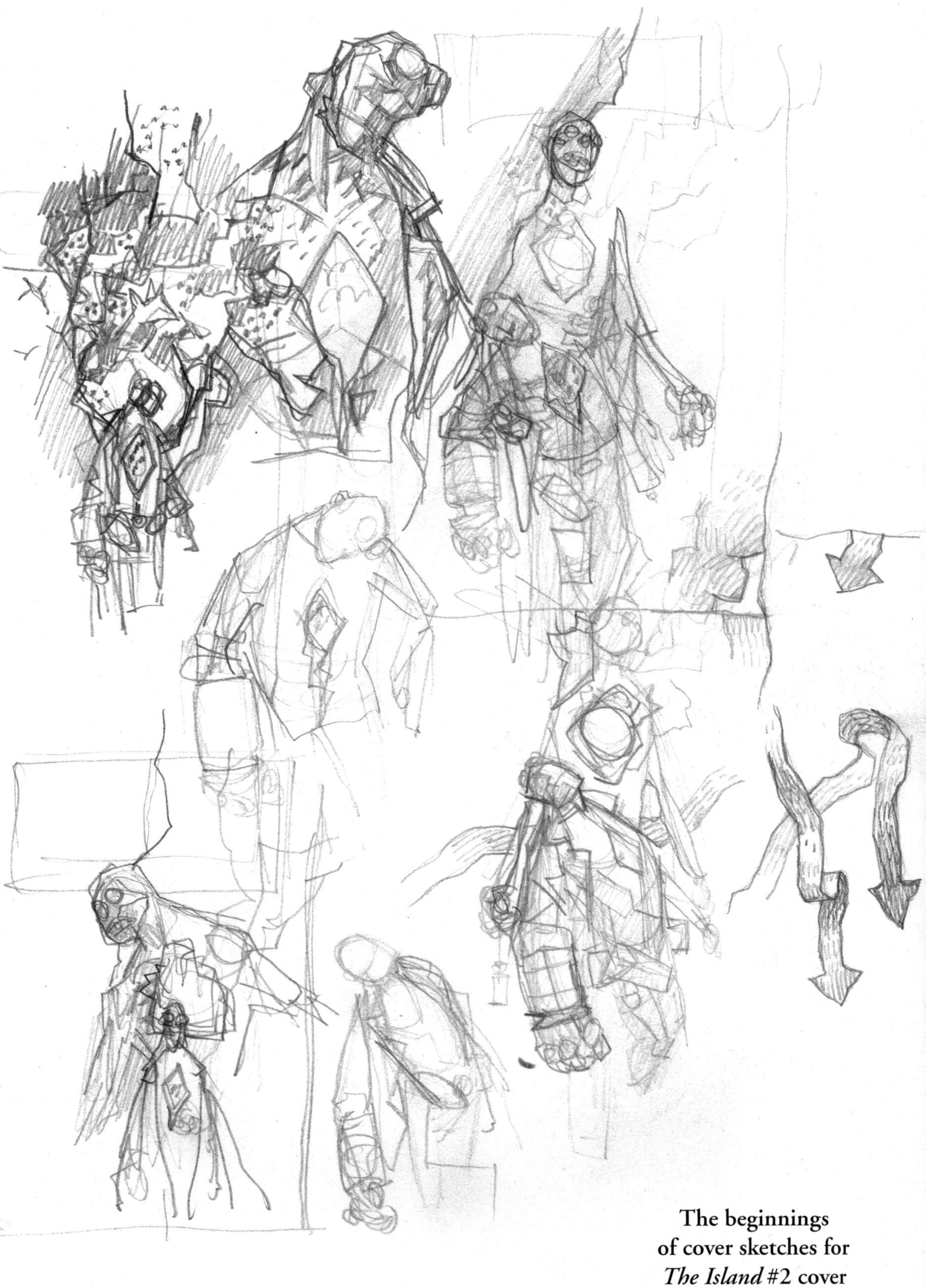

The beginnings
of cover sketches for
The Island #2 cover
(page 2 in this volume).

HELLBOY™

by MIKE MIGNOLA

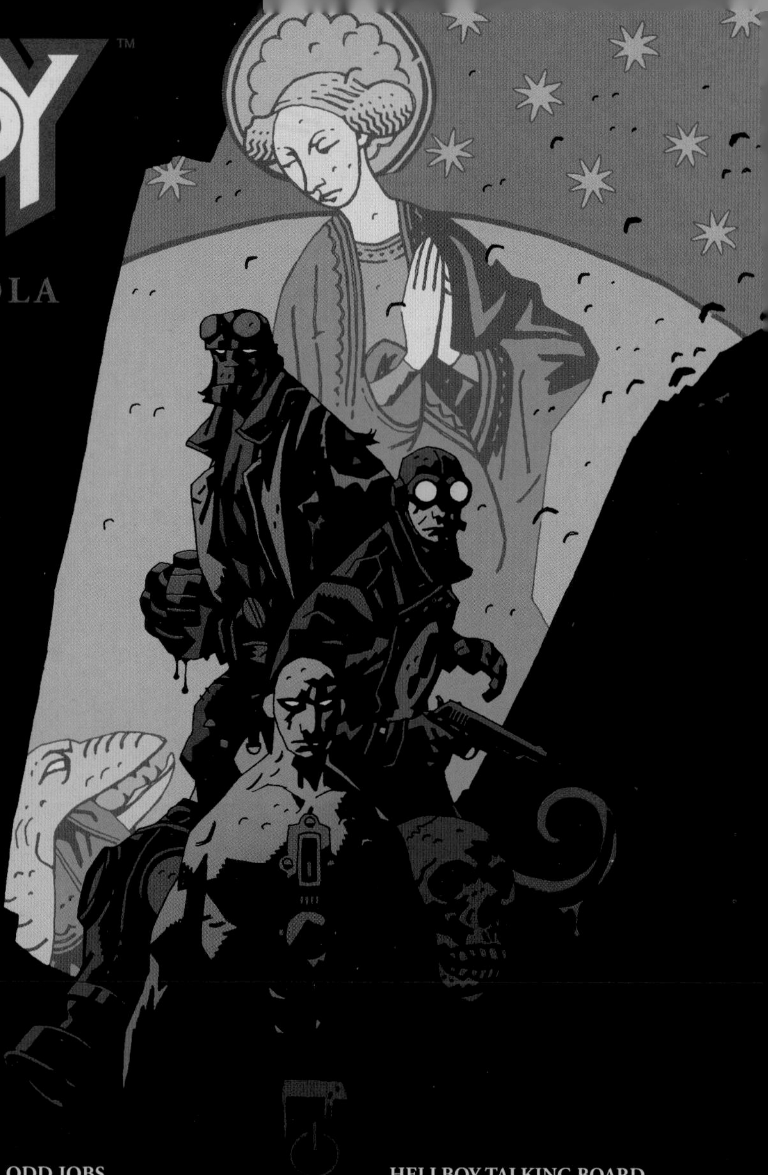

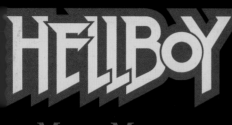